LONDON

Researcher-Writer
Christine Ann Hurd

Editorial Director
Claire McLaughlin

Research Manager
Christopher Holthouse

Associate Editor
Mackenzie Dolginow

Contents

HOW TO USE THIS BOOK

Chapters

In the next few chapters, you'll get to the meat of every *Let's Go* guide: the coverage chapters. Here's where we review where you should sleep in **Accommodations**; what you should see in **Sights**; (maybe most importantly) the best places to eat in **Food**; and the best places to go crazy—or relax with a glass of wine—in **Nightlife**. When you're looking to get a little more classy, **Arts and Culture** is there to help. And since our recommendations will help you save so many euro, you might want to do some **Shopping**. If London starts to get you down, Oxford, Cambridge, and Bath await in the **Excursions** chapter.

But that's not all, folks. We also have a few extra chapters:

CHAPTER	DESCRIPTION
Discover London	Discover tells you what to do, when to do it, and where to go for it. The absolute coolest things about any destination get highlighted in this chapter at the front of all *Let's Go* books.
Essentials	Essentials contains the practical info you need before, during, and after your trip—visas, regional transportation, health and safety, phrasebooks, and more.
Beyond Tourism	As students ourselves, we encourage getting more than the tourist experience. This chapter lists ideas for studying, volunteering, and working abroad with other young travelers to get the most out of London.

Listings

Listings—a.k.a. reviews of individual establishments—consti-tute a majority of *Let's Go* coverage. Our Researcher-Writers list establishments in order from **best to worst value**—not necessarily quality. (Obviously a five-star hotel is nicer than a hostel, but it would probably be ranked lower because it's not as good a value.) Listings pack in a lot of information, but it's easy to digest if you know how they're constructed:

ESTABLISHMENT NAME   TYPE OF ESTABLISHMENT $-$$$$
Address
☎phone number website

Editorial review goes here.

▶ *i* Directions to the establishment. Other practical information about the es-tablishment, like age restrictions at a club or whether breakfast is included at a hostel. Prices for goods or services. ⏰ Hours or schedules.

Icons

First things first: places and things that we absolutely love, sappily cherish, generally obsess over, and wholeheartedly endorse are denoted by the all-empowering 🖋**Let's Go thumbs-up.** In addition, the icons scattered at the end of a listing (as you saw in the sample above) can serve as visual cues to help you navigate each listing:

🖋	*Let's Go* recommends	☎	Phone numbers
i	General information	🕐	Hours

Price Diversity

A final set of icons corresponds to what we call our "price diversity" scale, which approximates how much money you can expect to spend at a given establishment. For **accommodations,** we base our range on the cheapest price for which a single traveler can stay for one night. For **food,** we estimate the average amount one traveler will spend in one sitting. The table below tells you what you'll *typically* find in Paris at the corresponding price range, but keep in mind that no scale can allow for the quirks of all individual establishments.

ACCOMMODATIONS	RANGE	WHAT YOU'RE LIKELY TO FIND
$	£25 or less	Campgrounds and dorm rooms, both in hostels and actual universities. Expect bunk beds and a communal bath. You may have to provide or rent towels and sheets.
$$	£26-45	Upper-end hostels and lower-end hotels. You may have a private bathroom, or a sink in your room with a shared hall shower.
$$$	£46-65	A small room with a private bath. Should have some amenities, such as phone and TV. Breakfast may be included.
$$$$	£66 or more	Large hotels, chains, and fancy boutiques. If it doesn't have the perks you want (and more), you've paid too much.
FOOD		**WHAT YOU'RE LIKELY TO FIND**
$	£8 or less	Street food, fast-food joints, university cafeterias, and bakeries (yum). Usually takeout, but you may have the option of sitting down.
$$	£9-16	Sandwiches, pizza, low-priced entrees, ethnic eateries, and bar grub. Either takeout or sit-down service with slightly classier decor.
$$$	£17-24	A somewhat fancy restaurant. Entrees tend to be heartier or more elaborate. Few places in this range have a dress code, but some may look down on T-shirts and sandals.
$$$$	£25 or more	Your meal might cost more than your room, but there's a reason—it's something fabulous, famous, or both. Slacks and dress shirts may be expected.

Discover London

London evades a one sentence summary besides the oft-trotted out maxim by Samuel Johnson: "When a man is tired of London, he is tired of life." That being said, a certain clump of neurons fires to the tune of "God Save the Queen" when the idea of "London" settles through the senses. If you haven't been before, your mind will of course fancy that it's all very much like *Sherlock Holmes, Harry Potter,* a Hugh Grant movie, or *Skins.* You wouldn't be wrong.

There is definitely the adventure of *Sherlock Holmes* in the city, a cold sort of mystery where people on the street have closed faces that need to be deduced. Seeing everything will be a fruitless chase, and you'll gape in awe at Holmes' eidetic, A-Z memory of the city after blankly not registering the Tube map in Heathrow Terminal 5 in a sort of sensory overload. For an aesthetic ideal, *Harry Potter* isn't a bad mental picture to hold. It's shocking to see Westminster Abbey and St. Paul's exceed the Ministry of Magic's grandeur, and the crowded Bank area seems just like Gringotts. The rows of identical houses in the books can appear cartoonized and unbelievable in the movies, but in Notting Hill and Chelsea, that's exactly what lines block after block.

As for the Hugh Grant canon, the residents do hold an embarrassed charm, although with less eyelash-fluttering. And you're very likely to meet Americans and go aimlessly shopping.

As for *Skins,* just head to Camden, Dalston, or Shoreditch. The grittier side to London exists all the same, with a clear divide between the posh, well-tailored skirt and heels crew and the black skinny jeaned ruffian type that haunts those neighborhoods.

Whether you're here for exhibitions of royal or imperial grandeur, an unparalleled theater scene, or a city that is becoming modern amidst its love of the past, London can only be approximated, for it contains multitudes.

ON A BUDGET

London may be one of the most expensive cities in the world, but armed with the right guide (this one) you can experience much of what it has to offer without having to pawn the family jewels.

Have Your Jellied Eels and Eat 'Em, Too

Don't worry, you don't need to resort to eels to eat cheaply in London.

- **Pie Minister:** This punny pie shop offers some of the best English eats in the city at some of the best prices; it's sure to leave you satis-pied.

- **Franco Manca:** Order an individual pizza at this South London pizzeria. It's just like stepping through a wormhole to Naples.

- **City Càphê:** Vietnamese bánh mì is your best bet for a delicious, cheap sandwich in the City.

- **Freebird Burritos:** We used to say it was impossible to find a good burrito in London. Then we found Freebird.

- **Le Mercury:** This is one of the best values in London; proof that good French food doesn't have to be expensive.

A Hostel Fit For the Queen

It can be hard to find budget accommodations in this notoriously pricey city. Good thing we've got you covered.

- **Palmer's Lodge:** This refurbished Victorian mansion (once home to a biscuit magnate), is one of the highest-rated hostels in the city.

- **Clink 78:** Ever wanted to sleep in a jail that you could check out of? This expertly renovated old jail and courthouse is a great place to make your dreams come true (though the "cells" aren't for the claustrophobic).

- **Astor Hyde Park:** Where else can you find hostel rooms with French windows and domed glass skylights? Aged grandeur and comfort mark this flagship of the Astor chain.

- **St. Christopher's Village:**   A proud party hostel with lots of amenities, organized activities, and local character.

Freebies

If you know where to go, it's possible to see some of the best London has to offer without paying a pound.

- **Museums:** Most of London's famous museums, including the British Museum, Tate Modern, and the National Gallery, are gloriously free.

- **Evensong:** Skip the ticket price and go to Westminster Abbey or St Paul's during Evensong. Just don't be a jerk and leave halfway through the service.

- **Parliament:** Instead of paying 15 quid for a tour, see democracy in action at a debate or committee session.

Pinching Pence

London may be one of the most expensive cities in the world, but armed with the right guide (this one) you can experience much of what it has to offer without having to pawn the family jewels.

- **Take the Tube:** Unless you're up to walking a marathon each day, the Tube will be your cheapest way of getting around. Plan efficient journeys to save money. The Piccadilly Line, which runs between Central London and Heathrow, is the cheapest way to get to and from the airport.

- **Oyster cards:** Get a reusable Oyster Card and save yourself up to 50% on all London public transportation. You can also buy 1- and 3-day passes, or weekly, monthly, and annual Travelcards that give you unlimited rides (within specific zones) for their duration.

- **Skip special exhibitions:** London's incredible free museums are big enough that you'll have plenty to see without shelling out for the special exhibits.

- **Skip touristy spots for similar, free alternatives:** For example, instead of going to the kitschy Tower of London (nearly £20), get your history on at the Museum of London (free).

WHAT TO DO

Museum Heaven On Earth

Luckily for budget travelers, many of London's world-class museums are completely free. Though there are countless great options, here are four that are unmissable. The British Museum's mind-blowing collection, ranging from the Elgin Marbles to the Rosetta Stone, will show you the full power of the British Empire. After that crash course in Western civilization, take another on Western art at the National Gallery, especially if you're a fan of Turner (not Tina). The Victoria and Albert Museum contains design exhibits on all cultures and time periods. Finally, the Tate Modern will show you all the big names of 20th-century art—including Duchamp, Pollock, and Warhol. And you can simply stroll into all of these museums without paying any admission fee.

Hold the Whole World In Your Stomach

Other than admiring the relics in the British Museum, the best way to experience the legacy of the British Empire is to tour London's many delicious ethnic eateries. The city is brimming with great Indian food, but Durbar (p. 69) in Notting Hill has been producing some of the best of it for 54 years. You can also fill up on spicy comfort food at Negril (p. 76), a great Afro-Caribbean joint in Brixton. Many swear Sufi (p. 76) in Shepherd's Bush makes the best Persian food in the city, while Mien Tay (p.

75) has the best price-to-quality ratio of East London's many Vietnamese eateries.

To Beer or not to Beer?

Feel like a challenge? Try counting all the pubs in London. Or, save yourself the time and just visit the best. Dove (p. 96) will make you feel truly English as you sample its local ales at a picnic table on the banks of the Thames. Cask (p. 84) can only be described as Beer Heaven. And at The Drayton Arms (p. 86), you can enjoy your ale while watching a play in the black-box theater or curled up in front of the fireplace.

Beyond Tourism

Ready to take a break from drinking Newcastle and counting churches? Get more involved with British culture by studying, working, or volunteering in London. You can legislate with a Parliamentary internship, hustle as a paid fundraiser for Greenpeace, or make the whole world your stage by studying acting at Shakespeare's Globe Theatre.

Planning Your Trip

To say that London is a sizeable city is to adopt the infamous British tendency for understatement. London is bloody massive. The central knot of museums, historical sights, shopping, and entertainment stretches along the Thames from the City of London (yes, a city within a city) through the West End to Westminster. The luxurious residential neighborhoods of Chelsea, Kensington, Notting Hill, and Marylebone lie to the north and west. Add in the university neighborhood of Bloomsbury and the culturally prominent South Bank, and you've got the whole of central London in a nice package.

These areas encompass most of Zone 1 in the Tube. Moving out to the second ring, a traveler will find less material wealth and more wealth of personality. These outer areas include ethnically rich South London (Brixton), artistically rich East London (Hackney), literarily and musically rich North London (Camden and Hampstead), and culturally rich West London (Shepherd's Bush and Hammersmith).

Navigating the sprawl of London can be incredibly frustrating. Fortunately, the ever-obliging Brits plaster the city center with maps, which can be found reliably at bus stops. If you don't want to leave your direction to chance, you can always shell out for the all-knowing A-Z city map.

WHEN TO GO

The first thing to know is that, in London, just about any day of the year can be warm, cold, or extremely wet. That said, the summer months offer the best odds of at least not being cold and wet at the same time. The city gets packed around late June, but empties out in late July as the British leave the city for summer homes and Majorca. If you're a fan of classical music, then July and August also host the BBC Proms, which includes dozens of concerts all throughout the two-month period. The low season (November through March) is when you can find the best deals on airfare and accommodations, so long as rainy (and sometimes snowy) weather doesn't cramp your sightseeing style too much.

NEIGHBORHOODS

The City of London

One of the oldest and most historic parts of London, the City of London, often referred to as "the City," is home to many of London's finest (and most crowded) tourist attractions as well as the city's financial center. The City holds many of London's Roman artifacts, including vestiges of the ancient London Wall. Next to these relics, the spires of famous churches are juxtaposed with the towers of powerful insurance companies. Because the City's real estate market was locked down sometime a couple of centuries ago, no one really lives in the area around Fleet St.—which lends the City a 28 Days Later vibe anytime other than the workweek. As you head farther north, the City fades into Farringdon and Clerkenwell, which is more reliably populated and provides something of a buffer zone from East London. Here you'll find a mix of the yuppie-gentrified City and the hipster-gentrified East; somehow, this turns out to be a magical combination, producing quirky pubs and terrific food.

The West End

The West End is one of the largest, most exciting parts of London. Its twin hearts are Soho and Covent Garden, but the neighborhood encompasses the area between Bloomsbury and the Thames, from the edge of Hyde Park to the City of London. Within that expanse are some of the city's best public museums (such as the National Gallery and the National Portrait Gallery), world-famous theater, interesting restaurants, loads of shopping, and vibrant nightlife. You can find just about anything you're looking for here (except maybe a good curry—Indian culture is strangely absent in this part of London).

Soho—most easily accessible via ⊖Tottenham Court Road—is one of the hipper and seedier parts of London. Home to one of the city's most prominent GLBT communities, Soho bursts at the seams with nightlife for gay and straight clubgoers alike. By day, this area (particularly Chinatown, located off Gerrard St.) is known for its excellent restaurants. North of Soho, Oxford Street is the high street to end all high streets, with department stores and cavernous flagships of major clothing chains. Smaller boutiques and many salons can also be found in this part of town. To the south and west, the buildings get fancier and the streets are quieter in regal neighborhoods like St James's. All in all, the West End feels like one of the most touristy parts of the city, but perhaps that's because it so conveniently encapsulates what London is (deservedly) famous for.

Westminster

Breaking this down into linguistic chunks, the "minster" comes from the Old English rendering of the Latin for monastery. The "west" comes from an Old English translation of "whist," which meant "a game played by Liberalus Democratiusin which a smaller party aligns itself with the controlling party and then traitorously raises university fees against their platform." Just kidding. It means west. But this area is the giant heart of the British power with all of its frantically beating aortic chambers: Buckingham Palace, Westminster Palace and the Houses of Parliament, and Westminster Abbey. The nearby West End is a much more exciting place to roam.

The South Bank

Back in the Puritan days, the South Bank was one giant den of sin. A trip across the river meant you and Satan would pal it up in the blasphemous theater district and maybe frequent a hooker or two while you were in the area. Now, it's a thoroughly un-gritty mecca of culture that hosts the biggest cinema in Britain, a half dozen theatres, the Tate Modern, and the fearsomely awesome Southbank Centre. Its purview extends—quite unsurprisingly—along the south bank of the Thames across from the City of London and Westminster. The main riverside path is called the Millennium Mile and stretches from the London Eye in the west eastward along the Thames, making for a beautiful walk, especially around sunset. No hookers though.

South Kensington and Chelsea

Welcome to the poshest part of London, where anything less than perfectly coiffed hair, a believable tan, and the flash of a Louboutin sole will earn you the curled-up lip of British disdain. Tired tourists—who flit in and out of the museums and buy only from the food section of Harrods—are easily distinguished from the fleet of glamazons who use cabs to travel mere blocks. So use the hostel iron for your best shirt and don't feel too bad when the staff of designer stores look at you you're wearing a Nazi costume—they're pretty much paid to hate on anyone who's not Madonna. This area—for our plebian purposes—extends from Cromwell Rd. down to the Thames and is enclosed by Sloane St. and Redcliffe Gardens.

Hyde Park to Notting Hill

Hyde Park is, we promise, actually a park and not terrible movie with Bill Murray. It's roughly rectangular with a Tube stop at pretty much every corner—Marble Arch, the incredibly unhelpfully named Hyde Park Corner, High Street Kensington, and Queensway. North of the park are a set of neighborhoods that get progressively nicer as you move west. Paddington, Edgware Rd., and Queensway mix fairly fancy houses on their back streets with main roads that have plenty of cheap ethnic eateries, souvenir shops, and stores of questionable legality that can unlock your phone, cash your checks, and wire your money across the world. Notting Hill has the mansions you would imagine, but popping out of the Tube at Notting Hill Gate may be a bit of a shock if you're expecting instant British charm—it's pretty much dull commercial real estate. Head slightly north, though, and you'll find the villas you were expecting. In the middle of that, Portobello Road has a market, antique stores, vintage clothing, and the kind of minimalist, hip cafes and restaurants that seem to appear anywhere you can get a secondhand prom dress or a pair of cowboy boots.

Marylebone and Bloomsbury

It doesn't get much more British than Marylebone—from the fact that Sherlock Holmes lived here to its mystifying pronunciation (it's Mar-leh-bone). Lush Regent's Park is surrounded by gleaming mansions, Marylebone Lane is lined with pubs, and the side streets are pocketed with clusters of Indian and Middle Eastern restaurants. The neighborhood stretches from Regent's Park south to Oxford St., and from Edgware Rd. east until it bleeds into Bloomsbury. While Marylebone is fun to poke around in, the prominence of fancy residential areas and spiffy office buildings means that good values here are hard to find.

Bloomsbury, on the other hand, is famous for its bohemian heritage. The namesake Bloomsbury Group included luminaries like Virginia Woolf, John Maynard Keynes, and E.M. Forster. Today, you can feel the continuation of all that cleverness emanating from the British Library and University College London—though creeping gentrification means there are few affordable garrets left for the burgeoning artist-intellectuals of today. Bloomsbury, centered on Russell Square, stretches east to King's Cross Rd., and is bounded on the north and south by Euston Rd. and High Holborn, respectively.

North London

Even though the area encompassing North London is only 3-4 miles from the city center, it boasts its very own self-contained Künstlerroman narrative. The hard rocker vibe the area staked its reputation on is now a mere kitschy shadow, but it hasn't yet been completely overrun with tourists searching fruitlessly for the "London Look" of the Stones. As the under-eye wrinkles of the insomniac university student become permanent, she might find herself in the northeast regions of Angel or Islington, which hosts both up-and-coming bankers and the outer regions of the Hackney hipster scene. So what happens when you've paid your dues/sold out? It's time to reward yourself with a several million pound house in Hampstead! While this beautiful, peaceful oasis of stately townhouses and kaleidoscopic gardens had been the residence of hundreds of not-yet-successful literati, it's now more of a "good job, ol' chap" prize for celebrities. Nevertheless, Hampstead's greatest resource—its marvelous heath—comes as freely as lines to Keats.

East London

Isn't it just so ironic that an area that was once a slum is now a completely choice place for artists trying to screw the man (and each other)? But really, the music scene is so authentic—nothing like those horrid megaclubs that are corporate fronts dishing out soma like candy. Did you know that they don't have Urban Outfitters here (except the one they do)? No, it's completely organic, local, microbrewed, ephemeral, a yawning Communist utopia with some of the absolutely best market steals. Fancy a free art gallery? And it's just absolutely brimming with diversity. Lots of immigrants here (even though it's relatively segregated to Brick Ln.--as you go north, it gets more homogenous). Why live anywhere else in a bougie, cloned London when you can thrive in a place that really understands that you're above that? Grab your Nietzsche, your tortoiseshells, your bleeding heart, and enjoy East London. If that's your sort of thing.

South London

South London has long been maligned as one of London's dodgier neighborhoods. While the area has enjoyed something of a renaissance in recent years, it's still not as safe as much of central London. Clapham is a good place to find pubs and restaurants full of young professionals. Clapham has also become a cultural hub as the home of the Battersea Arts Centre, renowned for its groundbreaking productions. Brixton is less quaint, but a bit more fun. Bible-thumpers preach the Apocalypse from convenience store pulpits, and purveyors of goods set up shop at the nearby Afro-Caribbean market, despite the overpowering smell of fish. Brixton is the place to come if you've started missing fast food, though some truly excellent restaurants peek out from between the fried-chicken stands. At night, it's a popular place to hear underground DJs and live reggae shows. The local Underground stations across the south of the city play classical music, thought by many to be a tactic for keeping young people from accumulating in the Tube, Clockwork Orange-style.

West London

West London is one of the most shape-shifting parts of the city. Shepherd's Bush is a hub of ethnic life, evident in the varied restaurants lining Goldhawk Rd., culminating in the veritable World's Fair of Shepherd's Bush Market. Shepherd's Bush is also home to Westfield's, a 43-acre ode to consumerism that makes American strip malls look like rinky-dink corner stores. Hammersmith, the neighborhood to the south of Shepherd's Bush, is quieter and more gentrified. It feels more like a seaside resort than London—once you get out of the thriving area surrounding the Tube station, that is. Farther south and west are Kew and Richmond, which have the luscious greenery of Kew Gardens and Hampton Court, two easily accessible places to escape the urban jungle.

SUGGESTED ITINERARIES

Cheap Date

Here's how to have an inexpensive, but romantic, night out in London.

- **Hampstead Heath.** Take a relaxing stroll through Hampstead Heath's 800 acres. You could easily pretend it's a walk in the English countryside. Then, climb Parliament Hill for one of the best views of the city.

- **Le Mercury.** Head to nearby Le Mercury for an incredible French meal. Impress your date with your intimate knowledge of the city's best eats at the best prices.

- **Blues, Booze, and Borderline.** Head to the West End then hit up the "best blues bar this side of the Atlantic" at Ain't Nothin' But, which has live music every night of the week (and £3.50 beer). If you need a beat to seal the deal, hit the dance floor at The Borderline.

How to Spend a Very British London Sunday

To have an authentically British Sunday, you should start off with a gray sky and a temperature around 50º F (or, if you want to be really British, 10º C). Ideally it will be drizzling, then raining harder and harder as the day goes on. Though it's possible to continue this very British Sunday without the appropriate weather, you may feel like an imposter.

- **Portobello Road.** Take the bus to Notting Hill. Walk down Portobello Rd. looking at the vintage stores and antiques markets. The narrow sidewalks and British manners will

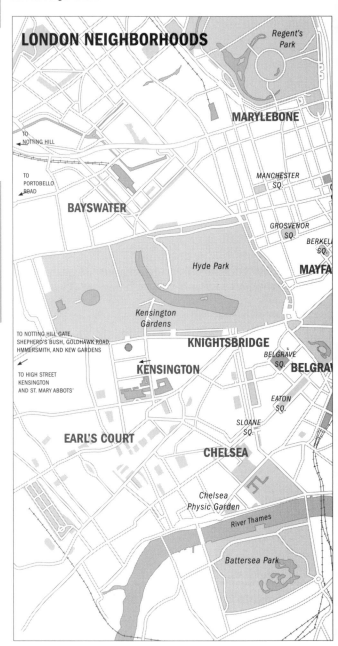

LONDON NEIGHBORHOODS

Regent's Park

MARYLEBONE

TO NOTTING HILL

TO PORTOBELLO ROAD

BAYSWATER

MANCHESTER SQ.

GROSVENOR SQ.

BERKEL SQ.

Hyde Park

MAYFA

Kensington Gardens

TO NOTTING HILL GATE, SHEPHERD'S BUSH, GOLDHAWK ROAD, HMMERSMITH, AND KEW GARDENS

KNIGHTSBRIDGE

BELGRAVE SQ.

BELGRA

TO HIGH STREET KENSINGTON AND ST. MARY ABBOTS'

KENSINGTON

EATON SQ.

SLOANE SQ.

EARL'S COURT

CHELSEA

Chelsea Physic Garden

River Thames

Battersea Park

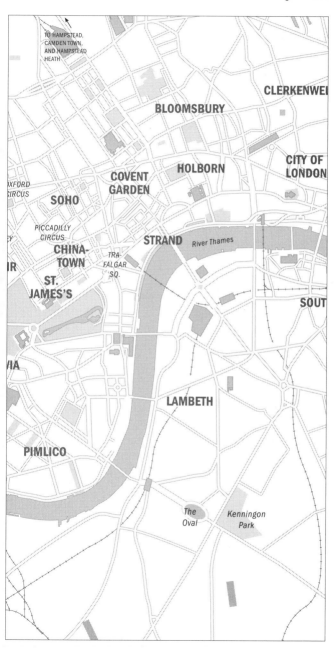

TO HAMPSTEAD, CAMDEN TOWN, AND HAMPSTEAD HEATH

CLERKENWEL

BLOOMSBURY

HOLBORN

CITY OF LONDON

OXFORD CIRCUS

COVENT GARDEN

SOHO

PICCADILLY CIRCUS

STRAND

River Thames

CHINA-TOWN

TRA-FALGAR SQ.

ST. JAMES'S

SOUT

IR

IA

LAMBETH

PIMLICO

The Oval

Kennington Park

mean that every time you encounter another person with an umbrella, an awkward dance of "oh you pass first," "no, you go ahead" will ensue.

- **Sunday Roast.** Consume a Sunday Roast at a cozy pub. Let's Go likes the slightly quirky take offered at Coach and Horses in the City of London. Learn to love the mushy vegetables like a real Brit.

- **Museum.** As the rain picks up, head inside one of London's many free museums. Feel properly imperial at the British Museum, get cozy with Shakespeare at the British Library, or see the men and women who built the country at The National Portrait Gallery.

- **Tea and the BBC.** Head back to your hostel, make yourself a cup of tea, and curl up with a book or the BBC. You're not going out tonight, because the rain is still thundering down. Everything's closed anyway.

A Three-Day Weekend in London

Day One

- **Head to Bloomsbury** for two of London's best sights. The British Museum exhibits the spoils of hundreds of years of empire, including such famous pieces as the Rosetta Stone and the Elgin Marbles. Don't miss it. Have yourself an exceedingly English lunch at Newman Arms. Just 15min. away is the British Library, where you can see everything from the Magna Carta and Shakespeare's First Folio to Beethoven's tuning fork and the original, handwritten lyrics to "A Hard Day's Night." If you're a Harry Potter fan, King's Cross Station is next door.

- **Take the Tube** into West London, and wander through the veritable World's Fair that is Shepherd's Bush Market for a taste of the city's ethnic diversity. For even more of a taste, head to Sufi for the best Persian food in London.

- **End the night** with a frothy pint on the banks of the Thames at Dove.

Day Two

- **Start your second day** with London's classic sights, clustered around the city's historical core, the City of London. Try stepping inside St Paul's Cathedral without exclaiming the Lord's name in vain. Climb to the top of the dome for an excellent view over the city's rooftops. Stroll through The Temple, an incredible architectural hodgepodge best seen on the labyrinthine paths through the complex. Take a gander at the Tower of London and Tower Bridge, but don't bother paying to go inside.

- **Have some lunch** at Clerkenwell Kitchen or City Càphê, then head down the river toward Westminster. Snap the requisite pictures of Big Ben and the Houses of Parliament, then spend some time admiring the spiritual center of London, Westminster Abbey.

- **Walk through St. James's Park** to Buckingham Palace then cross the river for a dinner at Pie Minster followed by cocktails at The Hide.

- **If you're not already asleep** on your feet, continue on to a blues show at Ain't Nothin' But or dancing at The Borderline, both in the West End.

Day Three

- **The Tate Modern** will make you repeat, yet again, "How can all these incredible museums possibly be free!?"

- **While you're in the neighborhood,** choose whether you're more interested in design or Shakespeare (a tricky decision, we know) and visit either the Museum of Design or Shakespeare's Globe Theatre (if you're here in the summer, try catching a 2:30pm matinee).

- **Continue on to Borough Market** and pick out a picnic lunch from the tangle of gourmet food stands under the old railway viaducts.

- **Make your way to Trafalgar Square** and conclude your museum tour of London with the National Gallery.

- **Get some dinner at Shibuya,** then bid farewell to London with a wild night out at the many excellent clubs in the West End.

Accommodations

To breathe the air of London, you're going to be shelling out more than you would in European capitals on the continent (excepting perhaps Paris). Except for East London's Hoxton, standard hotels are out of the budget range, starting at over £120 per night. Thus, for most travelers, it'll be a merry hostel life where, out of three categories (central location, markedly cheaper prices, and good amenities), you get to pick two. If you're in the city for a few days on a round-the-world tour, Bloomsbury, Paddington, and the South Bank have some good options that aren't that too far away from the main museums. If you're staying longer, West London and North London hostels (especially Palmers Lodge Swiss Cottage) reliably boast facilities like laundries and kitchens. For the light sleeper or introvert, there are a few B&Bs and budget hotels whose rates start around £50 for a single, and if you're traveling in a group, these hotels offer doubles, triples, and quads that go for just a little bit more than hostel rates.

THE CITY OF LONDON

⬜ YHA St Paul's   HOSTEL $

36 Carter Ln.

☎0845 371 9012 www.yha.org.uk

Most hostels play a game called "pick two," with your choices being good location, reasonable price, or killer amenities. Not so with this hostel, which is the former house for the St Paul's choir and, astoundingly, right across the street from the cathedral. Rooms come with ensuite washbasins and large lockers for your ever-accumulating horde of souvenirs; the premise also has laundry, an on-site restaurant, and blackboards thoroughly covered with upcoming events.

▶ *i* ✛St. Paul's. Go right down New Change, turn at the cathedral onto Cannon St., then take a left onto Carter Ln. Wi-Fi available on ground floor £1 per 20min., £5 for 24hr., £9 per week. Breakfast £4.99. Evening meals £6. Laundry facilities available. All dorms single-sex. 6- to 11-bed dorms £22-28; triples, quads, quints, and sextets all around £25 per person. ☼ Reception 24hr.

Fox & Anchor   HOTEL $$$$

115 Charterhouse Sq.

☎0845 347 0100 www.foxandanchor.com

The six rooms on top of this elegant pub are what a Victorian gentleman's bachelor pad must have looked like (admittedly, with more cigars and less flat screen TVs). Larger rooms—the "Superior" ones and the suites—have old-fashioned bathtubs right in the bedroom, and all are done up with luxurious fabrics and beautiful prints of the London skyline. With all the amenities of a luxury option, this hotel caters to more of a professional crowd. However, if you're just in London for the weekend, the rooms are a steal compared to weekday rates.

▶ *i* ✛Barbican. Turn left onto Aldersgate St., left onto Charterhouse St., then right onto Charterhouse Sq. Book at least a few weeks in advance for the weekend. Free Wi-Fi. On weekends, standard fro £117; superior from £140; suites from £188. Weekday rooms £205-280.

THE WEST END

The YHA option is a great deal for those who would rather spend their money on musical revivals and shows featuring Daniel Radcliffe (or the confluence of the two). However, if you're not chained to the idea of staying in Theatreland or couldn't get a hostel room there, consider staying in nearby Bloomsbury or the South Bank.

🏮 YHA Oxford St.   HOSTEL $

14 Noel St.

☎020 7734 1618 www.yha.org.uk

Oxford St. is crammed with enough shopping to easily wipe
out the most robust of accounts, so why spend extra for a room
that you'll merely need to hold your Topshop/Topman bags?
The hostel itself is clean, funkily neon, and limited to four-bed
dorms (so you won't feel like you're in a weird gulag with a 40-
bed quadruple bunk dorm). The staff organizes group events
like Camden pub crawls, and there's a spotless 24hr. kitchen for
your cooking machinations, but most travelers just set off into
the nearby streets for evening revelry and eats.

▶ *i* ⊖Oxford Circus. Turn left down Regent St., then left onto Noel St. Wi-
Fi available in the lounge and some rooms £5 per 24hr., £7.50 per 3 days.
Breakfast included. Book 2 months in advance for the summer. Laundry
available. 4-bed dorms £30-36; doubles £86; triples £117.

Fielding Hotel   HOTEL $$$$

4 Broad Ct.

☎020 7836 8305 www.thefieldinghotel.co.uk

Fielding Hotel is named after novelist Henry Fielding, who
worked next door at Bow St. Magistrate's Court, where Oscar
Wilde and Casanova were both defendants. The rooms' decor is
a cross between a contemporary earthen style (the outside looks
more flowery and continental your usual English hotel) and a
19th-century feel evoked by great gilt mirrors. However, the
boon that the Fielding offers is a great location that is simulta-
neously quiet—a rare find in the city.

▶ *i* ⊖Covent Garden. Turn right onto Long Acre, right onto Drury Ln., and
right onto Broad Ct. Free Wi-Fi. Single £90-100; doubles £140-180, depending on demand.

WESTMINSTER

🏮 Astor Victoria   HOSTEL $

71 Belgrave Rd.

☎020 7834 3077

The pros are a fairly central location (20min. walk from Westminster) and the communal spaces, including kitchen, movie
room, lounge, and a bustling doorstep that marks the Astor Victoria clearly as a hostel in an otherwise quiet, residential area.
The con is that it's an older building that doesn't deal well with
the heat in the summer (fans are provided, though). Otherwise,

dorms are rather spacious, with high ceilings and standard-issue bunk beds and lockers.

▶ *i* ⊖Victoria. Upon exiting the station, turn left onto Buckingham Palace Rd., then left onto Belgrave Rd. Free Wi-Fi. Breakfast included. Female-only dorms available. 4- to 8-bed dorm £20-28; singles £40-45; doubles £80-100.

Victor Hotel   HOTEL $$$$
51 Belgrave Rd.
☎020 7592 9853 www.victorhotel.co.uk

Belgrave Rd. is another London townhouse street with hotel options that generally vary only in logo (Copperplate or Times—take your pick). The Victor Hotel's rooms come about as cheap as you're going to find in this fairly well-off neighborhood, and they have a fresh, comfortable vibe that strikes a contrast with some of the heavier, stuffier options.

▶ *i* ⊖Victoria. Upon exiting the station, turn left onto Buckingham Palace Rd., and left onto Belgrave Rd. Free Wi-Fi. Breakfast included. Singles generally £60-85; doubles £85-150; triples £110-160. Check website for specific dates.

THE SOUTH BANK

▩ St. Christopher's Village   HOSTEL $
165 Borough High St.
☎020 7939 9710 www.st-christophers.co.uk

It takes a village to raise a party, and St. Christopher's is built for that purpose: in-house bar, restaurant, chill-out room, cinema room, condom machines on every floor, and a relatively unadvertised rooftop terrace. However, while some party hostels skimp on space in order to provide more amenities, the dorms are set up with the beds pushed against the walls, leaving the floor open as glorious space.

▶ *i* ⊖London Bridge. Walk down Borough High St. with the bridge at your back. Free Wi-Fi. Breakfast included. Luggage storage included. 4- to 22-bed dorm £12-37; doubles around £80.

Fresh @ The Steam Engine   HOSTEL $
41-42 Cosser St.
☎020 7928 0720 www.bestplaceinns.com

How much more British can it get when you're taking your lodgings above a pub? Especially a pub that looks right out of every rustic country bar scene ever (complete with pool table, older clientele, and jukebox). Granted, the lack of modernity has its downsides: there isn't the spaciness of the Tate Modern, and we're pretty sure that the invention of the triple bunk bed is not one for humanity's posterity. However, said beds are comfy, and the staff is as advertised: fresh.

▶ *i* ⊖Lambeth North. Exit down Kennington Rd. and turn right onto Cosser St. Free Wi-Fi. Breakfast included. 9- and 12-bed dorms in summer M- £20-25, Sa-Su up to £40; fall, winter, and spring M-F £16-18, Sa-Su up to £28.

SOUTH KENSINGTON AND CHELSEA

The ratio of budget to luxury accommodations in this neighborhood are comparable to the Greeks at Thermopylae against the Persians. However, there are a handful of decent options that will leave money over for special exhibitions at the V&A.

▨ Astor Hyde Park   HOSTEL $

191 Queen's Gate

☎020 7581 0103   www.astorhostels.co.uk

Location, location, location. However, that maxim of real estate implies that you'd be ecstatic in a trash heap as long as the post code is good, which would be uncharitable to this grandiose yet friendly hostel in the heart of the museum district. The flagship Astor hostel not only has sky-high ceilings, French windows, glass ceiling domes, and spacious dorms, but it also employs an energetic staff that organizes hostel-wide events like pub quizzes and beer Olympics every night.

▶ *i* ⊖High St. Kensington. Turn right onto Kensington High St., then right onto Queen's Gate. Ages 18-35 only. Free Wi-Fi. Breakfast included. Laundry available. Dorms £22-33; doubles £80-100.

Vicarage Hotel   B&B $$$

10 Vicarage Gate

☎020 7229 4030   www.londonvicaragehotel.com

If only all vicars lived so elegantly! This B&B—as unassuming as 12 Grimmauld Place in the adjacent townhouses—provides a warm and posh experience for visitors. The hotel is all iron metalwork, plush comforters, and gorgeous Victorian gilt. If you're traveling in a group or don't mind a shared bath, an absolute steal for the palace-proximal neighborhood (and a chance at seeing Prince Harry).

▶ *i* ⊖High St. Kensington. Turn right onto Kensington High St. and left onto Kensington Church St., which, perplexingly, turns into Vicarage Gate. Take the 2nd right, which is also named Vicarage Gate. Free Wi-Fi. Breakfast included. Single £65, with bath £110; doubles and twins £110/138; triples £140/180; quads £152/200.

YHA London Holland Park   HOSTEL $
20 Holland Walk
☎020 7937 0748 www.yha.org.uk

I am born. Shortly thereafter, I decide to stay at Holland Park.
Well, Dickens, Byron, and a cadre of literary greats all hung
out at the manor house (which makes up a tripartite compound
that now serves as a hostel proper, along with its "grounds").
The cultural ties can still be heard when opera and classical
music is performed in the park or seen when traipsing through
the fountain-laden gardens. The clean rooms are filled with
Jenga-stacked beds, and a kitchen is available for personal con-
coction as well as serving breakfast and dinner each day.

▶ *i* ⊖High St. Kensington. Turn left onto Kensington High St., then right
down Holland Walk in Holland Park. Look for signs for the hostel. Use night
gate at the rear after 10pm when the park closes. All rooms are single sex.
Laundry available. 1 week max. stay. 12- to 21-bed dorm £16-23.

Aster House   B&B $$$$
3 Sumner Pl.
☎020 7581 5888 www.asterhouse.com

While not exactly "budget" for a student traveler at over £100
per night, it does include the ultimate El Dorado in the city:
air conditioning. That's right. And when it comes down to it,
the amenities go far and beyond most accommodations for the
price: a sumptuous breakfast offering, free TV, free Wi-Fi, free
everything really, and if the Freon isn't enough to cool your hot
love, there's even an ice machine (these things must not be taken
for granted).

▶ *i* ⊖South Kensington. Exit to the right down Old Brompton Rd. and make
a left onto Sumner Pl. Free Wi-Fi. Breakfast included. Singles £125; doubles
£190; superior doubles and suites £235-270.

HYDE PARK TO NOTTING HILL

While hostels and hotels can serve as an oasis from the busier
parts of the city, if Edward Fortyhands is the name of your game,
we would recommend looking elsewhere: neighborhoods have
residential ordinances that crack down on riotous intemperance.

▨ Astor Quest   HOSTEL $
45 Queensborough Terr.
☎020 7229 7782 www.astorhostels.com

This hostel fulfills its name twice: its location is perfect for
tourist quester, as it lies within a 10min. walk of six Tube lines,
and many residents have fulfilled their personal quest to find an

Accommodations

inexpensive, potentially long-term abode. The decor is simple, but the light from the ceiling-high windows glances pleasingly off the candy-red lacquered bunk beds. Breakfast is served with a picture of Sex Pistols' Mssr. Vicious judging you, but the extroverted staff compensates with friendliness in full.

▶ *i* Reception 24hr.

Equity Point Hostel   HOSTEL $$
100-102 Westbourne Terr.
☎020 7087 8001 www.equity-point.com

Along the rows of white houses, a silent challenger to the party hostel appears. Despite its proximity to Paddington Station, this large-yet-intimate hostel lends itself to a quiet night's sleep and a day of relaxation, all facilitated by the bright rainbow-colored common spaces (which include an iridescent lounge downstairs and a loft-style library above the reception) and the warm, classical style of the dorms. And a hostel rarity—all of the dorms have ensuite bathrooms that are cleaned daily.

▶ *i* ⊖Paddington. Make a right onto Praed St. and a right onto Westbourne Terr. Wi-F £5 for 3-day pass. Continental breakfast included. 4- to 8-bed dorms £26-49; doubles £99; triples £120. Prices vary greatly within season; check the website before booking.

The Pavilion   HOTEL $$$
34-36 Sussex Gardens
☎020 7262 0905 www.pavilionhoteluk.com

All you really need to know about the Pavilion is that the most popular room is named "Honky Tonk Afro." Besides Blaxploitation, other rooms have motifs ranging from subtly-themed options like "Rhythm in Blues" to the ornate, jewel-toned "Indian Summer." Several of the rooms were used for a British *Vogue* photo shoot, and the hotel has hosted equally fashionable customers such as Kate Beckinsale and Helena Bonham Carter. Generally, the whole building feels like a psychedelic Victorian townhouse, with intensely colored velvet and stacks of oil paintings in ornate frames, giving the place an unforgettable oeuvre.

▶ *i* ⊖Paddington. Take a left onto Praed St., a right onto London St., then a left onto Sussex Gardens. Continental breakfast included. Small single £69, large £100; doubles £110; triples £130; family rooms (quads) £135. 4% surcharge with credit card.

Hyde Park Hostel   HOSTEL $
2-6 Inverness Terr.
☎020 7727 9163 www.smartbackpackers.com

The location is ideal, the rooms incredibly cheap, and if you're a minor, this is going to be one of your only hostel options in the entire city. If you don't mind teenagers or the 1-week max. stay clause, the simplicity of the dorms is perfect for the cash-strapped traveler passing through the city for a few days.

▶ *i* ⊖Bayswater. Take a right onto Queensway, a left onto Bayswater, and then a left onto Inverness Terr. 16+. 1-week max. stay. Linens included. 4- to 24-bed dorm £10-26. ⏰ Reception 24hr.

Garden Court Hotel   HOTEL $$$
30/31 Kensington Gardens Sq.
☎020 7229 2553 www.gardencourthotel.co.uk

If you're in London in the earlier part of the week for a brief visit, Garden Court is a tasteful deal for an Eden-like stay at blasphemously low prices (and as opposed to some hostels, here you'll never have to convince yourself that the mind can make a heaven or a hell of itself). The recently refurbished rooms have an aurora, nature-inspired theme of flowers that leaves your mind in a country B&B mindset even though you're quite intimately linked to the city.

▶ *i* ⊖Bayswater. Turn left onto Queensway, left onto Porchester Gardens, and right onto Kensington Gardens Sq. Free Wi-Fi. Breakfast included. Singles fro £50-90, with bath around £75; doubles £69-145; triples £125-150; family rooms £175.

The Admiral Hotel   HOTEL $$$
143 Sussex Gardens
☎020 7723 7309 www.admiral-hotel.com

Sussex Gardens is code for an impenetrable phalanx of hotels, and yet the Admiral sticks out for its blend between ultra-modern Japanese style and damask-loving, old-fashioned Britain. The rooms are well-lit and not oppressive; many of the bathrooms boast sleek designs, and the restaurant is a comfortable haven of guests munching happily on their baked beans and sausage.

▶ *i* ⊖Paddington. Left onto Praed St., right onto London St., left onto Sussex Gardens. Free Wi-Fi. Breakfast included. Single £52-80; doubles £80-120; triples £85-130; quads £110. Prices vary according to season and time of week; check website for specifics. Book 2 weeks in advance to be safe.

Bowden Court   HOSTEL $
24 Ladbroke Rd.
☎020 7727 5665 www.lhalondon.com

Primarily, people use Bowden Court as a temporary home while looking for a flat in the city. The weekly rates are about as cheap as you're going to find in the area (and include a membership to the on-site gym), but if you're looking for a group of friends to have splendid adventures with, you're probably going to find neither touristy nor pub-crawling types.

Accommodations

▶ *i* ⊖Notting Hill Gate. Exit north, take a right onto Pembridge Rd., and turn left onto Ladbroke Rd. Breakfast and dinner included, though serving hours are limited. Lockers and laundry facilities available. 2- to 3-bed dorm £27.50-30.50; singles £32.50. Weekly dorms £125-155 per week; singles £194. Min. 2-week stay for weekly rates to apply.

MARYLEBONE AND BLOOMSBURY

🗞 Clink78   HOSTEL $

78 King's Cross Rd.

☎020 7183 9400 www.clinkhostels.com

Two hundred years ago, Clink78's building was a disciplinary citadel of prison cells and courtrooms. Repurposed as a mega-hostel five years ago, it remains a living representation of why repeat offenders commit crimes to go back behind bars: every want and need is met with ease. The publicly intoxicated will love the Clashbar, a lovably dark affair named as such because The Clash stood trial at this courthouse for shooting a prize pigeon. Those prone to larceny will delight in the Wi-Fi—a complete steal for the hostel scene.

▶ *i* Reception 24hr.

Astors Museum Hostel   HOSTEL $

27 Montague St.

☎020 7580 5360 www.astorhostels.com

Astors Museum is the complete opposite of its namesake. While the Museum is filled with rambunctious school groups and chattering tours, the spacious dorms are quiet and calming. The sheer opulence and fussiness of millennia-old china is contrasted with clean, minimalist dorms that don't try to pack in as many beds as a WWII infirmary. And most importantly, while the guides in the British Museum wander around and try not to make eye contact, the staff of Astors is inviting and lives on site.

▶ *i* Reception 24hr.

Generator Hostel   HOSTEL $

37 Tavistock Pl.

☎020 7388 7666 www.generatorhostels.com

In the 90s, Generator catered to the party hostel scene with industrial decor and enough Jägermeister to fell a large elephant. Now, the mega-hostel has renovated itself and now embraces a calmer, more soothing image, with less neon and more Swedish modern style. Granted, it still has the amenities necessary for a small town, including a bar, travel shop, and lockers. However, the naturally quiet alcove off Tavistock Pl. where it stands makes the separation between sleep and play attainable.

▸ *i* Bar open 6pm-2am or later. Happy hour 6-9pm.

The George   HOTEL $$$
58-60 Cartwright Gardens
☎020 7387 8777 www.georgehotel.com

At three in the morning—when the door to the hostel dorm slams and your drunk bunkmate seems to be terminally burrowing into their covers—you'll crave womb-like privacy. Along with an included full English breakfast, the rooms have some creature comforts that exceed those of other hotels ofits price (thick duvets, high ceilings on the lower floors, stylish decor).

▸ *i* ⊖Russell Sq. Right across from the station is the entrance to Marchmont St. Continue for 5min. and turn left onto Cartwright Gardens. Call ahead for 1st fl. room. All rooms have a TV and safe. Discounts for 5 days or more. Single £65, with bath £90; doubles £90/115; triples £105/135; quads £125.

NORTH LONDON

🖼 Palmer's Lodge Swiss Cottage   HOSTEL $
40 College Crescent
☎020 7483 8470 www.palmerslodge.co.uk

"Swiss Cottage" implies that this hostel is some sort of alpine timeshare when really it's just the name of the nearest Tube station. But if Tube names were deterministic and there was an Angel in Islington or an Earl in a court, we'd recommend "Manor House" for this palatial, *X-Men*-style mansion that also happens to be a hostel. The set-up is bunks of dark-stained wood, with trunks underneath for storage, and bathrooms that are the cleanest we've seen in the London hostel gamut.

i ⊖Swiss Cottage. Take exit 2 from the station, turn left onto Eton Ave., then right onto College Crescent. Free Wi-Fi. Breakfast included. 18+. 4- to 28-bed dorm £18-37; doubles from £70.

St. Christopher's Camden   HOSTEL $
50 Camden High St.
☎020 7388 1012 www.st-christophers.co.uk

Camden Town is the setting of such cult portrayals of squalor and drinking lighter fluid as seen in *Withnail and I.* Nevertheless, in the 21st century, this area has moved away from a gritty arts scene and more toward friendly pub crawls, which the neighborhood is now known for. Therefore, if you're in the city for pleasure of the bitter variety, this St. Christopher's outpost offers both a good value and good atmosphere, with an in-house bar and guests who aren't wallflowers. As with most party hostels, the rooms have metal bunks with little other decoration, but each dorm includes an ensuite bathroom.

▶ *i* ⊖Camden Town. Turn left onto ⊖Camden High St. (walking away from the market). Free Wi-Fi. Breakfast included. 6- to 10-bed dorm £22-29.

EAST LONDON

▨ The Hoxton
HOTEL $$$

81 Great Eastern St.

☎020 7550 1000 www.hoxtonhotels.com

This taste of Shoreditch has eight specially demarcated "concept" rooms with modern and classic themes, but really, the whole set of 200 rooms is one large concept hotel for a yupster (yuppie + hipster) East End scene. Fast, free Wi-Fi for your Tumblr, fluffy duvets for your Byronic languor, a paper bag that you checkmark at night and is filled with breakfast in the morning, a mini-fridge for your absinthe—this list goes on. The biggest sell is that each night, five rooms go up for only £1, so call early if you know your travel dates.

▶ *i* ⊖Old St. Veer right at the roundabout, go down ⊖Old St., then turn right onto Great Eastern St. Free Wi-Fi. Breakfast included. 1hr. of free international landline calls per day. Room £59-199, depending on when you book.

Queen Mary University Campus Accommodations
DORM $

Mile End Rd.

☎020 7882 8177 www.accommodation.qmul.ac.uk

If you're eager to return to the comforting, IKEA-sponsored feng shui of "dorm room" or are going to be in the city for more than a few weeks, this is a solid option. In the space between the spring and fall terms, this East London university opens its rooms, all of which are arranged in six- to nine-person flats with access to a communal kitchen and living room. The flats are then arranged in a "student village," with laundry and other facilities that can be a headache to guarantee in a hostel. It is a bit far out but the great Tube location means you'll be in the city in less than 30min.

▶ *i* ⊖Mile End. Turn left down Mile End Rd. The campus is across the canal, on the right. The accommodations office is at point 4 on the campus map, on the main road. Breakfast included with B&B prices. Flats cleaned weekly during longer stays. B&B single £51-56; twins £72-77; weekly singles £182, with bath £203. Credit card only.

SOUTH LONDON

Journeys London Bridge Hostel   HOSTEL $

204 Manor Pl.

☎020 7735 6581 www.visitjourneys.com

South London is a budget area with surprisingly few accommodations, so Journeys is your only option for the neighborhood. It's close to the Tube, cheaper than a nice meal out, and has a kitchen open around meal times. The downsides are triple bunk beds and a dark color scheme that makes the rooms seem smaller than they are. Thankfully, privacy curtains make certain someone doesn't take a visual journey into your bunk.

▸ *i* ⊖Kennington. Make a left onto Braganza St., then a left onto Manor Pl. Female-only dorms available. 9- to 15-bed dorm £14-18; +£5 on weekends.

WEST LONDON

The Monkeys in the Trees   HOSTEL $

49 Becklow Rd.

☎020 8749 9197 www.monkeysinthetrees.co.uk

The London hostel scene is populated with flat-hunters, weekenders from the continent, and long-haul tourists (re: Australians on walkabout). The Monkeys in the Trees tends to attract more of the long-term sort and thus avoids the depersonalized revolving door feel of some of the hostels closer to the city center; conversations between residents are struck up friendly and easily. The dorms are serviceable, and the facilities include a downstairs bar that is at once comfy and classy.

▸ *i* ⊖Shepherd's Bush Market. Cross Uxbridge Rd. and make a right, then a left onto Becklow Rd. It's about a 15min. walk. Alternatively, take bus #207 or 260 to Galloway Rd. Free luggage storage. Dorms £13-20.

St. Christopher's Hammersmith   HOSTEL $

28 Hammersmith Broadway

☎020 8748 5285 www.st-christophers.co.uk

St. Christopher's recipe of in-house bar and prime location is exemplified at the Hammersmith branch. The place is right on top of the Tube station, and the bar is packed with residents and locals alike. If you're craving to get into the city, then you're looking at less than a 15min. sojourn on the Underground, but if you decide to stay in, you can enjoy the pleasant combination of elegant fireplaces, high ceilings, and modern bathrooms.

▸ *i* ⊖Hammersmith. Right above Tube entrance on Hammersmith Broadway. Female-only dorms available. Dorms £16-24; £5 more on weekends.

Accommodations

Sights

It's a known secret that while Americans coo over Kate Middleton's baby and tsk over the antics of Prince Harry, the Brits keep the royal family around as a tourist trap (and their palaces and residences are going to be the most expensive sights). It's definitely working: tourism accounts for about 8% of the UK's GDP. It's not that *everything* in London costs loads of money. In fact, many of the most famous historical and artistic sites—like The British Museum, National Gallery, National Portrait Gallery, Victoria & Albert, and Tate Modern—are free. Also, for St. Paul's Cathedral and Westminster Abbey, you can avoid the £16 ticket and visit during their Evensong services. However, the most overlooked set of free sights in the city is the lava game of parks and gardens that blanket London. We recommend Hampstead Heath whole-heartedly, as well as St. James's Park. Regent's and Hyde Park are more frequently traveled and provide a nice afternoon out, but the wilder heath types play up more of the Albion spirit that converts most non-Brits to Anglophilia. In terms of ticketed attractions, avoid the London Eye, the Tower of London, and Madame Tussaud's. Instead, if you're on budget, take the Tube out to Hampton Court or Kew Royal Gardens.

THE CITY OF LONDON

The only first tier sight here is St. Paul's. However, if you have a bit more time, the Museum of London and Tower Bridge are safe bets even if you're not particularly interested in history.

🖌 Saint Paul's Cathedral   CHURCH

St. Paul's Churchyard
☎020 7246 8350 www.stpauls.co.uk

⊠The upper levels of the cathedral are open to the hearty and hale. This means you'll be climbing enough stairs to practically ascend to heaven yourself. Two hundred and fifty-one steps up is the acoustically marvelous **Whispering Gallery,** where you can hear someone whisper to you from 32m opposite. For 119 steps more you can visit the outdoor Stone Gallery, then another climb will take you to the pinnacle Golden Gallery, which provides exquisite views of the city (although smokers and otherwise respiratorily-challenged visitors can zoom through the same views on the free video tour).

▶ *i* ⊖St. Paul's. Signs outside the station lead you to the cathedral. 1½hr. free guided tours are offered at 10am, 11am, 1pm, and 2pm. Briefer introductory tours run throughout the day. A handheld multimedia tour is included in the price of admission. £16, concessions £14, children £7. £1.50 discount if you book online. ② Open M-Sa 8:30am-4pm (last ticket sold). You can get in for free (though you'll have limited access) during church services. Matins M-Sa 7:30am. Eucharist M-Sa 8am and 12:30pm; Su 8am, 11am, and 6pm. Evensong M-Sa 5pm, Su 3:15pm. Free organ recitals Su 4:45-5:15pm. Service times subject to change; check the website or the signs outside the cathedral.

🖌 The Temple   HISTORICAL SITE

Between Essex St. and Temple Ave.
☎020 7427 4820

When Shakespeare gave the line "Let's kill all the lawyers" to an insurgent in *King Henry VI*, the Bard meant corrupt hooligans, not the upstanding barristers of The Temple, who premiered **Twelfth Night** for him here in 1602. We can sense your confusion: isn't this a church? Well, yes. The whole stunning complex of medieval, Elizabethan, and Victorian buildings was first established by the Knights Templar in 1185 as the English seat for the order (and catapulted into stardom by *The Da Vinci Code*). After the crusades proved a bit of a lost cause, The Temple stopped crusading for those who wore suits of armor and became the HQ for those who brought suits instead. Now, the site is devoted to two of London's Inns of Court, which are the location of legal offices and training grounds for baby lawyers. The gardens, medieval church, and Middle Temple Hall are occasionally open to the public. Middle Temple Hall is an excellent example of Elizabethan architecture, with its beautiful double hammer beam roof. The large gardens are perfectly manicured with lush shrubberies and provide a handy dell for a spot of quiet reflection.

▶ *i* ⊖ Temple. Go to the Victoria Embankment, turn left, and turn left again onto Temple Ln. Book 1hr. tours in advance. You can book to stay for lunch if you're appropriately dressed. Church admissio £4. Services Oct-Jul Su 11:15am. Organ recitals W 1:15-1:45pm. Tours Oct-Jul Tu-F 11am. 🕐 Middle Temple Hall open M-F 10am-noon and 3-4pm, except when in use. Hours for church vary, but are posted

🖿 Museum of London   MUSEUM

150 London Wall

☎020 7001 9844 www.museumoflondon.org.uk

The Museum of London is an incredibly thorough archeological and sociological survey of the city from its Celtic pre-history to its melting pot present. Some of the highlights include a gargantuan 19th-century map of the city, color-coded by class (including "criminal"), and the ruins of the original Roman wall that ran below the site of the present museum. Even if you're a modernist and don't enjoy the historical navel-gazing at which Brits excel, the end of the museum has a fascinating touchscreen projector that surveys problems the city will face in the future (like population growth, carbon emissions, and NHS solvency).

▶ *i* ⊖ St. Paul's. Go up St. Martins and Aldersgate. Free. 🕐 Open M-F 10am-6pm. 45min. tours at 11am, noon, 3pm, and 4pm.

🖿 Courtauld Gallery   MUSEUM

Somerset House, Strand

☎020 7872 0220 www.courtauld.ac.uk

Back in the '50s, when red was the new black, a fondness for Marx was quite commonplace in the academic sphere. Thus, infamous **KGB** double agent Anthony Blunt (spy code name: "Tony." Seriously.) served as director of this gallery for nearly 30 years despite suspicions of defection. Housed as part of the palatial Somerset House, the collection includes medieval and Renaissance art from the likes of Botticelli and Rubens—but it's most renowned for its delightful Impressionist and Post-Impressionist collection, featuring paintings by Degas, Monet, Manet (including **A Bar at the Folies-Bergère**), Seurat, and van Gogh.

▶ *i* ⊖ Temple. Turn right onto Temple Pl., left onto Arundel St., then left onto Strand £6; concessions £5, £3 on M. 🕐 Open daily 10am-6pm.

Tower Bridge   BRIDGE

Tower Bridge
☎020 7403 3761 www.towerbridge.org.uk

While the Golden Gate is the one that usually gets knocked down in apocalyptic films, Tower Bridge has its own history of action film moves, as when a bus driver not only minded the gap but sailed his passengers over it when the bridge began to rise without warning. Compared to London Bridge, Tower Bridge definitely wins on the aesthetic front (unless we're counting children's nursery rhymes). The exhibition you can pay to get into is enjoyable and runs through anecdotes and the history of the bridge's construction. Still, this might not be for those afraid of heights. On the whole, it's less of a tourist trap than the Tower of London, though you can skip the ticket price and just enjoy its stunning architecture for free.

▶ *i* ⊖Tower Hill. Follow signs to Tower Bridge £8, concessions £5.60, ages 5-15 £3.40, under 5 free. ⏲ Open daily Apr-Sept 10am-6:30pm; Oct-Mar 9:30am-6pm. Last entry 1hr. before close.

THE WEST END

Between the theater performances, comedy acts, and street performers, the West End is a prime place to spend the evenings. However, the day options are not too shabby themselves and include some of London's best museums.

▨ The National Gallery   MUSEUM

Trafalgar Sq.
☎020 7747 2885 www.nationalgallery.org.uk

When they say "National Gallery," it's not just code for "country's coolest collection." Really, the "National" stands for a distillation of British aesthetics and the "Gallery" means really famous art. Accordingly, you have the stunning slate of van Goghs (including *Sunflowers*) and Rubens. And then you have what seems like every painting of the Thames in existence. There's a gorgeous collection of Monet and Manet, and then you have Turner's 1001 ways to draw a naval fleet (the painting that Ben Whishaw and Daniel Craig discuss in *Skyfall* is indeed housed here). That's not to say that highbrow art and British sensibility never mix, but rather that aestheticians and Anglophiles alike will enjoy the expansive hall. The best way to explore is to buy a map £1) and pick and choose which rooms you want to peruse. For the undecided, we recommend the Dutch room and most of the **Sainsbury** wing, which includes some great examples of medieval art.

▶ *i* ⊖Charing Cross. Free. Special exhibits aroun £10. Audio tours £3.50, students £2.50. 1hr. guided tours daily at 11:30am and 2:30pm;

meet at Sainsbury Wing info desk. 10min. talks on individual paintings Tu 4pm. ⟨ℚ⟩ Open M-Th 10am-6pm, F 10am-9pm, Sa-Su 10am-6pm.

🖾 National Portrait Gallery   MUSEUM
St. Martin's Pl.
☎020 7306 0055 www.npg.org.uk

▶ Allow us to draw a comparison: the National Portrait Gallery is the Platonic ideal of Facebook. Everyone picks a flattering or interesting image (with the exception of Kate Middleton, whose portrait is merely creepy). You put it in one space that's easily accessible and free, there's no advertising, and you don't have to listen to said person's political opinions. It's just the faces of those you recognize, love, and love-to-hate. The NPG starts at sculptures of Tudor kings and works its way up to modern-day Last Supper parodies (news alert: Dame Judi Dench is immaculate not only in concept) and some definitely non-traditional representations of figures like Stephen Fry and Germaine Greer. Starting from the beginning of the collection, the early subjects are only royalty until the 1600s, when portraits of artistic figures such as Shakespeare and Milton are included as well. The larger political tableaus, such as Copley's *The Death of the Earl of Chatham,* are fascinating depictions of political bodies, but the most interesting is the 20th-century section—filled with images of Thatcher, McCartney, and Princess Diana—where familiarity intersects with a break from red-cheeked men in coiled wigs.

▶ *i* ⊖Charing Cross. Walk down Strand to Trafalgar Sq. and turn right. Free. Small special exhibit £6, large exhibits £12. Audio tours £3. ⟨ℚ⟩ Open M-W 10am-6pm, Th-F 10am-9pm, Sa-Su 10am-6pm. Open until 10pm on select nights; check website for details.

Trafalgar Square   HISTORICAL SITE
The Thames is a snottish brown, London puddles are murky pitch, and the Trafalgar fountain is as aquamarine as a cruise ship pool. Welcome to one of the world's most famous plazas, flanked by memorials to art, war, and God. From the designer of the Houses of Parliament, Charles Barry (this should be read in a deep movie announcer voice), Trafalgar Square commemorates **Admiral Horatio Nelson.** A sandstone statue of the military hero atop his eponymous column looks out toward the Thames to protect the English from the French/Germans/Russians/Immigrants, depending on the political flavor of the times. The **National Gallery** stands to the north of the square, and the surrounding perimeter is lined with various embassies and consulates. The sprawling center area serves as a meeting point, demonstration area, and the home of an annual Christmas tree (donated by Norway in thanks for service given in World War II, and we think to say "sorry" for Quisling).

Pinch-hitting for God is **St Martin-in-the-Fields,** whose spires peek out at the edge of the plaza.

▶ *i* ⊖Charing Cross.

St Martin-in-the-Fields   CHURCH

Trafalgar Sq.

☎020 7766 1100 www.smitf.org

Exhibiting the logic of "Look something pretty!", King Henry VIII significantly renovated the medieval version of this church to keep plague victims away from his palace. The strategy still works on tourists today, who visit for the Cafe in the Crypt and the concerts instead going to pray that things don't fall off. St Martin's is also the parish church of the royal family, but it's better known for its great musical tradition. Every Monday, Tuesday, and Friday at 1pm, the church holds a 45min."lunch-time concert," a classical recital from students at musical academies and colleges. In the evening, professional artists run the gamut of Mozart to modern works in the beautiful (for a Protestant church) space.

▶ *i* ⊖Charing Cross. It's on the east side of Trafalgar Sq. Jazz concerts W 8pm. Free. Lunchtime concerts £3.50 suggested donation. Reserved ticket for jazz £12, unreserved £9. ⏰ Open M-Tu 8:30am-1pm and 2-6pm, W 8:30am-1:15pm and 2-5pm, Th 8:30am-1:15pm and 2-6pm, F 8:30am-1pm and 2-6pm, Sa 9:30am-6pm, Su 3:30-5pm. Open at other times for services and concerts.

Institute of Contemporary Arts (ICA)   GALLERY

The Mall

☎020 7930 3647 www.ica.org.uk

Tradition: the Union Jack signal for "The Queen is here, look busy" waving in the breeze of the Thames, and the ICA messing it all up with its new-fangled notions of art. Because of its location smack dab in the middle of monuments to the status quo, it does occupy an uncomfortable space that the Whitechapel Gallery doesn't (because postal code or Tate Modern can combat with sheer Pollock and Rothko firepower). But that aside, the ICA is actually a neat, free treatment of some cutting-edge art. The cinema (not free) shows independent and world cinema with director Q and As and some live music gigs. Art exhibits include film, drawing, performance art, and sculpture.

▶ *i* ⊖Charing Cross. Turn left down Strand, go under the arch and continue down the Mall. The ICA is on the right. Exhibits rotate every 6-7 weeks. Free. Cinem £10, concessions £8. Film screenings usually after 6pm, with Sa and Su matinees. ⏰ Open Tu-Su 11am-11pm. Galleries open Tu-W noon-7pm, Th noon-9pm, F-Su noon-7pm.

WESTMINSTER

◪ Westminster Abbey   ABBEY, HISTORIC SITE
Off Parliament Sq.
☎020 7222 5152 www.westminster-abbey.org

No matter how maudlin the foundation, the church's day-to-day work is for the living, and it it is still primarily a functioning house of worship. Nearly all important British church ceremonies take place here—including William and Kate's wedding—with the notable exception of Diana and Charles's marriage, which took place in **St. Paul's** (p. 35). *Let's Go* almost automatically recommends attending a free service for touristy, ticketed cathedrals, but even if you pay admission, we recommend coming back for Evensong regardless. Seeing the Abbey in action with the accompanying sound of the choir is an experience you won't soon forget.

▶ *i* ↻Westminster. Walk away from the river. Parliament Sq. and the Abbey are on the left. The Abbey vergers offer 90min. tours £18, students and seniors £15, ages 11-18 £8. Verger-led tours £3. ☼ Admission M-Tu 9:30am-4:30pm, W 9:30am-7pm, Th-F 9:30am-4:30pm, Sa 9:30am-2:30pm. Last entry 1hr. before close. Verger-led tours M-F 10am, 10:30am, 11am, 2pm, and 2:30pm; Sa 10am, 10:30am, and 11am. Services: M-F Matins 7:30am, Holy Communion 8am and 12:30pm, choral Evensong 5pm (spoken on W); Sa 8am morning prayer, 9am Holy Communion, 3pm choral Evensong (5pm Jun-Sept); Su 8am Holy Communion, 10am choral Matins, 11:15am sung Eucharist, 3pm choral Evensong, 5:45pm organ recital, 6:30pm evening prayer.

◪ Churchill Museum and Cabinet War Rooms   MUSEUM
Clive Steps, King Charles St.
☎020 7930 6961 www.iwm.org.uk/cabinet

Winston Churchill is all things to all Britons: courageous prime minister, fearless leader, vivacious wit, amateur painter, not Neville Chamberlain. Really, he was a geopolitical Renaissance man. Britain doesn't produce that many multitaskers, and so what did they do to preserve and protect their best? Stick him underground in a bunker that oozes trapped anxiety from its windowless walls like a haunted house. Opened in 1939 a few days before the beginning of the long winter for Poland and France, the Cabinet War Rooms were used as a shelter for important government officers, and Churchill spent six years pacing around the map room, whose lights still burn brightly. Connected to the Cabinet War Rooms is the Churchill Museum. Visitors can step on sensors to hear excerpts from some of his most famous speeches and watch videos detailing the highs and lows of his career. Also on display are his alcoholic habits, which included drinks with every meal, and his signature

Sights

"romper," better known as a onesie. The interactive, touchscreen "lifeline" is phenomenally detailed; be sure to touch his 90th birthday and August 6th, 1945, but be prepared to draw stares from the other museum patrons. The memorialization grows a bit absurd: there's a lock of his hair on display, the possession of which is generally a universal sign for "stalker."

▶ *i* ⊖Westminster. Turn right onto Parliament St. and left onto King Charles St £15.45, students and seniors £12.35 (without voluntary donation), under 16 free. ⏰ Open daily 9:30am-6pm. Last entry 5pm.

Houses of Parliament   HISTORIC SITE
Westminster Palace
☎ www.parliament.uk

There are a number of ways members of the public can visit the Houses of Parliament. Debates in both Houses are generally open to the public; visitors can queue for admission during sitting times, though entrance is not guaranteed. Nor is it guaranteed that anything interesting will be going on—we recommend checking the website to see what bills are on the table. Prime Minister's Questions is a rowdy back and forth stand-up comedy session between the PM and the Shadow Chancellor, though tickets may only be reserved by UK residents, and foreign visitors can only take the rare leftover spaces. Finally, tours of the Houses are given throughout the year, but foreign visitors can only attend on Saturdays and during the Summer Recess (Aug and Sept).

▶ *i* ⊖Westminster. The public entrance is at Cromwell Green, on St. Margaret St., directly across from Westminster Abbey. Debates and committee sessions free. Tour £16.50, concessions £14, children £7. ⏰ When Parliament is in session, House of Commons open M 2:30-10:30pm, Tu 11:30am-10:30pm, W 11:30am-7:30pm, Th 9:30am-6:30pm, sometimes F 9:30am-3pm; House of Lords open M-Tu 2:30-10pm, W 3-10pm, Th 11am-7:30pm, sometimes F 10am-close of business. Tours leave every 15min. Aug M 1:15-5:30pm, Tu-F 9:15am-4:30pm; Sept Tu-F 9:15am-4:30pm; Oct-Jul Sa 9:15am-4:30pm (for UK residents).

Buckingham Palace   PALACE, MUSEUM, HISTORIC SITE
The Mall
☎020 7766 7300 www.royalcollection.org.uk

The interior of the palace is, for the most part, closed to the public—we can't imagine the Queen would be pleased with plebes tramping into her private chambers. From late July to early October, though, the royals head to Balmoral, and the **State Rooms** are opened to the public. As befits their status, the rooms feature fine porcelain, furniture, paintings, and sculptures by famous artists like Rembrandt and Rubens. In addition to the permanent pieces, the rooms often exhibit treasures from the Royal Collection—jewels, Fabergé eggs, and Kate Middleton's wedding dress. The **Royal Mews,** open most

Sights

of the year, functions as a museum, stable, riding school, and a working carriage house. The carriages are fantastic—especially the "Glass Coach," which carries royal brides to their weddings, and the four-ton Gold State Coach. Unfortunately, the magic pumpkin carriage used to escape from evil step-royals is only visible after midnight, but if you're in the Royal Mews when the clock strikes 12am, you have other problems (namely, how to scale the layers of barbed wire that surround the palace). Finally, the **Queen's Gallery** is dedicated to temporary exhibitions of jaw-droppingly valuable items from the Royal Collection. Five rooms designed to look like the interior of the palace are filled with glorious artifacts that the Queen holds in trust for the nation. They feature everything from Dutch landscape paintings to photographs of Antarctic expeditions to Leonardo da Vinci's anatomical drawings.

▶ *i* ⊖Victoria. Turn right onto Buckingham Palace Rd. and follow it to Buckingham Gate. Audio tour provided for State Rooms. State Room £19, students and seniors £17.50, ages 5-16 £10.85, under 5 free; Royal Mews £8.50/7.75/5.30; Queen's Gallery £9.50/8.75/4.80; combined ticket to Royal Mews and Queen's Gallery £16.25/14.90/9.10; Royal Day Out ticket (access to all 3) £33.25/30.50/18.85. ⏰ State Rooms open late Jul-Oct daily 9:30am-6:30pm. Last entry 4:15pm. Royal Mews open Apr-Oct daily 10am-5pm; Nov-Dec 22 daily 10am-4pm; Feb-Mar M-Sa 10am-4pm. Last entry 45min. before close. Queen's Gallery open daily 10am-5:30pm. Last entry 4:30pm.

St. James's Park
PARK

The Mall

While **Regent's Park** played host to the domestic intrigue of MI5, St. James's was where Russian and British MI6 spies came to "feed the ducks." Hyde Park is a bit tamer than this beautiful glen, which sort of a cross between a heath and a scene from Bambi. But even during the summer months, you can still find a quiet out-of-the-way spot to picnic, as tourists tend to skip straight from Buckingham to Green Park and leave the waterfowl in peace.

▶ *i* ⊖St. James's Park. Turn left off Tothill St. onto Broadway. Follow it until you hit the park. Free. ⏰ Open daily 5am-midnight.

THE SOUTH BANK

The Globe Theatre of Shakespeare's day was not the fun, middle-class night of historical edification it is now—rather a step up from the prostitution and animal fighting for which the South Bank was known. Now, the only cocks present are the skyline's phallic symbols, such as Tate Modern's obelisk tower and the Shard, a self-explanatory skyscraper that casts its blueish glaze over the entire bank. For those envious of the view, you can always buy a ticket for **The London Eye**, but at about £19 per ride, it's much more reasonable to just crane your neck on the plane flight down.

Tate Modern   MUSEUM, MODERN ART
53 Bankside
☎020 7887 8008 www.tate.org.uk

The movement of modern art as the worship of novelty has no better standard than Jackson Pollock—boldly painting what no man had painted before (namely, paint). And in addition to hosting one of Pollock's most famous works, Tate Modern is itself a novelty made concrete. The building is a converted power station whose insides are the sort of striking minimalism one would expect out of *1984*. Yet within the gallery rooms are Rothko and Picasso, Mondrian and Delvaux in glorious relief to such stark surroundings. The permanent galleries entitled **Poetry and Dream, Transformed Visions, Structure and Clarity,** and **Energy and Process** range from sculptures that touch the high ceilings to paintings of chaos to neon lighting and mirror work. Art exists for interpretation, so bring your open mind and free associate for a bit—or just stare at the Rothkos until your mind becomes a calm atmosphere in kind.

▶ *i* Open M-Th 10am-6pm, F-Sa 10am-10pm, Su 10am-6pm. Free guided tours of each permanent gallery 11am, noon, 2pm, and 3pm.

Imperial War Museum   MUSEUM
Lambeth Rd.
☎020 7416 5000 www.iwm.org.uk

Housed in what was once the infamous Bedlam insane asylum, the Imperial War Museum is mad for history. The exhibits start out with two massive naval guns standing sentinel over the imposing building's entrance. The first room is cluttered with enough war-making machinery to make any general salivate. Highlights include a Polaris A3 Missile, the first submarine-launched missile, a full-size German V2 Rocket, and the shell of a "Little Boy," the type of atomic bomb detonated above Hiroshima. Luckily, the bomb is non-functional, but it's still disconcerting when kids whack the casing. The third floor houses a haunting, expansive Holocaust exhibition, which traces the catastrophic injustice of WWII Nazi atrocities with cartographic precision, its miles of film exploring everything from the rhetoric of the Nazi party to the history of anti-Semitism. If this subject matter is too light for your fancy, take solace in the Crimes Against Humanity video exhibition one floor down. The first floor houses the exciting, if sensational, "Secret War" exhibit of WWII spy gadgetry, which provides a brief history of MI5 and the Special Operations Executive. Art nuts will enjoy the museum's unique art collection, called "Breakthrough."

The ground floor is devoted to the World Wars, with artifacts, models, videos, and the popular Blitz Experience and Trench Experience exhibits that recreate the feeling of hiding during an air raid and living in the trenches. Also down here is a section on post-1945 conflicts, sure to make you feel chipper about the state of the world.

▶ *i* ⊖Lambeth North. Exit the station and walk down Kennington Rd., then turn left onto Lambeth Rd. The Blitz Experience daily schedules downstairs; it lasts around 10min. Free. Special exhibit £6, students £5. Multimedia guides £4.50. ⏰ Open daily 10am-6pm.

Design Museum   MUSEUM
Shad Thames
☎020 7940 8790 www.designmuseum.org

Each item displayed here could inspire its own TED talk. When we visited, an exhibit called "United Micro Kingdoms" explored four types of fictional societies living in the same space—for example, how would "Communo-nucleists" structure their life given unlimited power yet a constant threat of attack from other micro-societies afraid of meltdown. The answer? A movable train of farms, pools, mountains, and living spaces three miles long (a Three Mile Island, anyone?). Also on show were the 99 winners of Designs of the Year 2013, from the Zombies, Run! app to re-designs of Ralph Ellison books to the grand winner: the UK government website redesign. The permanent collection includes more surveys of household objects than silicon-heavy technology. However, it is well-curated, and as the museum claims, everything that has been made has been designed.

▶ *i* ⊖Tower Hill. Cross Tower Bridge. Turn left onto Queen Elizabeth St., then left onto Shad Thames £11.85, concessions £10.70, students £6.50. ⏰ Open daily 10am-5:45pm. Last entry 5:15pm.

Shakespeare's Globe   THEATER, HISTORIC SITE
21 New Globe Walk
☎020 7902 1500 www.shakespearesglobe.com

When film producer and director Sam Wanamaker took his own tour to Britain in the 1940s, he traipsed over to the South Bank to pay homage to the patron saint of theater, only to find a sullen plaque that said, "Shakespeare wuz here." Or something like that. What commenced was a decades-long fundraising and construction project to recreate the Globe of Elizabethan glory. A ticket to the exhibitions and tour (for information on productions, see **Arts and Culture**) includes a 45min. walkthrough of the theater, chock full of anecdotes about bear-baiting, current productions, and the list of fire hazards that threatened the original Globe's integrity (namely, firing cannons inside a building with a thatched roof and the blazing oratory of Puritans that resulted in the closure of the theater during the English Revolution). The exhibits are a bit drier but a good starting point if you want to brush up on film and TV adaptations or Shakespeare's lesser-known works.

▶ *i* ⊖Southwark. Turn left onto Blackfriars Rd., right onto Southwark St., left onto Great Guildford, right onto Park St., then left onto Emerson St. The entrance faces the river, around the corner from the main entrance to the theater. Exhibition and Globe tou £13.50, students £11. 🕐 Exhibition open daily 9am-5:30pm. Tours M 9:30am-5pm, Tu-Sa 9:30am-12:30pm, Su 9:30am-11:30am.

SOUTH KENSINGTON AND CHELSEA

🏛 Victoria and Albert Museum   MUSEUM

Cromwell Rd.

☎020 7942 2000 www.vam.ac.uk

It is sadly political that female monarchs often tack on their husband's name (William and Mary as well) while the reverse never happens. Nevertheless, the V&A stands primarily as a fitting tribute to the 19th-century golden age of industrialization and art. Founded in 1851 at the Great Exhibition, the original museum focused more on manufacturing art than Dutch Old Masters—still seen today in such items as The Great Bed of Ware (that could sleep 12 people) and the exhibits on 19th-century dress straight out of Cranford and Jane Austen. Not that there's not your requisite dose of high-brow options, too. The Renaissance sculpture gallery has some beautiful examples of Samson strangling a Philistine and a Narcissus that looks like he's punching his own reflection, while St. George loosely holds what looks like Mushu in the back (British saints are so much more docile than those pagans, you know). Also worth your time is the giant room filled with the Raphael Cartoons (not TMNT)—prints of the tapestries in the Vatican that are as large as the School of Athens itself. The rotating ticketed exhibitions are drawn to please, the most recent crop including "David Bowie Is," a labyrinth of costumes and documents from Britain's favorite Starman.

▶ *i* ⊖South Kensington. Turn right onto Thurloe Pl. and left onto Exhibition Rd. The museum is to the right across Cromwell Rd. Free. Special exhibitions generall £6-10. Free daily tours available; check screens at entrances for times. 🕐 Open M-Th 10am-5:45pm, F 10am-10pm, Sa-Su 10am-5:45pm.

🏛 Saatchi Art Gallery   ART GALLERY

Duke of York Sq.

☎020 7811 3085 www.saatchigallery.co.uk

While Tate Modern certainly has the tourist monopoly on contemporary art in the city, the Saatchi embodies its spirit of edginess and wonder. Take the bottom floor gallery, for

Sights

example, hosting Richard Wilson's *20:50*. When you walk in, it looks relatively simple: a room has been painted in darker colors until the halfway point of the wall, and the lighter top half looks like a mirror image. Until you peer over the railing and notice that you are mirrored as well. You can even walk out on a steel platform so that the black liquid void surrounds you at waist level. Another brilliant piece shown when we visited was Annie Kevan's series of portraits of cruel dictators as children—notably, little Hitler is the only one painted to have blue eyes. While the exhibits are best approached with an open mind, we recommend buying the exhibition guide on the way out if you're an art aficionado (you can always come back, as the gallery is free!).

▶ *i* ⊖Sloane Sq. Go straight out of the Tube and continue onto King's Rd. The square is on the left. Free as the wind. Exhibition guides £13. ⏲ Open daily 10am-6pm. Last entry 30min. before close.

St. Mary Abbots   CHURCH
High St. Kensington
☎020 7937 5136 www.stmaryabbotschurch.org

Tucked away behind the usual slag of big-box fashion stores is a wooded grove with a pastoral flower shop outside. Behind the foliage and the flora, a church stands where churches have stood for over 1100 years, through which time Isaac Newton, Beatrix Potter, and Princess Diana all worshiped here. When you enter, the silence swallows you; all the better to notice the scorch marks from Satan prowling around (just kidding, WWII).

▶ *i* ⊖High St. Kensington. Turn right onto Kensington High St. and left onto Kensington Church St. Free. ⏲ Open M-Tu 8:30am-6pm, W-F 7:10am-6pm, Sa 9:40am-6pm, Su 8am-7pm.

National Army Museum   MUSEUM
Royal Hospital Rd.
☎020 7730 0717 www.nam.ac.uk

The four floors of NAM (no relation to Viet) are geared toward a slightly younger crowd than the Imperial War Museum, featuring coloring activities for "little soldiers" and a reliable company of youngsters excitedly pointing at all of the plaster figures with guns. However, for a museum about the distasteful subject of killing others, it is brutally honest about Britain's role in destruction (except for the fact that the exhibits start at 1642—no wars ever happened before Cromwell, that bastard). The highlights are a giant model of the Battle of Waterloo and an addicting pinball game that gives you your chances of surviving the war (answer: very, very low). As the timeline moves on into World War I and World War II, the mini-games disappear in favor of discussions of strategy more suited to the war buff.

▶ *i* ⊖Sloane Sq. Turn left onto Lower Sloane St. and right onto Royal Hospital Rd. Free. ⏲ Open daily 10am-5:30pm.

Science Museum
MUSEUM

Exhibition Rd., South Kensington

☎020 7942 4000 www.sciencemuseum.org.uk

Science museums: hands-on experiments, planes hanging from the ceilings, children hanging onto their parents. For the inner child, you'll easily amuse yourself as you run through exhibits on space, mathematics, medical history, and energy. Learn about Charles Babbage, the man responsible for mechanical calculators and water-walking shoes (Jesus really could have used the first to cater for the 5000). And if you're wondering what an inventor's brain looks like, they have Babbage's abnormally brilliant one in a**jar.** If you're looking for something a little less swarmed with youth, the IMAX theater screens theatrical and opera productions in addition to a series of cute informational films for the younger set.

▶ *i* ⊖South Kensington. Turn right onto Thurloe Pl. and left onto Exhibition Rd. The museum is to the left, just past the Natural History Museum. Free. IMAX show £10-20. ⏰ Open daily 10am-6pm. Last entry 5:15pm.

Chelsea Physic Gardens
GARDENS

66 Royal Hospital Rd.

☎020 7352 5646 www.chelseaphysicgarden.co.uk

The name implies fountains or other projectile landscape items are shooting in arcs across the green. However, this pharmaceutical botanical garden (named as such for "physician" and not as a code name for a marijuana field) is a calmer, more old-fashioned rendering of rock gardens, flowers, and over 5000 types of plants. A guided tour will walk you through the greenery and inform you of some of the medicinal properties of plants used to treat everything from Alzheimer's to a sore back.

▶ *i* ⊖Sloane Sq. Turn left onto Lower Sloane St. and right onto Royal Hospital Rd. Guided tours £9, students and children £6, under 5 free. ⏰ Open Apr-Oct M 11am-5pm, Tu-F 11am-6pm, Su 11am-6pm.

Chelsea Old Church
CHURCH

64 Cheyne Walk

☎020 7795 1019 www.chelseaoldchurch.org.uk

In the early 16th century, Thomas More made his home on the banks of the Thames in Chelsea. At the river's edge, he moored a barge that could take him to Westminster or Hampton Court (or the Tower of London) on official business. His patronage extended to Chelsea Old Church, where he and his family worshipped and where he erected a lovely private chapel that still stands today. The rest of the church was not so lucky, and during the Blitz, most of it was destroyed and later pieced back together (several of the tombs have long cracks running down them like jigsaw puzzles).

▶ *i* ⊖Sloane Sq. Turn left onto Lower Sloane St., right onto Royal

Sights

Hospital Rd., and right onto Cheyne Walk. Free. 🕐 Open Tu-Th 2-4pm for viewing, 8am and 12:15pm for Holy Communion, 10am for children's service, 11am for Mattins, 6pm for Evensong. Weekday mass Th 8am, F noon.

St. Luke's Gardens   PARK
Sydney St.

If you're in London for a long stay, then this hideaway a mere block from King's Rd. is perfect for a *private* repose. Because it's primarily in use for residents (and their too-young-for-daycare toddlers), it won't do to bring out the alcohol, 20 of your friends, and the speakers. You'll simply have to make due with the circlets of fiery roses laced around the towering Gothic church that overlooks this Arcadia.

▶ *i* ⊖Sloane Sq. Go down King's Rd. away from the Tube. Turn right onto Sydney St. 🕐 Open daily 7:30am-dusk.

Brompton Oratory   CHURCH
Brompton Rd.
☎020 7808 0900 www.bromptonoratory.com

"Look at that sumptuously *gorgeous* Puritan church," said no one ever. Luckily, the grand Brompton Oratory keeps holy the Roman Catholic tradition of beauty first, confession later. However, the marble-laden sanctuary also keeps up the pesky habit of the state being suspicious of Catholics: it was used as a drop point for KGB agents during the Cold War.

▶ *i* ⊖Knightsbridge. Turn left onto Brompton Rd. Free. 🕐 Open daily 6:30am-8pm. Services M-F 7, 8, 10am, 12:30, 6pm (in Latin); Sa 7, 8, 10am, 6pm; Su 8, 9, 10, 11am (Latin), 12:30, 4:30, 7pm.

Kensington Palace   PALACE
Kensington Palace Gardens
☎0844 482 7777 www.hrp.org.uk/kensingtonpalace

When William of "William and Mary" had one too many asthma attacks, he moved out to the 'burbs and into Kensington Palace. Since its establishment in the 17th century, it has played host to the likes of Georges I and II (after this, it became a home for minor royals like the pre-queen Victoria, Princess Diana and Charles, and, most recently, Will and Kate). A tour will take you through the state rooms done up as they were when the kings and queens were in residence. Also be sure to see the web of lace and Swarovski crystals in the center of the palace that look like something straight out of *Tron*. When you're finished with tour, stop by The Orangery to sip tea and method act your way into believing you could live here, too.

▶ *i* ⊖High St. Kensington. Turn right leaving the station and head down the road, then enter the park and make for the palace (it's kind of hard to miss) £15, concessions £11.40. ⏰ Open daily 10am-6pm.

Natural History Museum   MUSEUM
Cromwell Rd.
☎020 7942 5011 www.nhm.ac.uk

You might be thinking that once you've seen one Natural History Museum, you've seen them all. Rock collection, erect skeletons, stuffed animals, walk-in womb...wait, are we sure this museum is for children? Well, regardless, as the spawn of tired parents will jostle around you like 100 angry garden hoses, beeline for the back of the museum to see the unrepeatable Cadogan Gallery: a collection of British treasures including the most expensive book in the world (John James Audubon's "The Birds of America" at £7.3 million) and a moon rock so graciously given to Britain by a country that they used to own.

▶ *i* ⊖South Kensington. Turn right onto Thurloe Pl. and left onto Exhibition Rd. The museum is to the left across Cromwell Rd. Book early for tours of Darwin's special collections. Free. Special exhibits around £8; discounts for students. ⏰ Open daily 10am-5:50pm. Last entry 5:30pm.

HYDE PARK TO NOTTING HILL

Notting Hill provides no touristic sights save for navel-gazing at its posh dwellers and secretly hoping Hugh Grant will flutter his way down Portobello Rd. However, it's hard to visit the area without running into the Monaco-sized Hyde Park (literally, it's larger than Monaco, although the only gamble here is whether or not it will rain). The park's periphery is lined with various celebrations of the British military tradition and subtler tributes to free speech, such as the **Subway Gallery** and **Speakers' Corner.** If you'd care to rest your mind rather than stimulate it, visit **The Serpentine Boating Lake** for an easy afternoon out.

Speakers' Corner   HISTORICAL SITE, PERFORMANCE SPACE
Hyde Park, Park Ln.

In this alcove of free speech, London pays credence to its more democratic constitution: the Corner has been the stage for political, religious, and social debates for more than a century. In some ways, it's sort of like stand-up comedy, since you have to be quick on your feet to answer questions from the Corner regulars/hecklers (some of whom have frequented for decades). Famous speakers of yesteryear include Marx, Lenin, and George Orwell, but today you're as likely to find a fundamentalist Christian as a **Communist.** Anyone is welcome to speak, so young revolutionaries and Ciceros, prepare your oratory!

▶ *i* ⊖Marble Arch. Go through the arch into the park. The area where most people speak is the paved section between the arch and the beginning of the main grassy area. Free. 🕙 Hours vary, but around 9am-10pm in the summer.

Apsley House
HISTORICAL SITE, MUSEUM GALLERY

Hyde Park Corner

☎020 7499 5676 www.english-heritage.org.uk

Named for Baron Apsley, the house later known as "No.1, London" was bought by the Duke of Wellington in 1817 (his heirs still occupy a modest suite on the top floor and provide their best impersonations of Bill Nighy in contributions to the audio tour). The house is a stunning architectural triumph dotted with spoils from the Napoleonic Wars—including a beautiful collection of sabres abandoned in Napoleon's war carriage when he was on the run from Wellington—and gifts from grateful European monarchs. One of the unforgettable treasures is an 11ft. naked Napoleon statue at the foot of the staircase that the scourge of Europe was ashamed of because it made him look "too athletic." Other marvels include an original statue of Cicero hiding among 20 other reproduction busts, the key to the city of Pamplona (granted after the Duke captured the city), the death masks of Wellington and Napoleon, and a stunning 6.7m-long Egyptian service set given by Napoleon to Josephine as a divorce present. Scholars maintain that the dessert service was meant as a mean joke about Josephine's weight—it's huge. If you're an English history buff, the careful curation will delight you; otherwise, the exhibit pays for itself in droll audio tour commentary.

▶ *i* ⊖Hyde Park Corner. Jun 18 is Wellington Day, so check for special events £6.70, concession £6, children £4; joint ticket with Wellington Arch £8.60/7.70/5.20. Audio tour free. 🕙 Open Apr-Oct W-Su 11am-5pm. Last entry 30min. before close. Closed Nov 2013-Mar 2014 for refurbishment.

Serpentine Boating Lake
BOATING

Hyde Park

☎020 7262 1330 www.theboathouselondon.co.uk

If Hyde Park is already a cocoon from the traffic of the city, then Serpentine Boating Lake is its Russian nesting doll of tranquility. The prices are a bit too steep for you to fall asleep as the boat gently skims the water (and the waterfowl provide you escort), and you'll probably be a bit too conscious of the bystanders on the bank coveting your reprieve. Steer toward the north end for the Italian Gardens, a collection of fountains lined by gorgeous, white stone walls.

▶ *i* ⊖Hyde Park Corner. The boathouse is on the east side of the lake. Pedal boats and row boats £10 per person per 30min., £12 per person per hr. 🕙 Open daily Easter-Oct 10am-sundown.

Sights

Subway Gallery
GALLERY

Joe Strummer Subway

☎078 1128 6503 www.subwaygallery.com

This underground art space was founded on June 6, 2006 because of a love of palindromes and for no other reason, right? No matter. The exhibit is free and located in a neat glass compartment that stands amid more popular forms of underground art (graffiti). Exhibits change monthly—check the website for what's on now—and consider going earlier in the day, as it feels a bit deserted at night.

▶ *i* ⊖Edgware Rd. Take a sharp right down Cabbell St., turn left before the flyover, and then go down the stairs into Joe Strummer Subway. Free. Ⓩ Open M-Sa 11am-7pm.

The Wellington Arch
HISTORICAL SITE

Hyde Park Corner

☎020 7930 2726

If you're creating an art film that includes a fast time lapse of cars shooting around traffic circles, then congratulations! This sight is perfect for you. Otherwise, visitors are treated to a history of the arch and an unspectacular view from the observation deck, which is more or less tree-level with Hyde Park. Due to the better angels of our nature, the original statue of the Duke of Wellington was replaced with a symbol of peace—the angel Quadriga—in 1883 (and no fighting ever happened again!). However, despite the anti-climactic view, the Arch is worth it if you buy the joint ticket with Apsley House.

▶ *i* ⊖Hyde Park Corner. Adult £4, concessions £3.60, children £2.40; joint ticket with Wellington Arch £8.60/7.70/5.20. Ⓩ Open Apr-Sept W-Su 10am-5pm; Oct-Mar 10am-4pm. Last entry 30min. before close.

MARYLEBONE AND BLOOMSBURY

While the British Museum and the British Library are so similar in location and name, one could barely call the former "British," as at least 80% of the exhibits are of different cultures. Regardless, we suppose it is more British than the nearby Francophilic Wallace Collection, a decadent series of Rococo rooms dedicated to different *monarques*. But if we were to hold a competition, Regent's Park—dotted with Dalmatians and rugby matches—would only be second to the BBC Broadcasting Centre in representing the sceptered isle.

🖾 The British Museum   MUSEUM

Great Russell St.

☎020 7323 8299 www.british-museum.org

Another treasure is the **King's Library** on the eastern side of the ground floor, which holds artifacts gathered from throughout the world by English explorers during the Enlightenment. Some of the central display cases bear descriptions, but much of the collection is jumbled together without explanation—a curatorial choice meant to recreate the feel of collections from the period. We think it works pretty well. Mixed in with the artifacts are shelves full of books from the House of Commons' library—get your dork on and try to find an 18th-century copy of your favorite Roman poet or Greek historian.

▶ *i* ⊖Tottenham Court Rd., ⊖Russell Sq., or ⊖Holborn. Tours by request £5 suggested donation. Prices for events and special exhibitions vary, most £8-12. Excellent color maps with self-guided tours £2. Multimedia guide £5. Free daily tours in specific exhibition rooms 11am-3:45pm; check website for details. 20min. free spotlight tours F 5-7pm. Weekend tours £12, Sa-Su 11:30am and 2pm. ⏰ Museum open daily 10am-5:30pm. Select exhibitions M-Th 10am-5:30pm, F 10am-8:30pm, Sa-Su 10am-5:30pm.

🖾 The British Library   LIBRARY

96 Euston Rd.

☎020 7412 7676 www.bl.uk

The British Library is at once what a library would suggest—reading rooms, archives, member cards for UK residents, and, oh yes, a Gutenberg Bible thrown in just because. For tourists, the Treasures of the British Library is a compendium of scores, manuscripts, and illustrations that will register familiarity and awe. The literature section is comprised of words, words, words, not surprisingly focused on Shakespeare—although John Milton's common-place book, Oscar Wilde's *The Ballad of Reading Gaol,* and Jane Austen's reading desk are proffered non-Bard treasures. Even though Britain is not renowned for its musical tradition, the **Music** section makes due with circumstance and celebrates Vaughn Williams and Elgar; also included are several original Haydn scores, along with Beethoven's tuning fork and Mozart's marriage contract. However, the real highlights are related to God and Country, with one of 50 documented Gutenberg Bibles modestly hiding in the illuminated manuscripts section and the **Magna Carta** commanding its own exhibition room. Most of the treasures given space in the main room offer either something of visual beauty—as in the Armenian Bible or several illuminated Qu'rans—or historical significance, including a loving shout-out to the 1945 creation of the welfare state (admittedly not as flashy as the 2012 Olympics Opening Ceremonies). In addition to the permanent collection, the library has two rotating exhibition spaces, one free and located in the atrium outside of the Treasures gallery and the other a ticketed affair behind the museum shop. If you are aiming to become a luminary of your own, the cafe connected to the main floor has a majestic view of the 65,000 volumes that King George III assembled as a royal library. That shall surely inspire you as you greedily gorge on pastries and coffee without restraint, knowing that you are fighting intellectual death.

▶ *i* ⊖Euston Sq. or ⊖King's Cross St. Pancras. From Euston Sq., turn left. From King's Cross, turn right. Free Wi-Fi with registration. To register for use of reading room, bring 2 forms of ID, 1 with a signature and 1 with a permanent UK address. Free. Tours free. Group tours (up to 15 people) £85. Tours M-F 9:30am-6pm,Sa 9:30am-5pm, Su 11am-5pm, call020 7412 7639 to book. Individual tours M-Sa 10:30am and 3pm, Su 11:30am, call019 3754 6546 to book. 🕐 Open M 9:30am-6pm, Tu 9:30am-8pm, W-F 9:30am-6pm, Sa 9:30am-5pm, Su 11am-5pm. Reading rooms closed on Su.

🏛 The Regent's Park   PARK
☎020 7486 7905 www.royalparks.org.uk

While the Prince Regent (George IV) was a laudanum addict who amassed today's equivalent o £50 million in debt, his legacy now lies in some of the most aesthetically pleasing spaces in London. At the Queen's pleasure, the British and a smattering of internationals take to the 300 acres of the royal park for sport (football, rugby, and tennis are popular choices) or rest. The children at heart can wander through **The London Zoo,** and those who feel the same emotion for a flower or butterfly as they do a cathedral or picture will delight in **Queen Mary's Garden,** which boasts such plant species as "Conspicuous" and hosts over 40,000 roses, best viewed in early June. In the rain, the **Open Air Theatre** is your best bet to avoid muddy treks (although bring a waterproof raincoat, as Open Air is self-evident). If one craves solitude, rainy days are ideal for creepily standing by the pond MI6-style; however, even on sunny days, the farther you travel from the southern gates, the more number of baskers drops dramatically.

▶ *i* ⊖Regent's Park. Deck chair £1.50 per hr., £4 per 3hr., £7 per day. Boats £7.50 per hr., £5.50 before noon. Zoo £23, concessions £21, children £17. 🕐 Park open daily 5am-dusk. Zoo open daily 10am-5:30pm.

The Wallace Collection   GALLERY
Manchester Sq.
☎030 7563 9552 www.wallacecollection.org

If Netflix were to suggest a museum to you based on your love of 18th-century French period pieces, art with a strong naked female lead, and themes that deal with the transience of life, then the Wallace Collection would be front and center on your recommendation list. Housed in the palatial **Hertford House,** the collection is a multi-layered experience of silk wallpapered walls, whole furniture sets owned by Marie Antoinette, at least five clocks per room, symbolic busts of "Summer" and "Autumn," some requisite British paintings of hounds, and the exquisite *Francesa da Rimini* by Ary Scheffer that shows Dante and Virgil gazing upon the punishment of the lustful in Hell. The ground floor's four **Armoury Galleries** boast scads of richly decorated weapons and burnished suits of armor, while the **State Rooms** hold a collection of sumptuous Sèvres porcelain. On the upper floor, you'll find coral and cerulean rooms, dreamy paintings by artists like Rubens and some darker, sterner stuff by Rembrandt and van Ruisdael, as well as one of the collection's most celebrated pieces, Frans Hals's *The Laughing Cavalier* (who wasn't a cavalier at all).

▶ *i* ⊖Marble Arch. Turn left onto Oxford St., left onto Duke St., and right onto Manchester Sq. Gallery free; suggested donatio £5. Audio tour £4. 🕐 Open daily 10am-5pm.

BBC Broadcasting House   HISTORICAL SITE
Portland Place
☎037 0901 1227 www.bbc.co.uk/showsandtours/tours/bh_london

The BBC is a perfect distillation of the United Kingdom: droll, composed, calm, and, most importantly, at times hilarious. A tour of the old and brand new broadcasting center will have you producing your own radio play, sitting in the theater they use for intimate rock concerts (MUSE played for this venue of only 300), and looking down on the bustling news room that looks more like the New York Stock Exchange. Along the way, the tour guide explains different art installations (including why the Old Broadcasting House's identifying sight is a castrated boy). At the end of the tour, your allegiance to any other news company will have been exterminated.

▶ *i* ⊖Oxford Circus. Head north onto Regent St., round All Souls (the domed building ahead), and continue onto Portland Pl. The tour entrance is on the right-hand side, past the main entrance. Adult £13.50, concession £11.25, students £10. Schedule through the website or by phone. 🕐 Tours daily 10am-3:30pm.

NORTH LONDON

🏞 Hampstead Heath   PARK
Hampstead
☎020 7332 3030

These 1000 acres of unmanicured forest, fresh ponds, dusky grass, and silent dells are the most underrated attraction in London. Few tourists make it out here (probably because of the more centrally located park options like Regent's, Hyde, and St.

James), and the only "look, Facebook friends, isn't this cool?" photo opportunity involves climbing to the top of Parliament Hill and gazing upon the dusky, futuristic London below. As you move farther north up toward the Kenwood estate, the paths become more hilly and less touched by human hands (save for the odd champagne cork on the ground). The east part of the Heath features a slew of gender-separated bathing ponds. However, the best way to experience the widening brume is to start at the entrance near Hampstead and take as many side paths into the dark forest as possible, working your way through silence dearly purchased.

▶ *i* Bus #210 will drop you at the north of the Heath. Alternatively, get off at ⊖Hampstead, turn right onto Heath St., go up North End Way, turn left onto Inverforth Close, and left onto a path to arrive at the hill gardens. Bus #214 allows easy access to Parliament Hill. ⏰ Heath open 24hr. Hill Garden open daily 8:30am-1hr. before sunset.

Keats House   HISTORICAL SITE
Keats Grove
☎020 7332 3868 www.cityoflondon.gov.uk/keatshousehampstead

When the developers came round in 1920 and wanted to demolish this house to build flats, just imagine the lexicon of Keats quotes the council used to prevent its demise ("A thing of beauty is a joy forever," perhaps?). Now, fans of the tragic consumptive can appreciate the house and surrounding gardens where he wrote "Ode to a Nightingale." The house is comprised of historically preserved Regency-era rooms stocked with artifacts from his life (as well as those of his friend, Charles Brown, and fiancée, Fanny Brawne).

▶ *i* ⊖Hampstead Heath. Turn left onto South End Rd. and follow it until it hits Keats Grove £5, concessions £3, under 16 free. 45min. free guided tours; schedule varies. ⏰ Open Easter-Oct 31 Tu-Su 1-5pm; Nov-Easter F-Su 1-5pm.

Kenwood House   GALLERY
Hampstead Ln.
☎020 8348 1286 www.english-heritage.org.uk

Lord Iveagh, a barrister and Lord Chief Justice, lived here in the 18th century. Visitors to Kenwood House can now admire his fabulous art collection and see how the 18th-century elite lived. Iveagh's bequest fills the house with paintings that are essentially odes to the London of yore. The house is currently undergoing renovations and is scheduled to reopen in November 2013.

▶ *i* Bus #210 stops on Hampstead Ln. at the Kenwood House stop. The park is across the road. Free. Booklets £4. ⏰ Open daily 11:30am-4pm. Last entry 3:50pm.

EAST LONDON

🏛 Whitechapel Gallery   GALLERY
77-82 Whitechapel High St.

☎020 7522 7888 www.whitechapelgallery.org

In 1901, the Whitechapel Gallery began as an exemplar of *noblesse oblige*. Over a century later, the resident hipster swarm probably knows more about art (or seems to) than the elite ever could have imagined for their cute, East End charity cases. But even under the pall of its patronizing beginning, the space debuted Rothko, Pollock, and Kahlo to London audiences; it also served as the only British stop of Pablo Picasso's *Guernica*. Prepare yourself for challenging works of all media types as well as a few mid-career retrospectives.

▶ *i* ⊖Aldgate East. Turn left onto Whitechapel High St. Free. Special exhibits and events normally unde £10, £2 student discount. 🕐 Open Tu-Su 11am-6pm.

🏛 Geffrye Museum   MUSEUM
136 Kingsland Rd.

☎020 7739 9893 www.geffrye-museum.org.uk

Pemberley, Satis House, Brideshead, Downton Abbey—all accounts of these fictional houses are accompanied with obsessively lavish descriptions of their furnishings (re: indicators of yearly income) in a singularly British way. In the Geffrye Museum, you can see how domestic style evolved from 1630 to the present through a series of mock-up rooms. While it's a bit weird to imagine any British living room without a TV, the exhibits do a great job of putting you in the mindset to Bible read or play a good round of gin rummy.

▶ *i* ⊖Hoxton. Make a right onto Geffrye St., a left onto Pearson St., and a left onto Kingsland Rd. Free. Special exhibits aroun £5. 🕐 Open Tu-Sa 10am-5pm, Su noon-5pm.

The Royal Observatory   HISTORIC SITE, MUSEUM
Blackheath Ave.

☎020 8312 6608 www.nmm.ac.uk

Narcissists, small children, and millennials think that they're the center of the world. Seeing as Britain declared one of their delightful country villages the literal ground zero (0 0'0") of the planet and basically invented time, we think that this might be a helpful mirror to hold up to 19th-century imperialism. The eclectic towers of the Royal Observatory offer several boons to the wayfaring tourist: a lovely photo opportunity to straddle the Prime Meridian, a planetarium with dazzling shows, and more clocks than Doc Martin's house.

▶ *i* ⊖Cutty Sark. Turn left out of the station and continue onto College Approach; then turn right onto King William Walk and left onto Romney Rd. Trek toward the hill and then ascend it. Handicapped tourists should know that while there is parking on top of the hill, the hill itself is incredibly steep. Joint planetarium/museum ticke £11.50, concessions £8; planetarium shows £6.50/4.50. Guided tours free. ⏰ Open daily 10am-5pm.

SOUTH LONDON

South London Gallery   GALLERY
65 Peckham Rd.
☎020 7703 6120 www.southlondongallery.org

If you're tooling around London for an extended period of time, this contemporary gallery is a lovely way to use up a weekend afternoon. The in-house No67 cafe is almost more popular than the exhibition space itself, with locals and students sipping coffee and wandering in and out to check out the art and films. Be prepared for experimental videos with a local twinge and art focused on different senses rather than just sight.

▶ *i* ⊖Oval. Directly outside the station, take bus #36 or #436 east toward New Cross Way or Lewisham. Get off at Southampton Way. Free. ⏰ Open Tu 11am-6pm, W 11am-9pm, Th-Su 11am-6pm.

WEST LONDON

⛪ Hampton Court Palace   PALACE
East Molesey, Surrey
☎0844 482 7777 www.hrp.org.uk/hamptoncourtpalace

There's something slightly bizarre about being led through a historical audio tour by a more paranoid version of Francis Urquhart/Frank Underwood/Richard III (depending on your fourth wall experience). But then again, the whole of Hampton Court is an eclectic mix of architecture, curiosity, and historical appeal. The humongous palace was given by Henry VIII to Cardinal Wolsey and then abandoned until William and Mary gloriously restored it (well, actually, it's really just another episode of "Christopher Wren Strikes Again"). Outside of the walls lie the magnificent grounds, replete with hedge maze (portkey not included) and several gorgeously landscaped gardens.

▶ *i* Trains run from Waterloo to Hampton Court £5.50). The palace is just across the bridge from the train station. Alternatively, Richmond. Take the R68 toward Hampton Court. Audio and guided tours included with admission. £16, concessions £13.40, children under 16 £8; gardens only £5.72/4.84/free; maze only £4.40, children £2.75. ⏰ Open daily Jan-Mar 10am-4:30pm; Apr-Oct 10am-6pm; Oct-Dec 10am-4:30pm. Last entry 1hr. before close. Last entry to maze 45min. before close.

Sights

Royal Botanic Gardens, Kew   BOTANICAL GARDENS
Richmond, Surrey
☎020 8332 5000 www.kew.org

Combine a cultural legacy of landscaping and royal extrava-
gance, and you get Kew Gardens—a sprawling Shangri-la only
visited by the most thorough of tourists (even London locals
don't get out to it very often). These botanical gardens host
the largest collection of plants in the world, and visitors can
eat up gorgeous assemblages of roses, orchids, and cacti (or be
eaten up by the carnivorous plants). For those not so enamored
with flora, peacocks strut the 121 hectares at their leisure; for
architecture aficionados, the Asiatic pagoda and Kenyan-style
treetop walkways are funky contributions to an otherwise
solidly British collection of cottages and houses on the grounds.

▶ *i* ⊖Kew Gardens. Exit the station and walk down Litchfield Rd. to the
Gardens' Victoria Gate £14.50, concessions £12.50, under 17 free. ⏰
Open M-F 9:30am-6:30pm, Sa-Su 9:30am-7:30pm. Last entry 30min.
before close. Galleries close daily at 5:30pm. Free guided tours leave
Victoria Plaza at 11am and 2pm.

Food

British food doesn't have a great reputation. Yes, it is bad for you and no, it doesn't have complex flavors, but it is so intrinsically a part of British life that to forgo it would be a grave error for any visitor. Fish and chips, bangers and mash, tikka masala (a British invention), and warm ale are all different names for the same thing: comfort food. Neighborhoods like Brixton and Shoreditch serve up a span of ethnic cuisine, from Caribbean to Indian, while gourmet restaurants whip up inventive dishes. "Pub grub" still rules over everything. In case you hadn't noticed, Brits like to operate in certain set ways. There's a reason that old war propaganda line, "Keep Calm and Carry On," is plastered all over the place; there's a reason the Queen still rolls down the Mall every June; there's a reason the Brits always think England will win the Cup; there's a reason fair Albion still uses the pound; and for that same reason, you'll always be able to get a pie and a pint on any corner in London. Now eat your mushy peas—the cod's getting cold.

Food

THE CITY OF LONDON

A word of warning: the City of London completely clears out on the weekend. Therefore, if you dream of sipping your coffee on a Sunday morning in a happy pandemonium of British accents, stop. That being said, it's good to take into account the massive weekday lunch crowds that will show up from nearby offices.

🗽 City Càphê   VIETNAMESE $
17 Ironmonger Ln.
☎ www.citycaphe.com

During their lunch break, businesspeople in pleated pants and skirts quietly turn onto Ironmonger Ln. for one of the only non-chain restaurants in the area. The goods? Bánh mì and perfectly cooked rice noodle dishes. As opposed to the Vietnamese food stalls you'll find in Brick Ln. or Camden, this small, modern joint reflects its yuppie clientele in presentation (even though the prices don't require a Centurion Card).

▶ *i* ⊖Bank. Head down Poultry away from the stop, then turn right onto Iron-monger Ln. Bánh mì £4. Other dishes £4-6. ⏰ Open M-F 11:30am-3pm.

J&A Cafe   CAFE $
4 Sutton Ln.
☎020 7490 2992 www.jandacafe.com

The two young sisters who run this rustic hideaway (Johanna and Aoife) offer some rarities in British cafe culture: relatively long opening hours, a diverse menu, and a venue larger than an airplane aisle. It's easy to miss because of its off-road alleyway locale, which is filled with picnic benches and patrons. However, once settled in, you can spend hours nursing a coffee or one of their lemonades (that have extracts like rhubarb, elderflower, and pear).

▶ *i* ⊖Barbican. Turn left onto Goswell Rd., left onto Great Sutton St., and left onto Sutton Ln. Free Wi-Fi. Breakfast, sandwiches, and lunch dishes £4-8.50. ⏰ Open M-F 8am-6pm, Sa-Su 9am-5pm.

Coach and Horses   PUB $$
26-28 Ray St.
☎020 7278 8990 www.thecoachandhorses.com

London pub food evokes the same attitude that something like Rubinoff does: "Oh God. Never again...but I'll probably end up with it anyway after five drinks." Coach and Horses does not deal in mushy peas and food so oily it's a hazard to nearby aquatic wildlife—instead, the grub here is a foodie's take on the standard pub line-up. Try the venison ragout or an 8oz. West

Country steak or something simple like the delicious pea and ham soup.

▸ *i* ⊖Farringdon. Walk north on Farringdon Rd. and turn left onto Ray St. Appetizers £4.75-7.25. Main courses £11-15. ⏰ Open M-F noon-11pm. Kitchen open noon-3pm and 5-10pm.

The Clerkenwell Kitchen   BRITISH, SEASONAL $$
31 Clerkenwell Close
☎020 7101 9959 www.theclerkenwellkitchen.co.uk

Despite the trope of bad British cuisine and worse execution, the locally sourced movement has gained traction. Clerkenwell Kitchen, an IKEA-modern cafe, is a good example of the free-range/organic trend done without too much snobbery. The menu items are inventive—such as the squid with watercress and chili—and the waiters are a jovial bunch that will actually talk to you, either about the menu or your book (the rarest of rarities in socially-repressed London).

▸ *i* ⊖Farringdon. Turn right onto Cowcross St., right onto Farringdon Rd., right onto Pear Tree Ct., and right onto Clerkenwell Close. Walk straight as if still on Pear Tree Ct. If you see the church, you've gone too far. Main course £7.80-12. ⏰ Open M-F 8am-5pm.

Daddy Donkey   MEXICAN $
50b Leather Ln.
☎ www.daddydonkey.co.uk

Probably because Mexico was never a British colony, there's a definite dearth of quesadillas and assorted spicy goods in the city. In 2005, Daddy Donkey opened the first Mexican food cart in the city, and in 2013, they moved on up to nearly the exact same location and bought up a proper shop. As a leftover from the food cart days, there's not a large seating area, but Leather Ln. has benches and some garden areas to the south that suffice.

▸ *i* ⊖Farringdon. Turn right onto Farringdon Rd., left onto St. Cross St., then left onto Leather Ln. Burrito £5.50-6. ⏰ Open M-Sa 11am-4pm.

THE WEST END

▨ Kulu Kulu   SUSHI $$
76 Brewer St.
☎020 7734 7316 www.kulukulu.co.uk

Kulu Kulu is an onomatopoetic play on "Kuru Kuru," the noise that conveyer belts apparently make. And that is what you'll get here: a steady stream of small sushi dishes whirling around the runway while discerning businesspeople pluck them for consumption. Different plates indicate different prices; when you're ready to pay, a waiter will come over and add up your plates. Granted, you're not going to get über-modern low-lighting and black lacquered bars like you will at some uppity West End joints, but the prices here are more competitive than even what you'll find at Tesco's.

▶ *i* ⊖Piccadilly Circus. Go down Glasshouse St., keep right onto Sherwood St., and turn left onto Brewer St. Dishe £2 (4-5 dishes make a good meal). Sushi combos from £6. ☺ Open M-Sa noon-10pm.

▨ **Monmouth Coffee Company**   CAFE $

27 Monmouth St.

☎0872 148 1409 www.monmouthcoffee.co.uk

The English have a more estranged relationship with filter coffee than the States, no better evidenced by the fact that the only variety of black coffee offered in most brand-name shops is the Americano. However, Monmouth is one of the few places in the city where you can buy individually filtered coffee, and the resulting heaven can power you through an entire morning of Covent Garden tourism. There's limited seating available, but most customers take a coffee and croissant either to work or to wait outside one of the nearby theaters for rush tickets.

▶ *i* ⊖Leicester Sq. Turn right and then left onto Upper St. Martin's Ln., which becomes Monmouth St. Coffe £2.50. Baked goods £1.50-2. ☺ Open M-Sa 8am-6:30pm.

Fortnum&Mason   TEA $$$$

181 Piccadilly

☎020 7734 8040 www.fortnumandmason.com

Fortnum&Mason is basically the Malfoy family's ideal of what Hogsmeade should look like: specialty tea, truffles, champagne, picnic hampers filled with china, roulette sets, fancy cologne, and animal-topped canes. However, a more universal highlight is the tea service that includes scones, sandwiches, cakes, and options like Scotch Egg and Welsh Rarebit. Admittedly, this is all quite expensive, so a good option for those with a budget is The Parlour, for a less formal tea experience (£5.75 per pot), or the lowest floor, where you can grab a solitary cuppa (£1.80).

▶ *i* ⊖Piccadilly Circus. Turn left down Piccadilly. Afternoon tea £40-50 per person. ☺ Open M-Sa noon-9pm, Su noon-8pm.

Fernandez and Wells Cafe   CAFE, SANDWICHES $

73 Beak St.

☎020 7287 8124 www.fernandezandwells.com

Let's just say that for a cafe in the middle of the West End, it's not actually that pretentious. Okay, the sandwiches are all-natural and organic, lacking in preservatives, and served on slabs of wood that look like they just did some time on *Barefoot Contessa*. But the baristas are quite friendly, and the small, intimate environment is a nice change from the sprawling corporate Pret and Costa stores.

▶ *i* ⊖Piccadilly Circus. Turn right down Shaftesbury Ave., left onto Lexington St., and left onto Beak St. Coffe £2.50. Sandwiches £5-6. ⏲ Open M-F 7:30am-6pm, Sa 9am-6pm, Su 9am-5pm.

Rossopomodoro   ITALIAN $$
50-52 Monmouth St.
☎020 7240 9095 www.rossopomodoro.co.uk

The best way to recognize a budget restaurant in the West End is by the outdoor chairs and tables. Leather? Marble? Glass? Don't bite unless you want to fork out. Similarly, the light metal chairs outside this well-regarded Neapolitan pizza chain betrays its budget prices, but the food definitively does not. We're not talking Domino's here; Rossopomodoro offers exquisite pizzas and pastas with only the finest ingredients, including buffalo mozzarella specially flown in from Italy.

▶ *i* ⊖Leicester Sq. Make a left onto Upper St. Martin's Ln., which becomes Monmouth St. Pizz £8-15. Pasta £10-13. ⏲ Open daily noon-11:30pm.

WESTMINSTER

▨ Poilâne   BAKERY $
46 Elizabeth St.
☎020 7808 4910 www.poilane.com

As you wander through the traveler's gauntlet of plastic-wrapped sandwiches, it's easy to forget what bread is like. Not "vessel for my jam" or "clamp for my ham and cheese." Actual, thick, chewy, crispy, soft, warm, salty bread. There's literally one option in the city for a heavenly manna experience: the only non-French branch of the famous Parisian bakery chain, Poilâne. Like the cobbling elves that help the shoemaker at night, many of the bakers live upstairs and cook through the night so the bread is fresh for the die-hard morning crowd. Interestingly enough, they bake the bread in the same model that was responsible for burning down half of London once upon a time.

▶ *i* ⊖Victoria. Turn left onto Buckingham Palace Rd., then right onto Elizabeth St. Loaves generally fro £4-10. Walnut bread £4.50. ⏲ Open M-F 7:30am-7pm, Sa 7:30am-3pm.

Food

⚄ Pimlico Fresh   CAFE, MEDITERRANEAN $

86 Wilton Rd.

☎020 7932 0030

Even though a dish like fish and chips has a simple composition *technically,* British food sometimes seems confusing and excessive. Why does this potato have so much stuff in it? Who eats baked beans for breakfast/ever? Is it normal that my plate has enough oil left over to be the next Deepwater Drilling scandal? Pimlico Fresh is a rare bird in that it freshens up British staples and ignores the "acquired taste" options, like oil, tuna, mayo, and cress.

▶ *i* ✆Victoria. Wilton Rd. runs behind the station, toward Pimlico, away from Buckingham Palace. Takeout available. Main dishe £5-7.50. Coffee from £2. ⏲ Open M-F 7:30am-7:30pm, Sa-Su 9am-6pm.

Jenny Lo's Teahouse   ASIAN FUSION $$

14 Eccleston St.

☎020 7259 0399 www.jennylo.co.uk

As most tea-drinking Brits live a quiet, domestic life where the kettle is never that far away, there are surprisingly few tea-centric spots in the city. And when there are, it's usually for minor royalty who should be congratulated on not drinking something stronger at 2pm. However, this unassuming tea shop is the original deal (remember: imperialism), with an equally good menu of Thai and Vietnamese options as well. And the best part is that the tea doesn't come with stony British judgment.

▶ *i* ✆Victoria. Turn left onto Buckingham Palace Rd., then right onto Eccleston St. Takeout and delivery available. Tea £2-4. Main courses £8-10. Cash only. ⏲ Open M-F noon-3pm and 6-10pm.

THE SOUTH BANK

The South Bank is home to the terrific **Borough Market.** Located just south of London Bridge, it's a tangle of stalls and shops where you can get prime cuts of meat, organic vegetables, and fragrant cheeses. If you want a more structured meal, this is generally a pretty good neighborhood to find a deal, as prices are lower here than they are in the city center.

⚄ Pieminister   PIES $

Gabriel's Wharf, 56 Upper Ground

☎020 7928 5755 www.pieminister.co.uk

The South Bank is lined with refuge for the diaspora of tourists coming from Tate Modern, the London Eye, and London Bridge. Avoid anything saying "Fish and Chips" and head straight to the best pies in London (but actually—no demon barbers and psychotic mistresses running this happy joint). These fist-sized pies are a healthier take on the British staple, with options such as the Heidi (sweet potato and goat cheese) alongside comfort favorites like kidney and beef. Enjoy them outside during the summer or as takeaway in the winter, since there's no indoor seating.

▶ *i* ⊖Waterloo. Walk toward the main roundabout and onto Waterloo Rd., then turn right onto Upper Ground. Pie £4.25; with gravy, mashed potatoes, and mushy peas £5.95. ☼ Open daily 10am-6pm.

Tsuru   JAPANESE $
4 Canvey St.
☎020 7928 2228 www.tsuru-sushi.co.uk

Some of the packages looks suspiciously like dressed-up Tesco sushi, but as soon as you indulge, you can taste the handmade, succulent difference. The interior is not very large, but there are large seating areas outside on the closed street. If you're hungry before seeing a production at The Globe (p. 44) or the National Theatre (p. 98), just try one of the takeaway boxes that sometimes goes for half-price in the early evening.

▶ *i* ⊖Southwark. Walk down Blackfriars Rd. toward the river, then turn right onto Southwark Rd. and left onto Canvey St. Sushi boxe £4-6. Katsu £6. ☼ Open M-F 11am-9pm, Sa noon-9pm.

SOUTH KENSINGTON AND CHELSEA

It's hard to swing a gold-tipped cane without hitting £40 per plate restaurant. However, Old Brompton Rd., High St. Kensington, and King's Rd. are cradles of not *too* pricey eateries.

▨ Buona Sera Jam   ITALIAN $$
289A King's Rd.
☎020 7352 8827

Chelsea is a neighborhood where the disheveled traveler will be looked down upon: if you're not in a suit or similar finery, you'll be marked as a tourist. Now, however, you can look down on them. Climb up a ladder to one of the second-story stacked booths of Buona Sera and enjoy your affordable risotto while you feel like you're a T-block in a giant Tetris game.

▶ *i* ⊖Sloane Sq. Exit the Tube and head straight down ⊖Sloane Sq. Turn onto King's Rd., which slants gently off to the left. Alternatively, take bus #11, 19, 22, 211, or 319. Salads £5. Pasta and risotto £9. Meat and fish entrees £14. ☼ Open M-F noon-11pm, Sa-Su noon-10:30pm.

Food

Bumpkin
BRITISH $$$

109 Brompton Rd.

☎020 7341 0802 www.bumpkinuk.com

Bumpkin has the same hearth and earth feel of a country pub, but that's about as "bumpkin" as it gets. Of course, they *are* referring to their patriotic menu of nosh only hailing from British farm, field, and shore (notable exceptions are most of the items on the wine menu and the coffee, but we think that's better for all involved). As the patronage views tennis matches and feasts on duck and pudding, we declare them successful and also recommend the eggs royale if you find yourself in a brunching mood.

▶ *i* ⊖South Kensington. Exit down Old Brompton Rd. The restaurant is on the right. Appetizer £5.50-10. Main courses £11-22. ⏰ Open daily 11am-11pm.

My Old Dutch Pancake House
DUTCH $$

221 King's Rd.

☎020 7376 5650 www.myolddutch.com

While IHOP attempts diplomatic overtures, this tucked away pancake diner is unapologetically Dutch. For example, the 12in. pancakes (roughly, crepes) are served on blue and white porcelain emblazoned with windmills. How quixotic then that the diner hosts "Monday Madness," where you can choose a sweet or savory option for onl £5. Tuck into the vermeer pancake (sugar pancake with ice cream and shot of vermeer; £6.75), a delicious pearl on the menu.

▶ *i* ⊖Sloane Sq. Exit the Tube and go straight down ⊖Sloane Sq. The street slanting gently left is King's Rd. Pancakes £5-9. ⏰ Open M-F 10am-9:30pm, Sa-Su 9am-9:45pm.

Thai Square
THAI $$

19 Exhibition Rd.

☎020 7584 8359 www.thaisquare.net

The Museum district is, quite simply, one giant exhibition of "Look at how much the humans will pay for bottled water!" However, count on this popular Thai chain to remain sane in the midst of such gouging. Provided with the usual favorites of spring rolls, curries, and vegetarian options galore, you won't even have to sacrifice comfort or decor: the delicate floral patterns and homey interior more than provide a haven for you to rest your weary, museum-milling feet.

▶ *i* ⊖South Kensington. Turn right onto Thurloe St. and left onto Exhibition Rd. Appetizer £3-5. Main courses £7-12. ⏰ Open M-Sa noon-4pm and 5:30-11pm, Su noon-4pm and 5:30-10pm.

Food

The Marketplace   EUROPEAN $$$

125 Sydney St.

☎020 7352 5600 www.marketplacerest.com

Oh how the city-dwellers do so crave the country! Let us take out our checkered tablecloths and dine on the natural fruits of Earth. And we shall dine not on cold chicken and watermelon, but on ribeye steak, hummus, and goat cheese. More charitably, the food is delicious, even if it is a bit laughable to claim that it's more wholesome than bougie. Probably the best thing about this outdoor eatery is that it's heated in the winter, so head on over regardless if anything local is actually growing outside.

▶ *i* ⊖Sloane Sq. Walk down King's Rd. and turn right onto Sydney St. Main course £11-23. ⏰ Open daily 9am-8pm.

Whole Foods Market   GROCERY, BUFFET $

63-97 Kensington High St.

☎020 7368 4500 www.wholefoodsmarket.com

After your fifth cheese and onion box sandwich of the week further buoys the profits of Tesco, this American chain will restore your faith in grocery stores. Far and away, the biggest draw here is the diversity, as the upstairs floor is filled with mini-restaurants that run the gamut—BBQ, sushi, pizza, gelato, coffee, and alcohol (along with one of the most diverse salad bars we've come across). Sit in one of the alcoves, munch on some fresh food, and don't forget to take advantage of your two hours of free Wi-Fi.

▶ *i* ⊖High St. Kensington. Turn right down the road. Buffe £1.91 per 100g. ⏰ Open M-Sa 8am-10pm, Su 11am-6pm.

The Orangery   CAFE $$$

Kensington Palace Gardens

☎020 7376 0239

Tea. It's at Starbucks and Costa. In the hostels and the souvenir shops. On the number one list of things that it means to be British, it's choosing the subtlety of the leaf over the cocaine-equivalent bean. Thus, how better to celebrate this mild caffeinator than with a tea service that lauds and extols its being? The service comes with sandwiches, scones, clotted cream, and even champagne on some menus. Pinkies up.

▶ *i* ⊖High St. Kensington. Turn right down Kensington High St. and head through the park toward Kensington Palace. The Orangery is on the far side. Tea menus £22-33. ⏰ Open daily Mar-Sept 10am-6pm; Oct-Feb 10am-5pm.

Food

Crémerie Crêperie
CREPERIE $$

2-6 Exhibition Rd.

☎020 7589 8947 www.kensingtoncreperie.com

There are cupcake boutiques and designer smoothie bars that have enough vitamins pumped into them to nutritionally rehabilitate a village. Then there are creperies, which occupy the same space of novelty and high prices for a single food; however, for its location right off of Exhibition Rd., this house of crepes inexpensively serves truly special designs, such as the delicious toffee crepe (toffee dulce de leche, banana, coconut, and vanilla ice cream; £6.75).

▶ *i* ⊖South Kensington. Turn right onto Thurloe St. and left onto Exhibition Rd. Crepe £6-9. Sundaes £6. ⏰ Open M 11am-11:30pm, Tu-F 10am-11:30pm, Sa-Su 9:30am-11:30pm.

HYDE PARK TO NOTTING HILL

If you're in search of a cheap, filling meal, Queensway is lined with generic Chinese, Persian, and Lebanese options (and also has the highest density of supermarkets for the DIY eater). As you head west on Westbourne Grove, the area quickly gentrifies into novelty restaurants and expensive cafes. Turning south onto Portobello Rd. as it turns into Pembridge Villas, a recent cropping of open-late gelato, pizza, and bakery offerings serve the bright young things of Notting Hill on their posh night out.

🖼 Otto
PIZZA $

6 Chepstow Rd.

☎020 7792 4088 www.ottopizza.co.uk

Otto's confidence in its cornmeal pizza crust is exemplified by a map of continental America with arrows pointing to Alaska, Hawaii, and apparently the 51st state: Otto. Then again, with the sound of Mumford & Sons and the smell of delicious hope wafting through the dining area, this restaurant has enough popularity to level such a claim. Pick one of eight or so options (we recommend the No. 114) and enjoy the crispy crust and piled-on toppings. The commitment-phobic can order the Chef's Taster—which has six different slices—and even the seminal pizza hater can order a broccoli, black bean, and mushroom salad that makes a great side dish as well.

▶ *i* ⊖Notting Hill Gate. Make a right down Pembridge Rd., which will turn into Pembridge Villas, and then a left onto Chepstow Rd. Takeaway available. Gluten-free and vegetarian options always available.Slice £3.85-4.95; half pizza £10; whole pizza (serves 2-3) £18. ⏰ Open M-F noon-3pm and 5:30pm-11pm, Sa noon-11pm, Su noon-10pm.

Food

▨ Durbar Restaurant INDIAN $
24 Hereford Rd.
☎020 7727 1947 www.durbartandoori.co.uk

It's hard to resist the warm smells from the kitchen of Durbar, where the same family has served up Indian specialties for the last 54 years. This was a popular Indian restaurant before Indian restaurants were popular, and—in a city now brimming with this kind of food—it still manages to be one of the best values. The menu ranges across India, with a collection of favorites and some unexpected dishes, such as the Brinjal Jalfrezi—an entire eggplant spiced with chilies.

▶ *i* ⊖Bayswater. Turn left onto Queensway, left onto Moscow Rd., and right onto Hereford toward Westbourne Grove. Starter £2-5. Main courses £6-9. Lunch special £4.50. ⏲ Open M-Th noon-2:30pm and 5:30-11:30pm, F 5:30-11:30pm, Sa-Su noon-2:30pm and 5:30-11:30pm.

Snowflake Gelato GELATO $
43 Westbourne Grove
☎020 7221 9549 www.snowflakegelato.co.uk

A constant stream of customers slip in and out of this über-modern gelateria in the heart of Hyde Park. The signature flavor—Snowflake—is a feathery mix of white chocolate, coconut, and almond that transcends ice cream and lands somewhere between whipped, frozen nectar of the gods and really great gelato. Takeaway is a popular option, but the pure white leather booths and delicate lighting makes you feel like you're eating in the Snow Queen's palace (happily, the mirrors remain on the wall instead of as a shard in your eye).

▶ *i* ⊖Bayswater. Turn left out of the station onto Queensway, then turn left again onto Westbourne Grove. The gelateria is on the left. 1 scoo £3, 2 scoops £4, 3 scoops £5. ⏲ Open M-Th 10:30am-11:30pm, F-Sa 10:30am-12:30am, Su 10:30am-midnight.

Bloody French FRENCH $$$
149 Westbourne Grove
☎020 7727 7770 www.bloodyfrench.com

Despite the pejorative title, respect of French cooking and service predominates at this eatery on the gentrified side of Westbourne Grove. The long communal tables, small dining space, option to bring your own bottle of wine (M-Th, Su), and laid-back atmosphere means this is a perfect spot for a night out with friends—intricate knowledge of French table manners not required.

i ⊖Notting Hill Gate. Turn right out of the station and turn immediately right again onto Pembridge Villas. Walk 10min. and turn left onto Westbourne Grove. The restaurant is on the left. Appetizer £3, 3 for £7.50. Entrees £6-9. Plates £12-16. Dessert £5.50-7. ☎ Open M-Th 5:30-10:30pm, F 5:30-11pm, Sa 11am-11pm, Su 11am-10:30pm.

Charlie's Portobello Road Cafe   CAFE $
59A Portobello Rd.
☎020 7221 2422 www.charliesportobelloroadcafe.co.uk

The name sounds more like an American roadside diner, but the breakfast is decidedly English, the decor French continental, and the cappuccino good enough to be Italian. If you're staying in one of the nearby hotels on Portobello Rd. or perusing antique, floral-printed upholstered chairs at the market, this shop provides a complimentary mood of knot-unwinding relaxation to accompany your stay in Notting Hill.

i ⊖Notting Hill Gate. Take a right onto Pembridge Rd. and then a left onto Portobello Rd. Free Wi-Fi. Sandwiches £3.75-4.50. Salads £6-8. Full English breakfast £9.50. ☎ Open M-Sa 9am-5pm, Su noon-3pm.

MARYLEBONE AND BLOOMSBURY

The leathery, weathered hipsters of University College London and the yuptastic, rat-racing businesspeople dressed in Westwood make eternal battle over whether the streets of Marylebone and Bloomsbury should be filled with cheap, delicious ethnic eateries or fantastic, modern testaments to capitalism.

🍴 La Fromagerie   CHEESE $
2-6 Moxon St.
☎020 7935 0341 www.lafromagerie.co.uk

Cheese. Everywhere. In the cheeseroom. In the cafe. On your plate. In your stomach. Oh there *is* a reason heroin is nicknamed as such, and while *Let's Go* does not condone drug use, you can quit che—alright, we shall enable you. Sample one of the cheese plates (we recommend the British one) from the quaint, rustic cafe; then pick out some cheese from vault-like cheese room. Then buy some of La Fromagerie's special cheese crackers. Then, declare madness. For how can you claim sanity when you think there is no way your cheese can be better than last time, when, in fact, it is and will be with each bite, you fool!

▶ *i* ⊖Baker St. Turn left onto Marylebone Rd., right onto Marylebone High St., and right again onto Moxon St. Cheese prices vary wildly. Small cheese plat £8.75; large £13.50. Wine pairings by the glass £5-10. ☎ Open M-F 8am-7:30pm, Sa 9am-7pm, Su 10am-6pm.

⬚ Speedy's Café   CAFE $

187 North Gower St.

☎020 7383 3485 www.speedyscafe.co.uk

Because of the commercialization of Baker St. proper, North Gower St. has become the new home of Sir Arthur Conan Doyle's hero in the deerstalker (or shall we say ear hat?). Despite its newfound fame due to its prominence in BBC's *Sherlock,* Speedy's and its delicious sandwiches remain cheap £3-5), and the decor very modestly acknowledges its role in the series with only a few pictures and drawings of the cast. Moreover, the friendly staff couldn't possibly include someone that would lead on Mrs. Hudson while having wives in Doncaster and Islamabad. Enjoy your own 7% solution (of coffee beans) and a sarnie after a visit to the British Library—a resource we're admittedly not sure could help with cataloging 243 different types of tobacco ash.

▶ *i* ⊖Euston Sq. Take the Euston Rd. exit, turn right onto Euston Rd., then right onto North Gower St. Speedy's is on the left. Entree £6-8. ⏰ Open M-F early-3:30pm, Sa early-1:30pm.

⬚ Newman Arms   PIES $$

23 Rathbone St.

☎020 7636 1127 www.newmanarms.co.uk

Newman Arms recently faced the wrath of the Westminster City Council, which decreed that it must serve its pies "more slowly" as a strategy to reduce the number of after-work drinkers milling on the street outside. However, the fact that this is even a problem is just good testament to the charm of the three-centuries-old purveyor of pies. Head upstairs to the Pie Room to try such delicacies as lamb and rosemary or beef and Guinness. Afterward, do not make the mistake of thinking Spotted Dick has anything to do with your cutaneously-challenged ex-boyfriend (or his member). It's simply vegetable pie with currants. And delicious.

▶ *i* ⊖Goodge St. Turn left onto ⊖Tottenham Court Rd., left onto Tottenham St., left onto Charlotte St., and right onto Rathbone St. Enter through the corridor next to the entrance to the pub. Pie £10-12.50. Desserts £4.50. Pints from £3.50. ⏰ Open M-F noon-3pm and 6-10pm.

⬚ Shibuya   JAPANESE $$

2 Acton St.

☎020 7278 3447 www.shibuyalondon.co.uk

In the city proper, sushi this fresh would cost a sum thrice that of Shibuya's offerings. The restaurant's atmosphere is a modern zen haven filled with the lilting birdsong of light J-pop hits and natural fresh light (that streams through some heraldry stained glass). Enjoy one of the sake choices, and if sushi is too raw/too bougie for your taste, select a curry or rice dish. Admittedly, Shibuya does cater to yuppies that seemingly teleport through the less-coiffed St. Pancras area from business-formal Marylebone. However, Shibuya remains a wonderful place to clear your palate and your head and ultimately emerge unsullied by the suited, hunched patrons surrounding you.

▸ *i* ⊖King's Cross St. Pancras. Make a left leaving the station, stay on Euston as it turns into Pentonville Rd., then make a right onto King's Cross Rd. The restaurant is on the corner with Acton St. Sushi fro £3.80. Sushi combos from £15. Entrees £9.50 £10. ⏰ Lunch M-F noon-3pm. Dinner daily 6pm-10:30pm.

Fairuz   LEBANESE $$

3 Blandford St.
☎020 7486 8108 www.fairuz.uk.com

Fairuz—named as such for the Lebanese singing sensation—is the ideal for the indecisive who have made friends with their fellow noncommittal brethren. The set menu lets patrons choose 10 things from dozens of starter options (we recommend the Lamb Sambusak and Shankleesh) with emphases on juicy lamb and the thick hummus. Keeping with the healthy oeuvre of the area, dessert options include fresh fruit (but also baklava).

▸ *i* ⊖Bond St. Turn left onto Oxford St. and right onto James St., which eventually turns into Thayer St. Then make a right onto Blandford St. Takeaway available. Starter £5.50-6.50. Main courses £13-18. ⏰ Open M-Sa noon-11pm, Su noon-10:30pm.

Firebox   CAFE $

106-108 Cromer St.
☎078 5017 7637 fireboxlondon.net

During the good ol' days of Occupy, Firebox stood as a liberal citadel in the heart of Bloomsbury. Now that the radical passions have calmed, the cafe still serves up tasty sandwiches and baked goods (hang around for the poetry slams and free Wi-Fi for the student crowd of UCL). A small corner is devoted to texts by Marx and Lenin that serve as intellectual food for the next vanguard.

▸ *i* ⊖Russell Sq. Turn right onto Bernard St. Then turn left onto Brunswick Square; in a mere 5min., it will switch names from Hunter St. to Judd St. Turn right onto Cromer; the cafe is on the left. Free Wi-Fi. Breakfast item £1.50-6. Sandwiches £4-4.50. Smoothies £3.20. ⏰ Open M-F 8am-6pm, Sa 11am-6pm.

Alara

ORGANIC, VEGETARIAN $

58-60 Marchmont St.
☎020 7837 1172 www.alarashop.com

Alara, a health food store that provides welcome relief from processed food, plays with such British staples (try the brie and apple sandwich £2.50). Instead of the jacket potato and shepherd's pie, however, Alara's hot buffet offers roasted potatoes and other such vegetarian hits like ratatouille.

▶ *i* ⊖Russell Sq. Veer right when exiting the station and head up Marchmont St.Buffet £1.19 per 100g. 🕗 Open M-F 9am-8pm, Sa 10am-7pm, Su 11am-6pm.

NORTH LONDON

⬛ La Crêperie de Hampstead

CREPERIE $

Around 77 Hampstead High St

Hampstead natives swear that this creperie saves a trip across the Channel. Hampstead natives also hit the level of privilege where going across the Channel merely for some crepes isn't that strange. Regardless of its posh patrons, you can snag a delicious, filling crepe here in a cone for unde £5 with little to no wait; then, take it to the Heath (p. 54).

▶ *i* ⊖Hampstead. Turn left onto Hampstead High St. No seating. Most crepes fro £3.90-4.50. 🕗 Open M-Th 11:45am-11pm, F-Su 11:45am-11:30pm.

⬛ Le Mercury

FRENCH $$

140A Upper St.
☎020 7354 4088 www.lemercury.co.uk

Complete your English experience by expatriating your palate to France. In London, your Gaul options are usually limited to Michelin star restaurants and Pret a Manger. Le Mercury strikes a happy medium, with low prices (all dishes unde £9) and ambitious items like *Poir pochee et bleu* (white wine poached pear, blue cheese and roast walnuts) and slow-roasted pork belly with celeriac confeit. Enjoy them in the yellow interior dotted by flickering candlelight.

▶ *i* ⊖Angel. Exit and turn right onto Upper St. Starter £4. Main courses £9. Desserts £3. 🕗 Open M-Sa noon-1am, Su noon-11:30pm.

Mango Room

CARIBBEAN $$

10-12 Kentish Town Rd.
☎020 7482 5065 www.mangoroom.co.uk

Stables Market is filled with black-clad teenagers arguing through mouthfuls of dried-out stall rice about who is faker (the girl with the avian-themed dress or the boy with the

Food

horn-rimmed glasses?). Ignore that "scene" and head to a truly authentic restaurant dominated by bright paintings, reggae, and delicious Caribbean dishes—like ackee and saltfish, jerk chicken, and curries.

▶ *i* ⊖Camden High St. Turn left onto ⊖Camden High St., left onto Camden Rd., and left onto Kentish Town Rd. Lunch entree £7.50-9. Dinner entrees £11-15. ⏰ Open daily noon-11pm.

Gallipoli   TURKISH $$
102 Upper St.
☎020 7359 0630 www.cafegallipoli.com

More successful than the British military forays referenced in its name, Gallipoli is a warren of hanging bronze lamps, painted plates, and wooden knick-knacks that make this restaurant feel like a Turkish bazaar. The food—tangy feta, smoky grilled meats, and delicately spiced pilafs—feels no less convincing. Choose from a selection of mezze or order a more traditional main course.

▶ *i* ⊖Angel. Turn right onto Upper St. Mezz £4-5.50. Entrees £9-12. ⏰ Open M-Th 11am-11pm, F 11am-midnight, Sa 9:30am-midnight, Su 9:30am-11pm.

EAST LONDON

Brick Lane is one long banquet table of ethnic eateries and coffee shops. Bengali and Vietnamese joints are plentiful, and the brand name caffeine distributors (COSTA, Starbucks, Nero) are happily absent, although we're sure they'd still get business as an "ironic statement."

📵 Cafe 1001   CAFE $
91 Brick Ln.
☎020 7247 9679 www.cafe1001.co.uk

After you've picked up some avian-emblazoned apparel at Old Spitalfields Market (p. 111), walk over to this alleyway coffee shop whose patrons converse enough to rival Scheherazade. At night, the salad bar transitions to a real bar, and the back room becomes a venue for up-and-coming bands and DJs. Bloc Party filmed their video for "The Prayer" here; in their apt, immortal words, "East London is a vampire."

▶ *i* ⊖Aldgate East. Turn left onto Whitechapel Rd., left onto Osborn St., then continue onto Brick Ln. Free Wi-Fi. Live bands on Tu (rock) and W (folk and jazz). Swing dancing classes Th 11am-5pm. Club night F-Su 7pm-midnight. Cove £3-5 after midnight. Burger and chips £5. Coffee £1.20-2. ⏰ Open daily 7am-midnight, often stays open all night F-Su.

Mien Tay
VIETNAMESE $

122 Kingsland Rd.

☎020 7729 3074 www.mientay.co.uk

What Brick Lane is to Bengali food, this stretch of Kingsland Rd. is to Vietnamese cuisine. Mien Tay sets itself above the rest the hackneyed options with low prices and high-quality, crispy spring rolls, fragrant *pho,* and tasty noodle dishes (try the lemongrass and curry noodles). The service is swift, and the dining room is bright and roomy. We recommend coming before or after a visit to the nearby Geffrye Museum (p. 56).

▸ *i* ✆Hoxton. Make a left after leaving the station, then a right onto Cremer St., and a left onto Kingsland Rd. Starter £2-5. Main courses £5-9. ⟁ Open M-Sa noon-11pm, Su noon-10pm.

Aladin
BANGLADESHI $$

132 Brick Ln.

☎020 7247 8210 www.aladinbricklane.co.uk

Pass by the line of restaurant hawkers and head straight for Aladin. Their touts are less aggressive, probably because their Bangladeshi food is so legitimately good that they don't need special deals to attract customers. The waiters are happy to offer suggestions, both about what sort of curry or dish you should order and which nearby off-license you should visit to find the cheapest beer. The restaurant has even been praised by HRH Prince Charles himself on LBC Radio (Aladin will play you the tape if you ask).

▸ *i* ✆Shoreditch High St. Make a right after leaving the station, go down Sclater St., and turn right onto Brick Ln. No alcohol served, but you can BYOB with no corkage charge. Main course £7-12. Curries from £5. ⟁ Open M-Th noon-midnight, F-Sa noon-1am, Su noon-10:30pm.

SOUTH LONDON

◪ Franco Manca
PIZZERIA $

Unit 4, Market Row

☎020 7738 3021 www.francomanca.co.uk

It's not the most inviting of scenarios, winding your way through the back alley corridors of a Brixton shopping complex to reach Franca Manca. Nevertheless, the boisterous flow of Italian and divine smells of pizza toppings other than "cheese" are worth the strange approach. The crust is a light sourdough concoction, the olive oil is organic, and the toppings include some bold choices like courgettes and aubergines (that's zucchini and eggplant, y'all) and yellow peppers. If we have not yet

Food

convinced you, the bottles of libation are quite liberally priced, all unde £20.

▶ *i* ⊖Brixton. Make a left leaving the Tube, a quick left onto Electric Ave., then a right onto Electric Ln., and a left onto Market Row. Pizz £4.50-7. ⏰ Open M noon-5pm, Tu-Sa noon-11pm, Su noon-10:30pm.

🗒 Negril   CARIBBEAN $$
132 Brixton Hill
☎020 8674 8798

Brixton is famous for its Afro-Caribbean food, and Negril is the place to sample some of its greatest hits. You can try regional specialties like callaloo (a leafy green), saltfish fritters, and goat curry or go with something more familiar, like roasted chicken or barbeque ribs (as well as smoothies). They also have quite a few vegan options, in accordance with the traditional Rastafarian diet. The weekend brunch is very popular and allows patrons to spread out on Negril's picnic benches for hours.

▶ *i* ⊖Brixton. Make a left leaving the Tube and continue as the road becomes Brixton Hill. Delivery and takeaway available. No alcohol served, but you can BYOB for £2.50 corkage charge per person. Entrees £7-12. ⏰ Open M-F 5-10pm, Sa-Su 10am-10pm.

The Common Café & Bistro   CAFE $
21 The Pavement
☎020 7622 4944

The Common is a simple, French-style cafe across from Clapham Common that can cheaply cater your picnicking goals. If you prefer maintaining the sun exposure level of Nicole Kidman, hang out on one of the two levels of seating or visit at night, when they serve bistro-style dishes (steak, pasta, etc.). However, they're known for their abundant breakfast and brunch, which includes everything from granola with yogurt and fresh fruit to a full fry-up.

▶ *i* ⊖Clapham Common. Go left from the station and continue along The Pavement toward the park. Sandwiche £2-4.50. Brunch and breakfast dishes £4-7. Entrees £7-12. ⏰ Open daily 8am-10pm.

WEST LONDON

🗒 Sufi   PERSIAN $$
70 Askew Rd.
☎020 8834 4888 www.sufirestaurant.com

Nestled in the streets connecting Goldhawk Rd. and Uxbridge Rd. is what many locals will swear to be the best Persian food in London. It's a small place with a nice but ultimately unmemorable façade and decor (excluding the dozens of award stickers hanging near the bottom of the window), but the delights within will blow away first impressions. Sample the saffron ice cream after your meal for only £3 more.

▶ *i* ⊖Shepherd's Bush Market. Make a right down Uxbridge Rd. when leaving the station, then walk about 15min. and make a left down Askew Rd. You can also take Bus #207 to the beginning of Askew Rd. Starter £2-4. Entrees £7-13. ⏰ Open daily noon-11pm.

The Gate   VEGAN, GLUTEN-FREE $$$

51 Queen Caroline St., 2nd fl.
☎020 8748 6932 www.thegate.tv

London isn't really vegetarian *unfriendly* per se. The preponderance of over 20 major produce markets in the city, combined with the ethnic influence of Indian and Asian food, means that if your empathy extends to animals, you're not going to starve. However, vegetarian/vegan exclusive restaurants are a bit of a rarity. Helpfully, The Gate has a series of delectable options for herbivores, from lavender crème brûlée to the couscous-crusted aubergine. If you're going to catch a show afterward at The Apollo (p. 98), the pre-theater menu is great option even if you don't adhere to a specific diet.

▶ *i* ⊖Hammersmith. Take the south exit from the Hammersmith shopping center toward the London Apollo and follow Queen Caroline St. Reservations recommended 3 days in advance. Mezze 1 fo £4, 3 for £10, 5 for £15. Entrees £11-14. ⏰ Open M-F noon-2:30pm and 6-10pm, Sa 6-11pm.

Patio   POLISH $$

5 Goldhawk Rd.
☎020 8743 5194

"Hey! Wanna go out for Chinese, Thai, or Italian?" exclaimed the young traveler. "Polish," deadpanned the expert. It's not conventional, but excellence rarely is. Patio is owned by a former Polish opera singer and full of warm carpets, over-stuffed chairs, and the smell of grandmotherly cooking. Diners enjoy traditional Polish fare like stuffed pancakes, veal, and cucumber and dill salad. There's even a dusty-sounding piano for guests to bang out a tune and occasional gypsy fiddlers.

▶ *i* ⊖Shepherd's Bush. Cross Uxbridge Rd. and turn right onto Shepherd's Bush Green. Follow it until it becomes Goldhawk Rd. Entrees £8-13. 3-course meal £15. ⏰ Open M-F noon-3pm and 5-11pm, Sa-Su 6-11:30pm.

Nightlife

If you're looking for an "authentic British drinking experience," you're best off just steadily day drinking. Simply put, the British drink a lot. However, in terms of institutionalized, well-mannered frivolity, three different experiences distinguish themselves: the pub, the club, and the speakeasy. The pub scene is relatively standardized, right down to the fonts that advertise the Sunday roasts, so what we've endeavored to do is tap the ones with the most local crowds and the cheapest prices. Befitting its status as a world capital, the club scene here has seen hundreds of world famous DJs at venues such as Fabric and Ministry of Sound. And strangely enough, even though Britain never banned alcohol outright like the States, there are hidden "speakeasy" cocktail joints that rely on mixology to bring in their customer base. Whichever your modus operandi, all three serve as antidotes against London's sometimes dark mood.

THE CITY OF LONDON

Pricey pubs filled with *American Psycho* (or British psycho) types are a dime a dozen in the City, but your options improve as you head north toward **Clerkenwell.**

◙ Fabric   CLUB

77A Charterhouse St.

☎020 7336 8898 www.fabriclondon.com

It feels like the space-time fabric is bending underneath you at London's most famous club. Oh wait, that's just the vibrating dance floor. The biggest contributor to this club's legitimacy is the soundtrack: they eschew not only top 40 but more mainstream DJs like Tiësto and Paul Oakenfeld as well. The space—a renovated warehouse full of deconstructed industrial decor—is equally serious (especially compared to the fun-loving dance crowd). If you're over 21, you'll probably feel a bit old, as the bulk of the clientele are teenagers drinking £10 rum and cokes to their newfound clubbing freedom.

▶ *i* ✪Farringdon. Turn left onto Cowcross St. and continue until you hit Charterhouse St. Cover F-S £15-20, Su up to £10. Get discounts by buying tickets in advance. Beer £4.50. ⏰ Open F 10pm-6am, Sa 11pm-8am, Su 11pm-6am.

◙ The Jerusalem Tavern   PUB

55 Britton St.

☎020 7490 4281 www.stpetersbrewery.co.uk

The Jerusalem Tavern is the kind of London pub where you might be convinced you're back in the 18th century (or turn of the BCE Jerusalem for all we know). The tavern is as bare as they come: it's just a narrow, wooden interior without any music playing. It's the only tavern in London to offer all of the St. Peter's ales. These specialized brews are enough to renounce your prior beer preferences. Then again, if you don't want the walk back to seem like a Calvary trudge, we recommend multiple trips.

▶ *i* ✪Farringdon. Turn left onto Cowcross St., left onto Turnmill St., right onto Benjamin St., and left onto Britton St. Pints fro £3. ⏰ Open M-F 11am-11pm.

The Slaughtered Lamb PUB

34-35 Great Sutton St.

☎020 7253 1516 www.theslaughteredlambpub.com

Don't be put off by this pub's macabre name (or the pentacle logo)—it's merely a remnant of the district's old meat-packin' days. The Slaughtered Lamb feels a bit like a gigantic old gentleman's club, with leather couches, comfy armchairs, and framed pictures around a fireplace...and a hip hop soundtrack. Downstairs, the music continues with frequent live shows and occasional comedy acts.

▶ *i* ⊖Barbican. Turn left onto Goswell Rd. and left onto Great Sutton St. Pints aroun £4. ⏰ Open M-Th 11:30am-midnight, F-Sa 11:30am-1am, Su 12:30-10:30pm.

The Betsey Trotwood PUB

56 Farringdon Rd.

☎020 7253 4285 www.thebetsey.com

The namesake Betsey Trotwood was a colorful, man-hating character in Dickens's *David Copperfield*. The pub has retained the verve of Dame Maggie Smith and done away with the sexism, so most patrons just quietly enjoy a pint of one of many cask ales. The space opens out onto the street, and sunshine streams in through the large windows, creating a comfortable lazy vibe in summer. Various events, like bluegrass shows and poetry readings, are held downstairs.

▶ *i* ⊖Farringdon. Turn right onto Cowcross St. and right onto Farringdon Rd. Pints fro £3.50. ⏰ Open M-F noon-11pm, Sa noon-11:30pm, Su noon-10:30pm.

Ye Olde Cheshire Cheese PUB

145 Fleet St.

☎020 7353 6170

There's nothing we hate more than tacking "Ye Olde" onto something built in the late '90s. But here we have a genuine article: the Cheshire Cheese has been serving pints since the 17th century. Charles Dickens was once a regular patron, and now it's filled with the perfect ratio of bankers, tourists, and students procrastinating on their revisions. Mind your head on your way down to the basement bar; people were a lot shorter back when they built this place.

▶ *i* ⊖Temple. Go up Arundel St. and turn right onto Strand, which becomes Fleet St. Pints from £3.50. ⏰ Open M-F 11am-11pm, Sa noon-11pm, Su noon-7pm.

THE WEST END

The West End is home to not only the theater district and the red light district, but the nightlife district as well. The wealthy have memberships to private clubs, so public options sometimes leave Londoners and tourists trying a bit too hard. Nevertheless, there's no place more trafficked on a Friday night, and your nicest high heels and/or dress shirt will probably still not be enough for the scene's judgmental gaze. The West End also is home base for London's GLBT scene, which provides a nice smorgasbord of cocktail clubs and dance venues.

◪ The Borderline   CLUB

Orange Yard, off Manette St. http://venues.meanfiddler.com/borderline/home
☎020 7734 5547

Though Borderline is essentially a bare basement with the same drunken dancing as you'll discover at any London club, the all-important variable is the playlist of indie artists like Joy Division, The Smiths, The Kooks, and Vampire Weekend. The crowd is quite devoted to the music, and you can't help but get into the spirit of things when everyone is shouting lyrics to purposely obscure songs. The club also hosts live music, for those who have the "Christopher Columbus saw it first" approach to performers (or, as a true hipster would say, Leif Erikson).

▶ *i* ⊖Tottenham Court Rd. Turn right onto ⊖Charing Cross Rd. and right onto Manette St. Punk on W. Student night on Th. Indie rock and Brit pop on F-Sa. Cover W-T £5, F-Sa £7. Frequent £2 drink specials. ⦿ Open W-Sa 11pm-4am.

◪ Dirty Martini   BAR, CLUB

11-12 Russell St.
☎0844 371 2550 www.dirtymartini.uk.com

Martinis: the ode to gin made by James Bond and countless other debonair sirs. This club in the heart of Covent Garden does not relinquish this tradition, even though the cool, tuxedoed, cigar-smoking associations have metamorphosed into tightly dressed women and their suit jacket-less friends. Society has traded in fussiness for accessibility, and that's great for the student traveler, as the expert mixology is a steal compared to other clubs charging the same for a lousy, too-sweet mojito.

▶ *i* ⊖Covent Garden. Head down James St. to the ⊖Covent Garden Piazza, turn left and go around it until you come to the corner of Russell St. Happy hour M-Th until 10pm, F-Sa until 8pm, Su all day. Cove £5 high-capacity weekend. Beer £4. Cocktails £8-9. ⦿ Open M-W 5pm-1am, Th 5pm-3am, F 4pm-3am, Sa noon-3am, Su 1-11pm.

Nightlife

▨ Ain't Nothin' But...   BAR, LIVE MUSIC

20 Kingly St.

☎020 7287 0514 www.aintnothinbut.co.uk

Has your wife left you? Has your dog died? Has your life been nothing but a meaningless parade of drivel-filled observations? Well then, dear, the blues are your anthem, and in an area filled with pop hits of the later '00s, this R&B stalwart provides a haven for both good times and bad. Most patrons lounge around the bar, but the back room hosts live music, so you can really sink your teeth into the existential pain of your plight.

▶ *i* ⊖Oxford Circus. Head down Regent St., turn right onto Great Marlborough St., then right onto Kingly St. Cove £5 F-Sa after 8:30pm. Beer from £4. ☾ Open M-Th 5pm-1am, F 5pm-2:30am, Sa 3pm-2:30am, Su 3pm-midnight.

▨ Heaven   CLUB, GLBT

Under the Arches, Villiers St.

☎020 7930 2020 www.heavennightclub-london.com

Loudly announcing that heaven is in a Tube Station is a one-way ticket to being committed. Nay, the paradise we refer to is one of London's largest gay clubs, replete with giant video screens, a warehouse for a dance floor, and enough campy men to staff a production of *La Cage Aux Folles*. Mondays have "Popcorn," a student-friendly event with good drink specials and a welcoming door policy; the music varies from hip hop to techno to classic dance tunes. Thursday through Saturday, the club is run by G-A-Y, London's biggest GLBT party organization. Friday night brings "Camp Attacks"(with amazingly cheesy disco music) and performances by famous pop stars.

▶ *i* ⊖Charing Cross. Turn right from the station and head down Villiers St. The club is under the archway about halfway down. Cove £5; usually free before midnight or if you sign up on the guest list. ☾ Open M 11pm-3am, Th 11pm-3am, F-Sa 11pm-5am.

Freud   BAR

198 Shaftesbury Ave.

☎020 7240 9933

Freud said in *Interpretation of Dreams*that dreaming of staircases was indicative of sexual suppression. Well, climb on down into your mother's womb—er, a totally normal West End bar. The place is more Kafkaesque than Freudian, with no chaise lounges and a lot of concrete, but the drinks are clever (Slippery Nipple, anyone?), and the prices are right.

▶ *i* ⊖Piccadilly Circus. Turn right onto Shaftesbury Ave. Bee £3.50. Mixed drinks £5.50-7.50. Credit card min. £10. ☾ Open M-Th 11am-11pm, F-Sa 11am-1am, Su noon-10:30pm.

Village
BAR, GLBT

81 Wardour St.

☎020 7478 0530 www.village-soho.co.uk

Early in the evening, Village looks like just another after-work bar with a happily iridescent logo. Then the go-go dancers climb up onto their perches, and a veritable parade of attractive men—and their equally attractive flame dames—swarm in to enjoy the night (with associate flame dames as well). Throughout the week, you can expect drag queens, karaoke (Tuesdays and Wednesdays), and more.

▶ *i* ✆Piccadilly Circus. Turn right onto Shaftesbury Ave. then left onto Wardour St. Cocktail £6-7. 🕑 Open M-Sa 4pm-1am, Su 4-11:30pm.

Candy Bar
BAR, CLUB, GLBT

4 Carlisle St.

☎020 7287 5041 www.candybarsoho.com

Candy Bar is London's premier—and certainly most popular—lesbian bar and club. Working our way down, the top level is a lounge and bag check, the ground floor is a mirrored bar with LCD TVs playing top 40 hits, and the basement is a dance club (where boys are not allowed when dancers are performing). To Candy's credit, the patrons are some of the most diverse in terms of ethnicity and age in London.

▶ *i* ✆Tottenham Court Rd. Turn left onto Oxford St., left onto Dean St., and right onto Carlisle St. Cove £5 F-Sa after 10pm. Drinks £1.50-6. 🕑 Open M-Th 5pm-3am, F-Sa 4pm-3am, Su 4pm-12:30am.

Lowlander
BAR

36 Drury Ln.

☎020 7379 7446 www.lowlander.com

No, this isn't the Highlander's favorite place to nurse a drink when down. Rather, its name comes from its Belgian theme (think cavernous ceilings and Art Nouveau-type posters), and Lowlander is the place to go if you can't stand another row of taps pouring exclusively British ale. Catering to a pre- and post-theater crowd, it's one of few bars where people actually eat meals.

▶ *i* ✆Covent Garden. Head right down Longacre and turn left onto Drury Ln. Pints fro £4. Tasters £7.50-15. 🕑 Open M-W 11:30am-11pm, Th-Sa 11:30am-11:30pm, Su noon-10:30pm.

Nightlife

Club 49 CLUB

49 Greek St.

☎020 7439 4159 www.club49soho.com

Club 49 is in many ways the classic West End club. Girls in strappy, glittery, sky-high heels teeter with drink in hand. They are soon joined by suited men whose ties—the ultimate untapped potential for diversity—even look the same. Nevertheless, the staff is friendlier than the average, tired set, and the gyrating revelers always seem to be having fun. Finally, you can enjoy the competitively priced drinks in the mirrored upstairs lounge if you don't feel like dealing with the sloppy result of precarious footwear and inebriation.

▶ *i* ⊖Tottenham Court Rd. Turn left onto Oxford St., left onto Soho St., left around Soho Sq., and left onto Greek St. Cove £4-10. Cocktails £8-10. ⏰ Open M-F 5:30pm-3am, Sa 7pm-3am.

Thirst BAR, CLUB

53 Greek St.

☎020 7437 1977 www.thirstbar.com

Given that alcohol and Andy Murray are the only thing we've seen melt British stoicism, we have to give credit to Thirst's enabling of the former. For at this stylish pub, it's usually either "stupid" hour (half-price drinks) or happy hour (when they're £2 off). The scene can be a bit subdued at times, but the decor of stainless steel and low lights can make conversation intimate even during more crowded hours.

▶ *i* ⊖Tottenham Court Rd. Turn left onto Oxford St., left onto Soho St., left around Soho Sq., and left onto Greek St. Cover (usually after 10pm) £3-5. "Stupid" prices are £4.25-4.50, "happy" around £6, normal £8. Credit card min. £10. ⏰ Open M-Sa 5pm-3am. "Stupid" hour daily 5-7pm. Happy hour M-W 7:30pm-close, Th 7:30-9pm.

WESTMINSTER

It's good to remember that Westminster is a metonym for the English government. And where does the English government go to drink? Not anywhere you're invited to, unless Ed Miliband is among our readers. Therefore, there are no tucked away bars in Whitehall, but as you go toward Pimlico, there's an affordable, quiet pub scene to be discovered.

◪ Cask BEER HEAVEN

6 Charlwood St.

☎020 7630 7225 www.caskpubandkitchen.com

Maybe you're not a beer person, and maybe you're bitter about not knowing why everyone orders a "lager." Cask is a great introduction to this expansive world of acquired taste, and would you want your first great nicotine experience to be with a pack of Lucky Strikes behind a KFC or a Cuban cigar? The beer "menu" is actually a binder full of hundreds upon hundreds of bottled beers from around the world. A couple dozen more are on tap, and they rotate the selection so they can accommodate as many rare and novel brews as possible. Eager to induct another to the bro-fold of beer, the staff is always ready to make recommendations and refrain from snobbery when responding to even the most basic questions and silliest mispronunciations.

▶ *i* ⊖Pimlico. Turn right onto Tachwood St.; Cask is on the right, at the corner with Charlwood St. Free Wi-Fi (as if you needed an excuse to spend more time here). Pints start aroun £4, but vary wildly from there. ☒ Open M-Sa noon-11pm, Su noon-10:30pm.

Brass Monkey PUB

250 Vauxhall Bridge Rd.
☎020 7834 0553 www.brass-monkeybar.co.uk

Vauxhall Bridge Rd. can be a bit intimidatingly run-down as it prepares to shoot over the Thames. However, this charming, twinkly pub stands out as a solid option, especially if you're staying in the area. It's not a rowdy scene, and a good indicator of calm is that a decent proportion of patrons enjoy food with their drink.

▶ *i* ⊖Victoria. Turn right onto Vauxhall Bridge Rd. Win £5-6. Pints around £4. ☒ Open M-Sa 11am-11pm.

THE SOUTH BANK

▩ The Hide BAR

39-45 Bermondsey St.
☎020 7403 6655 www.thehidebar.com

The isolated elements of The Hide would hint at pretention: fancy cocktails with snarky descriptions, red velvet curtains, obscure jazz, and suited men in various state of dishevelment. However, it's mostly a local crowd that's just as happy with a modern concrete bar and mood lighting as an old-fashioned wooden one with fringe lamps. The cocktails are quite good: try your liver at the Parliamentary Brandy (Jensen's Old Tom Gin, cubed sugar, Peychaud's bitters £9), modeled after a moonshine recipe used during one of the temperance periods.

▶ *i* ⊖London Bridge. Walk toward the bridge and turn right onto Tooley St., then right onto Bermondsey St. Most spirit £4. Beer from £4.80. Cocktails £9-10. ☒ Open Tu 5pm-midnight, W-Th 5pm-1am, F-Sa 5pm-2am, Su 5pm-10:30pm.

Nightlife

Southwark Tavern   PUB

22 Southwark St.

☎020 7403 0257 www.thesouthwarktavern.co.uk

You can try your hand at the certifiably hokey London Dungeon "experience," or you can drink in Southwark Tavern's basement—a series of converted prison cells that exceed their original charm (then again, it often seems as if half the South Bank is a prison and the other half a brothel). The ground floor is your standard warm welcome with some surprises: would you like some quail eggs, ox cheek, or edamame with that pint?

▶ *i* ⊖London Bridge. Exit down Borough High St.; the pub is where Southwark St. splits off. Quiz night on Tu. Pint £4. ② Open M-W 11am-midnight, Th-F 11am-1am, Sa 10am-1am, Su noon-midnight.

Ministry of Sound   CLUB

103 Gaunt St.

☎087 0060 0010 www.ministryofsound.com

In club years, this staple of the EDM scene is ancient and has hosted world-famous DJs like Tiësto, Armin van Buuren, Afrojack, and Deadmau5 for over 20 years. Now, the scene is a mix of techno die-hards and dilettantes in Jeffrey Campbell high heels and plaid shirts that use the trance interludes to take selfies. Your music options are the main dance floor with go-go dancers, smoke hoses,and light shows; the smaller boutique floor on the second floor; the VIP lounge; and the outside patio that streams in music from the main floor.

▶ *i* ⊖Elephant and Castle. Exit toward the roundabout, walk down Borough High St., and turn left onto Gaunt St. Cover £13-20; £5 discount with student ID. ② Open F 10:30pm-6am, Sa 11pm-7am. Weekday hours vary; check the website.

SOUTH KENSINGTON AND CHELSEA

🔲 The Drayton Arms   PUB

153 Old Brompton Rd.

☎020 7835 2301 www.thedraytonarmssw5.co.uk

The Drayton Arms is a aesthete's pub, with a sun-catching wall of windows that breaks the mold of the typically dark and cloistered London joint. It's really the perfect mix between its post code (chandeliers and leather booths) and a liberal spirit (in-house theater and a not exclusively yuppie crowd). The theater hosts five nights a week of comedy, film, and drama.

▶ *i* ⊖Gloucester Rd. Turn right onto Gloucester Rd. and right onto Old Brompton Rd. Theater productions Tu-Sa. Quiz night M £1 buy-in). Pints around £3.70. Wine £4-7. Cocktails £6-7. ② Open M-Sa noon-11pm.

🞀 The Troubadour Club   LIVE MUSIC, BAR

263-267 Old Brompton Rd.

☎020 7370 1434 www.troubadour.co.uk

A Troubadour is a sublime thing to call an artist: it means a poet who puts lyric to music. But instead of merely a pretty name, this bar has earned its title, playing host to Bob Dylan, Joni Mitchell, Paul Simon, and Jimi Hendrix. More recently, it was the site of Adele's first gig. The adjacent bar and cafe is intimate with coffee cups and wine glasses hanging from the ceiling and a strip adjacent to the bar packed with aspiring artists themselves.

▶ *i* ⊖Gloucester Rd. Turn right onto Gloucester Rd., then right onto Old Brompton Rd. Live music most nights. Poetry night every other M. Friday shows 21+. Happy hour Tu-Su 8-9pm. Cover usuall £6-12. Cash only. 🕐 Cafe open daily 9am-midnight. Live music M-W 8pm-midnight, Th-Sa 8pm-2am, Su 8pm-midnight.

Azteca Latin Lounge   LATIN BAR

329 King's Rd.

☎020 7352 4087 www.aztecalatinlounge.com

Azteca is a perfect cocktail itself. Mix together sultry Latin music, giant party drinks that serve four, salsa lessons, and cheap, delicious food. Within this absurdly colorful environment, Chelsea's residents take a welcome respite from the chatting on bar stools with a pint in hand and switch it out for shooting tequila on comfy couches.

▶ *i* ⊖Sloane Sq. It's a 10-15min. walk from the station, so you can also take bus #11 or 22. Salsa lessons Tu 7:30-8:30pm. Beer fro £3. Cocktails from £6. Party cocktail (serves 4) £25. 🕐 Open M-Th 5pm-midnight, F-Sa 5pm-3am, Su 5pm-midnight.

The Blackbird   PUB

209 Earl's Court Rd.

☎020 7835 1855

The Blackbird is your friendly neighborhood pub with all of the infrastructural necessities: long bar, lots of booths, cheap drinks, soft rock, and healthy local contingent. The food runs the gamut from roasts to British staples and is served up quick. Stop here for a calm night instead of rushing to the self-proclaimed "local English pubs" to the east.

▶ *i* ⊖Earl's Court. Just across the road from the station, slightly to the right. Pints fro £3.50. 🕐 Open M-W 8:30am-11pm, Th-Sa 8:30am-11:30pm, Su 8:30am-10:30pm.

Nightlife

Janet's Bar   BAR

30 Old Brompton Rd.

☎020 7581 3160

Janet's is the dive bar you did not think Kensington was capable
of supporting. Yet within its kitsch walls—plastered in pen-
nants and photographs—stand some of the area's professional
sort that is clearly tired of the predictable football game/lager/
muttering that typifies the British pub scene. Join in for a
Beatles sing-along or rejoice in the fact that here you can drink
publicly past midnight.

▶ *i* ⊖South Kensington. As you exit the station, Old Brompton Rd. is across
the street. Live music Tu-Su after 9:30pm. Beer aroun £4.50. Cocktails
£6.50-8.50. Credit card min. £3. ⏰ Open M-W 11:30am-1am, Th 11:30am-
1:30am, F-Sa 11:30am-2:30am, Su 11:30am-1am.

Zuma   BAR

5 Raphael St.

☎020 7854 1010 www.zumarestaurant.com

Hidden away behind the hectic Knightsbridge area is one of the
best (read: expensive) Japanese restaurants in London, replete
with a mind-blowing bar. If you've ever wanted to try sake or if
you've refined your palate to expert-level tasting, a selection of
over 40 varieties await your taste buds and soon-to-be-warmed
throat. They also serve deliciously complex cocktails like the
rubabu (rhubarb-infused sake shaken with vodka and fresh passion fruit) that put mojitos to shame. Granted, the only party to
be found here is when one of the business-casual patrons loosens
his tie a bit, so put on those nice clothes and imbibe.

▶ *i* ⊖Knightsbridge. Walk left down Brompton Rd., take right onto Lancelot
Place, and a right onto Raphael St. Cocktails £10-12. ⏰ Open daily noon-
3pm and 6-11pm.

HYDE PARK TO NOTTING HILL

Of course you're not going to want to drink alone in Hyde Park
every night. Thank heavens then for the quiet nightlife scene
divided between the younger, trendy cocktail sippers and their
parents, who prefer a well-decorated pub. Every option here is
on the tony side, but raising a pint for £3-4 is a pretty universal
standard to which you can repair.

◙ Notting Hill Arts Club   CLUB
21 Notting Hill Gate
☎020 7460 4459 www.nottinghillartsclub.com

As you burst forth into the club's urban grotto, you would never suspect its well-to-do neighborhood would condone such gritty revelry. The concrete walls reverberate hard-hitting techno as 18- to 25-year-olds kick back absinthe and dance precariously on the stage. Art installations include words projected onto the lounge couches, resulting in patrons' smiling faces imprinted with words like "sweet sounds memory" in a new level of Insta-gram nostalgia. Of course, you can always just have a pint and a conversation, but with the level of visual performance around here, relaxation is achieved more through sensory overload.

▶ *i* ⊖Notting Hill Gate. Walking up from the subway, it is on the right side of the road between two segments of the A204 (look for the large triangular crosswalks). The door isn't well marked, but look for the smoking area and metal fences keeping the entrance line in place. 18+, be sure to bring proof of age. Check the website beforehand for specific opening times and events. Cover varies, generall £5-8. Beer £3. Cocktails from £8. ⌚ Open M-W 7pm-2am, Th 7:30pm-2am, F 7pm-2am, Sa 8pm-2am, Su 6pm-1am.

◙ Portobello Star   BAR
171 Portobello Rd.
☎020 7229 8016 www.portobellostarbar.co.uk

The Portobello Star has gentrified itself from a old-timey, Modest Mouse "Float On" aesthetic to a yuppie affair, but the cocktails remain fearsomely good. We recommend taking a friend and splitting the strongest drink on the menu—the W11 Zombie (four types of rum, Pernod absinthe, and an exotic medley of passion fruit, grenadine, and pineapple; £15). Enjoy it as the DJ (posted at the bar with a laptop) spins pepped-up R&B and rock; take your drink to the back lounge room if the trussed-up crowd near the front starts networking too enthusiastically.

▶ *i* ⊖Notting Hill Gate. Take a right onto Pembridge Rd., then a left onto Portobello Rd. Cocktails £7.50-15. ⌚ Open M-Th 11am-11:30pm, F-Sa 11am-12:30am, Su 11am-11:30pm.

Portobello Gold   PUB
95 Portobello Rd.
☎020 7229 8528 www.portobellogold.com

Portobello Gold is an old-fashioned pub with live music and a patronage that sings along to rock hits (and includes Bill Clinton). The front is your traditional, wood-paneled bar with pub-dwellers ranging from 18 to 80; the back is a sort of green-house, with candles and plants shielding patrons from prying eyes (although ears can pick up all manner of accents in this multi-culti bar). If you can wrangle it, try to snag the one table upstairs that overlooks the bar: romance personified.

▶ *i* ⊖Notting Hill Gate. Turn right onto Pembridge Rd., then left onto Portobello Rd. Live music Su 7pm. Pints fro £3.50. Wine £4-6. ⌚ Open M-Th 9am-midnight, F-Sa 9am-12:30am, Su 9am-11pm.

Sun in Splendour   PUB
7 Portobello Rd.
☎020 7792 0914 www.suninsplendourpub.co.uk

As the summer solstice nears, the apex of this fun pub is its secret beer garden (which sadly closes up shop when the sun does at 9:30pm). Otherwise, take a drink in the main room bedecked with wood-latticed windows, giant mirrors, gold chandeliers, and faux-distressed Victorian wallpaper. The crowd tends towards a mixed bunch of well-worn regulars, youth, and professionals that seem to all enjoy the electronic rock soundtrack in kind.

▶ *i* ⊖Notting Hill Gate. Take a right onto Pembridge Rd., then a left onto Portobello Rd. Free Wi-Fi. Pints £4-6. Wine £3-6. Spirits from £3. ⌚ Open M-Th noon-11pm, F 10am-midnight, Sa 9am-midnight, Su 10am-10:30pm.

The Champion   PUB
1 Wellington Terr.
☎020 7792 4527 www.thechampionpub.co.uk

No gimmicks. No one-word definition besides "local." The Champion serves a grown-up set that has transitioned from five pints of beer to one or two glasses of non-house wine. The fringe chandeliers and candles on the tables give the place a more serious vibe to accommodate the late-20s to early-40s crowd, and when it comes to places where you want to drink in peace contemplatively, then this pub wins (although we regret that it does not serve breakfast).

▶ *i* ⊖Notting Hill Gate. Exit the station and walk down Bayswater Rd. toward Hyde Park; the pub is on the corner with the main road. Pub quiz on W. Live music every other Su. Pints fro £3. ⌚ Open M-Th noon-11pm, F-Sa noon-midnight, Su noon-10:30pm.

MARYLEBONE AND BLOOMSBURY

▨ The Social   BAR, CLUB
5 Little Portland St.
☎020 7636 4992 www.thesocial.com

During the evening hours, the pubs of Bloomsbury play host to clutches of students waving about their pints with well-meant frivolity. The Social is a welcome energy outlet: downstairs, hip hop and dance music blasts through the quiet oeuvre of the alley. Upstairs, the intimate bar plays Motown numbers (quirkily enough, pictures of birds à la The Audubon Society lined the walls when we visited). Weekly events include Bashment, a Jamaican dance set on Wednesdays, and Hip-Hop Karaoke on Thursdays.

▶ *i* ⊖Oxford Circus. Turn right onto Regent St. then turn right onto Little Portland St. Live acts on the ground fl. most nights. Student cards will get you discounts on most covered nights. Cove £5-7. Pints £4-5. Cocktails £8.50. ⏰ Open M-Sa noon-midnight, Th-Sa noon-1am.

▧ **Purl** BAR
50/54 Blandford St.
☎ www.purl-london.co.uk

Designed to look like an Al Capone speakeasy—interesting if only for the fact that Britain has never prohibited alcohol—Purl caters to a posh modern crowd that's probably never broken a nail much less someone's legs. Sipped by patrons in the darkened, intimate labyrinth of nooks and crannies, the drinks are less a cobbling of lighter fluid and rubbing alcohol and more a creation from an MIT lab. Liquid nitrogen, ice cream, grape jelly, and candied bacon make appearances in the cocktails and work together splendidly (try the Corpse Reviver #1, which mixes grape jelly and blue cheese foam).

▶ *i* ⊖Bond St. Turn eft onto Oxford St. and right onto James St., which eventually turns into Thayer St. Then turn right onto Blandford St. Reservations recommended for tables; book online through the website. Cocktail £9-12. ⏰ Open M-Th 5-11:30pm, F-Sa 5pm-midnight.

▧ **The Golden Eagle** PUB
59 Marylebone Ln.
☎020 7935 3228

There are plenty of spots in London where leaning against the bar, tossing or flipping your hair with that devilish charm, and playing it cool is encouraged. Or you can do something truly spectacular and sing along with the boozy crowd to bespectacled Tony "Fingers" Pearson on the piano every Tuesday, Thursday, and Friday; have fun with old-timey hits that weren't old-timey when the crowd was your age. Given the cheap pints and your resulting inebriation, you just might be the one belting out tunes the loudest.

▶ *i* ⊖Bond St. turn right onto Oxford St. and left onto Marylebone Ln. Music Tu 8:30pm, Th-F 8:30pm. Pint £3.50-4. Wine from £3. ⏰ Open M-Th 11am-11pm, F-Sa 11am-midnight, Su noon-7pm.

Nightlife

The Fitzroy Tavern   PUB

16A Charlotte St.
☎020 7580 3714

By our count, there are at least 30 "oldest" pubs in London
and dozens more that had famous patrons—although Britain's
density of well-known thinkers and their personal drinking
levels means that that claim is a little less impressive. But the
Fitzroy has some genuine history to keep the old and comedy
shows to bring in the new. The walls of the pub are lined with
some hilarious memorabilia from the war (including a poster
saying "We're here for the duration, we hope" and another one
with a white box in a field of black that served as directions for
finding the pub in a blackout).

▶ *i* ⊖Goodge St. Turn left onto Tottenham Ct. Rd., left onto Tottenham St.,
and left onto Charlotte St. Comedy night W 8:30pm. Pints aroun £2.50-3.
Burgers from £6. ⟁ Open M-Sa 11am-11pm, Su noon-10:30pm.

Scala   CLUB

275 Pentonville Rd.
☎020 7833 2022 www.scala-london.co.uk

Repurposed from a cinema, this simply cool, four-level club
has seen acts from Coldplay to The Scissor Sisters to Lionel
Richie. The place is popular with a younger crowd that makes
its presence known on the dance floor, and the older patrons
congregate more toward the bar. Both dance floors are usually
packed on a club night, but leave the high heels at home, as
some patrons can be a bit over exuberant.

▶ *i* ⊖King's Cross St. Pancras. Head left when leaving the station. Cover
varies, usuall £8-16. Club nights F-Sa 10pm-4am or later. ⟁ Opening
hours depend on the night; check website for details.

The Rocket   PUB

120 Euston Rd.
☎020 7388 5796 www.therocketeustonroad.co.uk

This pub has shifted its clientele from primarily youngsters to a
more professional/student mix. Inside, wrought iron chandeliers
support multicolored light bulbs, and patrons pass barbs at each
other near the warmly lit bar. Outside is a bit harsher, as the
pub's location on Euston Rd. means that traffic and pedestrians
streaming from King's Cross might put a damper on your night
out with friends.

▶ *i* ⊖Euston. Make a left down Euston Rd. Pints around £3. Wine £3-5. ⟁
Open M-W 11:30am-midnight, Th-F 11:30am-2am, Sa-Su 10am-2am.

NORTH LONDON

Camden Town and the area around **Angel** come alive at night, but the scene is primarily limited to pubs and bars. Camden is also home to some important live-music venues.

▓ 69 Colebrooke Row   BAR

69 Colebrooke Row

☎075 4052 8593 www.69colebrookerow.com

69 Colebrooke Row's advertising of the venue as "The Bar with No Name" sounds like a bad secondary title, yet the effort put into their mixology makes the hokeyness a bit more acceptable. Of the cocktails, we liked the "Death in Venice" (Campari with grapefruit bitters topped with prosecco). Popular among Islington yuppies and cocktail connoisseurs, the bar's vibe is saved from pretension by the impromptu ditties played by patrons on the upright piano.

▶ *i* ⊖Angel. Turn right after leaving the station and stay to the right as you pass Islington Green. Then turn right onto Colebrooke Row. It's number 69. Cocktail £9. ⏰ Open M-W 5pm-midnight, Th 5pm-1am, F-Sa 5pm-2am, Su 5pm-midnight.

Slim Jim's Liquor Store   BAR

112 Upper St.

☎020 7354 4364 www.slimjimsliquorstore.com

It sounds like a convenience store that never has any cars parked in front of it, but it's actually an American dive bar with enough bras hanging from the ceiling to clothe a feminist commune (you can add yours if you'd like). A nice selection of bourbons and beers make this a solid option even if you don't have any particular love of rockabilly style; however, the music scene is surprisingly vibrant and popular with young Brits.

▶ *i* ⊖Angel. Turn right and continue up Upper St. Bourbon and scotc £3-10. Pints from £3.75. ⏰ Open M-W 4pm-2am, Th 4pm-3am, F-Sa noon-3am, Su noon-2am.

Duchess of Kent   PUB

441 Liverpool Rd.

☎020 7609 7104

The actual Duchess of Kent largely disappeared from public life after being the first royal to convert to Catholicism since the 17th century. This pub is similarly estranged from the city proper, but this creates an authentic, local haunt feel. Lots of arm chairs and couches are available for you to settle in with a cheap pint from the extensive, rotating array of beers. They host a fantastic pub quiz on Monday nights, with a first prize of four free dinners at the pub's restaurant.

▶ *i* ⊖Highbury and Islington. Turn left down Holloway Rd., left onto Furlong Rd., and left onto Liverpool Rd. Pub quiz M 8pm. Pints fro £3. Wine from £4.50 🕐 Open daily noon-11pm.

EAST LONDON

🏷 The Book Club   BAR, CLUB
100 Leonard St.
☎020 7684 8618 www.wearetbc.com

We don't even want to know what a Book Club in this part of town would look like. Ironically reading Dan Brown? Commentary on how every Nicholas Sparks novel boils down to pretty people finding each other in the rain? Thankfully, this cafe/bar/lecture hall/dance club/art installation is more about how to live like F. Scott Fitzgerald than how to read him. During the week, events range from speed dating ("Are you a fan of Soviet-era film? Me too! Let's have sex. Capitalism hates sex."), drawing classes ("The body is merely a canvas for our pain."), and beer pong ("Alcohol!"). Thursday through Saturday are usually reserved for dancing the depression away.

▶ *i* ⊖Shoreditch High St. Make a left after leaving the station, then a right onto Great Eastern St., and a left onto Leonard St. Cover varies from free t £12; on most weekends, it's £5 after 9pm. 🕐 Open M-W 8am-midnight, Th-F 8am-2am, Sa 10am-2am, Su 10am-midnight.

🏷 Strongroom Bar   BAR
120-124 Curtain Rd.
☎020 7426 5103 www.strongroombar.com

Did you know that in order to be a "cool" bar, you have to be in an alleyway? So goes the East London nightlife scene, young imbiber. The Strongroom makes understandably less use of its dark, sparse indoors than the umbrella tables in the space between brick buildings. The crowd is a bit older than the expected cadre of "Dalston Superstars" but has some concessions, like a great series of cocktail options and late hours during the weekend.

▶ *i* ⊖Shoreditch High St. Make a left after leaving the station, then a right onto Great Eastern St., and a right onto Curtain Rd. Pints aroun £4. 🕐 Open M 9am-11pm, Tu-W 9am-midnight, Th 9am-1am, F 9am-2am, Sa noon-2am, Su noon-10pm.

Callooh Callay   BAR

65 Rivington St.

☎020 7739 4781 www.calloohcallaybar.com

After your first time trying Callooh Callay's cocktails, we bet you'll jabber away to your friends about how the drinks are made of high-quality booze, are sometimes served in gramophones, and are perfectly titled for a Shoreditch crowd like "Respect Your Elders." The Upstairs Bar isn't Lewis Carroll-themed (e.g. you don't have to go through the looking glass to go to the bathroom), but rather changes every six weeks from themes like "Dutch Gin House" and "Havana Nights." The crowd tends to be a bit more upper crust than other places in the area, but the chummy bartenders create a comforting den.

▶ *i* ⊖Old St. Make a right down Great Eastern Rd., then a left onto Rivington St. Cocktail £9. Upstairs bar closed on M and Su. Make a table reservation if you don't want to stand at the bar. ⏰ Open M-W 6pm-midnight, Th-Su 6pm-1am.

SOUTH LONDON

Brixton's nightlife is luckily centered around Tube stations (for convenience and safety's sake), so a quick wander around will reliably unearth several well-priced pub options. When an area begins to gentrify, its residents find themselves unable to consume lager and soon require large amounts of cocktails in order to breathe properly; therefore, it's so lovely that Clapham provides mixed drinks for its yuppie ecology.

▨ Hootananny   BAR, CONCERT VENUE

95 Effra Rd.

☎020 7737 7273 www.hootanannybrixton.co.uk

Hootananny during the day is a bit like what we'd imagine the downtime bar for circus workers would be. For example, there are the swaths of fabric draped big top-style in the back alcove, the red velvet booths, the pool tables, and the celebratory tone that the bright red house brings to the drab surrounding area—it's as if something magical could happen anytime. Well, it *is* magical, as Hootananny hosts musicians and DJs playing everything from death disco to Central Asian folk melodies— you can almost feel the East End's envy of authenticity.

▶ *i* ⊖Brixton. Make a left as you exit the station and continue on Effra Rd. as it forks off. 21+. Most shows are free; occasiona £5 cover. Shows W-Su start at 8 or 9pm. Beer from £3.80. ⏰ Pub open M-W 3pm-midnight, Th 3pm-2am, F 3pm-3am, Sa noon-3am, Su noon-midnight. Hours vary

The White Horse   PUB

94 Brixton Hill

☎020 8678 6666 www.whitehorsebrixton.com

There's a sort of childish glee about The White Horse that separates it from the Hog's Head Inn-quality of many English pubs. The pápier mâché lotus flowers hanging in the window and from the ceiling loosen up the patrons to root for their favorite football and rugby teams with abandon. During weekday evenings, the pub attracts a young professional crowd for no-fuss drinks, while DJs liven things up on the weekends with hip hop, funk, and house. Sunday afternoons host live folk and jazz.

▸ *i* ⊖Brixton. Make a left leaving the station and stay on the road as it turns into Brixton Hill. Pints abou £3.50. Wine from £4. ⏰ Open M-Th 5pm-midnight, F 4pm-3am, Sa noon-3am, Su noon-midnight.

WEST LONDON

❧ Dove   PUB

19 Upper Mall

☎020 8748 9474

The only thing recognizing the existence of this bar to a Ulysses of pub crawls is an arrow pointing into an alleyway near the Thames. Through the stone walls lies the best riverside pub for the cheapest prices you're going to find in the city. Another bonus is the fact that only locals frequent the Dove, and pints and comforting pub grub litters the tables as the conversation continues into the night. In the summer, sit out on the river patio and try to snag a set in the upper balcony.

▸ *i* ⊖Ravenscourt Park. Make a left down Ravenscourt Rd., cross King St. (you'll need to go under the road in the subway) onto Rivercourt Rd., and make a left onto Upper Mall. Pints aroun £4. ⏰ Open M-Sa 11am-11pm, Su noon-10:30pm.

Nightlife

St. Paul's Cathedral, City of London, London

Westminster Abbey, Westminster, London.

Imperial War Museum, South Bank, London.

Hampton Court, West London, London.

The Shard, South Bank, London.

Portobello Road market stall, Notting Hill, London.

Greenhouse in Kew Gardens, West London, London.

Flowers in Kew Gardens, West London, London.

View of the River Cam from Clare College, Cambridge.

Mercury Fountain in the center of the Great Quadrangle, or "Tom Quad," Christ Church, Oxford.

King's College Chapel, Cambridge.

Arts and Culture

For both cultural connoisseur and dilettante, London offers a truly terrifying spectrum of performance art. With Shakespeare's word-smithing running through all of the English language, the **Globe Theatre** pays due homage to the dramatic poet. The theater scene then spreads to include musicals and their revivals, off-beat British comedies, experimental works, and some celebrity showcases (staffed by a cadre of British actors whose stage presence eclipses the film roles for which they're generally known). But, of course, it's not all sitting in a dark auditorium in regulation cocktail attire, for Britain is also known for its incredible rock music tradition. British singers and bands almost always begin their journey to stardom in the London circuit of cafes and small performance venues. It's this divide between centuries-old and seconds-old art that approximates a city—with its reliance on the past and the contrarian reaction against it fighting each other on the battlefield of art.

THEATER

Ah, "theatre" (thee-ya-tah) in London. The city is renowned for its affordable performances—tickets for big musicals in the **West End** can be had for as little a £25, a pittance compared to the $100 tickets sold on Broadway. Only buy discounted tickets from booths with a circle and check mark symbol that says **STAR** on it; this stands for the Society of Tickets Agents and Retailers, and it vouches for the legitimacy of a discount booth.

▨ Royal Court Theatre   SOUTH KENSINGTON AND CHELSEA
Sloane Sq.

☎020 7565 5000 www.royalcourttheatre.com

The Royal Court has built its reputation as the antidote to all the orchestral swoons and celebrity cameos sweeping through the West End. The Royal Court's 1956 production of John Osborne's *Look Back in Anger* (not to be confused with the Oasis song) is credited with single-handedly launching modern British drama. Royal is primarily writers' theater, purveying high-minded works for audiences that will appreciate them.

▶ *i* ⊖Sloane Sq. Tickets £10, Tu-S £12-28. Student discounts available on day of performance. ☒ Box office open M-F 10am-6pm or until the doors open, Sa 10am-curtain (if there's a performance).

▨ The National Theatre   THE SOUTH BANK
Belvedere Rd.

☎020 7452 3400 www.nationaltheatre.org.uk

Okay, it looks a bit like a Kafkaesque prison, especially when the brutalist structure displays Helvetica advertisements fo £12 Travelex tickets that can be seen from the other side of the river. Prison structure aside, the National Theatre's multiple stages host new and classic British drama, including many premieres, revived lost classics from around the world, and a standard repertoire of Chekhov and Ibsen.

▶ *i* ⊖Waterloo. Turn right onto York Rd. and left onto Waterloo Rd. Ticket £12-44. ☒ Box office open M-Sa 9:30am-8pm, Su noon-6pm.

▨ The Old Vic   SOUTH LONDON
The Cut

☎0844 871 7628 www.oldvictheatre.com

This famous, stately theater was built in 1818 and has hosted the likes of Ralph Richardson and Laurence Olivier. Though showcasing a huge range of styles, the Old Vic focuses on the classics, including star-studded Shakespeare productions. Kevin

Spacey—when he's not playing men in mid-life crises—serves as artistic director (and has since 2003).

▶ *i* ⊖Southwark. Turn right onto The Cut. Ticket £11-52. 🕐 Box office open M-Sa 10am-7pm on show days, 10am-6pm on non-show days.

The Young Vic
SOUTH LONDON

66 The Cut

☎020 7922 2922 www.youngvic.org

▶ Formerly the studio space for the Old Vic, the Young Vic now puts on a variety of shows and is generally edgier and more exciting than its decorous parent theater down the road. Between its main stage and two studio spaces, the Young Vic also provides greater flexibility in stagings.

Shakespeare's Globe
THE SOUTH BANK

21 New Globe Walk

☎020 7401 9919 www.shakespearesglobe.org

There are definitely two tribes that attend Globe Performances: groundlings and non-groundlings. Since the Globe is a near replica of the original theater, an open roof and standing area are available for said "groundlings." An experience of being so close to the actors that you can see the spit fly from their perfectly dictating mouths, this special opportunity can be yours fo £5. The other seats are spread across three semi-circled tiers around the stage, which can become fairly uncomfortable if you don't shell out for a cushion as well. The Globe stages works not only by the Bard, but also two new plays per season. Understandably for an open-air theater, the season runs from Apr-Oct, although the recently opened Sam Wanamaker Playhouse hosts performances year-round.

▶ *i* ⊖Southwark. Turn left onto Blackfriars Rd., right onto Southwark St., left onto Great Guildford St., right onto Park St., then left onto New Globe Walk. Standin £5; seat £15-35, under 1 £12-32. 🕐 Box office open M-Sa 10am-8pm, Su 10am-7pm.

Hackney Empire
EAST LONDON

291 Mare St.

☎020 8985 2424 www.hackneyempire.co.uk

With bold sandstone letters announcing its presence on another wise nondescript block, the Hackney Empire is an old variety theater that once showcased the talents of **Charlie Chaplin** and **Harry Houdini.** All faded grandeur and vaudeville-esque decor, the Hackney hosts everything from comedy gigs to concerts to productions by the Royal Shakespeare Company.

▶ *i* Take the Overground to Hackney Central (in East London). Turn left onto Graham Rd., then right onto Mare St. Ticket £10-25, student £8-21. 🕐 Box

Arts And Culture

office open M-Sa 10am-6pm, show days 10am-9:30pm.

Battersea Art Center (BAC)   SOUTH LONDON
176 Lavender Hill, Old Town Hall
☎020 7223 2223 www.bac.org.uk

Located in the old Clapham Town Hall, the Battersea Art Center makes for a strange theater experience. Throw in the BAC's reputation for hosting young producers and new companies, and you get some truly cutting-edge and bizarre theater. The BAC holds performances in all of its 72 rooms, ranging from closets to more traditional spaces. One of the best parts about the BAC is the SCRATCH program, in which artists show works in progress and get feedback from the audience.

▶ *i* ⊖Clapham Common. Take bus #345 toward South Kensington and get off at Lavender Hill. Ticket prices vary, generally aroun £12, concession £9. SCRATCH performances are often pay-what-you-can. ☼ Box office open M-F 10am-6pm, Sa 3-6pm.

CINEMA

London is teeming with traditional cinemas, the most dominant of which are **Cineworld** (www.cineworld.co.uk) and **Odeon** (www.odeon.co.uk). But the best way to enjoy a film is in one of the hip repertory or luxury cinemas like **Everyman** or **Curzon**. *Time Out* publishes show times, as does www.viewlondon.co.uk.

▨ BFI Southbank and IMAX   SOUTH BANK
Belvedere Rd.
☎020 7928 3232 www.bfi.org.uk

There are two reasons the BFI is awesome. First, it has the BFI Southbank, which is a champagne-drinking, bougie madhouse hidden under Waterloo Bridge. It showcases everything from early premieres to challenging foreign works and runs themed "seasons" that focus on the work of a particular director, cinematographer, or actor. Also, their Mediatheque is free and allows you to privately view films from their archives. The second reason is that the largest screen in all of Britain—the BFI IMAX—is just down the street, meaning you can see your favorite arthouse film and then catch the latest rock-'em-sock-'em comic book adaptation in a sensory overload chamber of win.

▶ *i* ⊖Waterloo. Follow the signs to either BFI Southbank (along the river) or the IMAX theater (so large you can't miss it). Note: you must go underground to reach the IMAX theater. Several exits spin off from it like wheel spokes. £11, concession £8.50, matine £6. ☼ Open daily 11am-11pm. Mediatech open Tu-F noon-8pm, Sa-Su 12:30-8:30pm.

Riverside Studios   WEST LONDON
Crisp Rd.
☎020 8237 1111 www.riversidestudios.co.uk

Frequently showing films in old-school double features, Riverside Studios specializes in foreign films, arthouse flicks, and classics. The building is a hotbed for other culture as well, featuring an exhibition space, live theater performances, a popular cafe, and a bar.

▸ *i* ⊖Hammersmith. Take the south exit and pass the Hammersmith Apollo. Continue to follow Queen Caroline St. and turn left onto Crisp Rd. Ethernet access in cafe. Tickets £4-9.50. ⏰ Open M-F 8:30am-11pm, Sa 10am-11pm, Su 10am-10:30pm. Box office open daily noon-9pm.

COMEDY

The English are famous for their dry, sophisticated, and sometimes ridiculous ("We are the knights who say 'Ni!'") sense of humor. This humor thrives in the stand-up and sketch comedy clubs throughout the city. Check *Time Out* for listings, and be warned that the city virtually empties of comedians come August, when it's Fringe Festival time in Edinburgh.

◪ Comedy Store   THE WEST END
1A Oxendon St.
☎0844 871 7699 www.thecomedystore.co.uk

Hands-down the most famous comedy venue in London, the Comedy Store made a name for itself in the '80s as a home for up-and-coming comedians like Jennifer Saunders, Dawn French, and Mike Myers (who was one of the founding members). Nowadays, visiting comics perform Thursday through Saturday, and the resident sketch-comedy team takes the stage on Wednesdays and Sundays. Tuesdays have stand-up on recent topical events, while the last Monday of the month hosts would-be comedians who are either encouraged or heckled by the audience. Famous comedians like Eddie Izzard have been known to pop in from time to time for impromptu performances.

▸ *i* ⊖Piccadilly Circus. Turn left onto Coventry, then right onto Oxendon. Ticket £14-20. ⏰ Box office open M-Th 6:30-9:30pm, F-Sa 6:30pm-1:15am, Su 6:30-9:30pm. Doors open daily 6:30pm. Shows usually 8 and 11pm.

Hen & Chickens Theatre   NORTH LONDON
109 St. Paul's Rd.
☎020 7704 2001 www.unrestrictedview.co.uk

You'll be treated to some of the most hilarious and quirky comedy around in this 50-seat venue, located above an Islington pub. Acts vary from stand-up to sketch comedy groups. Past performers have included the Unexpected Items, a group that includes the originator of the "Gap Yah" video. Come in July to see comedians try out the material they're taking up to Edinburgh. Head down to the pub to enjoy a pint with the performers after the show.

▶ *i* ⊖Highbury and Islington. Turn right and go down the road past the green. Ticket £6-8. ⏰ Performances usually start at 7:30 or 9:30pm.

DANCE

As with everything else in London, the dance scene is diverse, innovative, and first-rate. And more of a luxury given that in some other countries, ballet is the only thing you can normally understand due to the language barrier.

Sadler's Wells   NORTH LONDON
Rosebery Ave.
☎0844 412 4300 www.sadlerswells.com

Sadler's Wells is renowned for stunning dance shows, including traditional ballet, contemporary dance, and dazzling Cuban ensembles. With multiple performance spaces, they might even all be on at the same time.

▶ *i* ⊖Angel. Turn left onto Upper St., then right onto Rosebery Ave. Some shows offer student discounts. Ticket £10-55. ⏰ Box office open M-Sa 9am-8:30pm.

POP AND ROCK

Clubs are expensive, and many pubs close at 11pm. Especially given the current economic climate, fewer young people are willing to shell ou £10-15 to get into a club, especially since beers inside cost an additiona £4-5 apiece. To find the heart of London's nightlife, you have to scratch beyond the pub-and-club surface and head into the darkened basements of bars and seismically loud music clubs. With a history of homegrown musical talent—including **The Rolling Stones, Radiohead,** and **The Clash,** all of the bands from the infamous **"British Invasion,"** and many of the best '90s pop groups—London's fantastic music scene goes way back.

🏛 Koko   NORTH LONDON
1A Camden High St.
☎0870 432 5527 www.koko.uk.com

Koko's isn't a typical rock and roll venue. Originally a theater, then a cinema, then one of the BBC's first broadcasting loca-

Arts And Culture

tions, and then the famous Camden Palace Nightclub, Koko holds a 110-year history within its music-soaked red walls and gilded balconies. Bringing in mostly big-name indie acts, along with some pop and rock acts (they've had everyone from Madonna to Usher to Justice), Koko is one of the premier venues in London. It also hosts an indie night with DJs and dancing on Friday.

▶ *i* ⊖Mornington Crescent. Turn right onto Hampstead Rd. Koko is on the right. Tickets sold online. Concert £10-30. Bee £3.50-4. Cash only for in-person purchases. ⊘ Box office open M-Th noon-4pm, F noon-5pm.

▨ **Borderline** THE WEST END

Orange Yard, off Manette St. http://venues.meanfiddler.com/borderline/home
☎020 7734 5547

This simple venue (which is also a fantastic club) lacks the outlandish Art Deco trappings of other London concert halls, but it oozes the spirit of rock and roll from every beer-soaked wall and ear-blowing speaker. Big-name artists often play the Borderline when starting solo careers. Townes Van Zandt played his last show here; Eddie Vedder, Jeff Buckley, and Rilo Kiley have played here; and **Spinal Tap** performed here right after the movie came out. The amps go up to 11, the music's piping hot, and the location is prime.

▶ *i* ⊖Tottenham Court Rd. Turn right onto ⊖Charing Cross Rd., and right onto Manette St. Ticket £3-30. ⊘ Doors open daily 7pm. Tickets available at the Jazz Cafe box office M-Sa 10:30am-5:30pm.

HMV Apollo WEST LONDON

15 Queen Caroline St.
☎020 8563 3800 www.hmvapollo.com

Like many of the big, architecturally stunning venues in London, the Art Deco HMV Apollo used to be a cinema. It was originally called the Hammersmith Odeon and was the site of Bruce Springsteen's 1975 concert film. It's also hosted big acts like Oasis, R.E.M., Elton John, the Rolling Stones, and even the Beatles.

▶ *i* ⊖Hammersmith. Apollo is opposite the Broadway Shopping Centre. There are plenty of signs leading to it. Call ☎08448 44 47 48 for tickets. Ticket prices vary; check online for more info. ⊘ Box office open on performance days 4pm-start of the show.

O2 Academy Brixton SOUTH LONDON

211 Stockwell Rd.
☎020 7771 3000 www.o2academybrixton.co.uk

Home to Europe's largest fixed stage, the O2 Academy Brixton's set list is rife with the big names of our generation—past acts include MGMT, Morrissey, Pavement, LCD Soundsystem, and

Wiz Khalifa. They also occasionally host club nights. You can also check the lineups at the other O2 Academies in Shepherd's Bush and Islington.

▶ *i* ⊖Brixton. Turn right onto Brixton Rd. and left onto Stockwell Rd. Ticket prices vary, generall £20-35. Pint £4. Bar cash only. 🕐 Box office opens 2hr. before doors on gig nights.

CLASSICAL MUSIC

🎵 Royal Opera House   THE WEST END
Bow St.

☎020 7304 4000 www.roh.org.uk

Admittedly, the glorious glass façade of the Royal Opera House makes it look like a train station (albeit a nice one). However, the only tracks running out of this Opera House are world-class arias. Tickets go on sale about two months before performances, and it's a good idea to book early. Or you can wait for standby tickets, which are offered 4hr. before performances for half price and are onl £15 for students. The ROH also sponsors free outdoor film screenings. Performances also included classical ballet.

▶ *i* ⊖Covent Garden. Turn right onto Long Acre, then right onto Bow St. Ticket £4-150. 🕐 Box office open M-Sa 10am-8pm.

Royal Albert Hall   SOUTH KENSINGTON AND CHELSEA
Kensington Gore

☎0845 401 5045 www.royalalberthall.com

Deep in the heart of South Kensington, the Royal Albert Hall (commissioned by Prince Albert) has been one of the biggest purveyors of the London arts scene since 1871. The hall hosts some of the city's biggest concerts, including the spectacular month of the **BBC Proms** classical festival (see **Festivals**) and a range of other phenomenal musical events. If you're in the city in July and August, this is not something to miss.

▶ *i* ⊖Knightsbridge. Turn left onto Knightsbridge and continue onto Kensington Rd., which becomes Kensington Gore. Tickets fro £10. 🕐 Open daily 9am-9pm.

The London Coliseum   THE WEST END
33 St. Martin's Ln.

☎0871 472 0600 www.eno.org

Home to the **English National Opera,** the London Coliseum showcases new, cutting-edge ballet and opera. They also perform unique reworkings of classic opera productions, like a version of Donizetti's *L'Elisird' Amore* set in a 1950s diner.

▶ *i* ⊖Charing Cross. Walk toward Trafalgar Sq. on Duncannon St., turn right at the square onto St. Martin's Pl., and St. Martin's Ln. splits off to the right. Sometimes students and other concessions can get discounted tickets 3hr. before the performance. Ticket £15-90. ⏰ Box office open M-Sa 10am-8pm on performance days, 10am-6pm on non-performance days.

JAZZ

🛇 Ronnie Scott's   THE WEST END
47 Frith St.
☎020 7439 0747 www.ronniescotts.co.uk

Ronnie Scott's has been defining "hip" in Soho for the last 51 years. It was the first British club to host American jazz artists, and everyone from Chick Corea to Tom Waits (ok, not jazz, but who's complaining?) has played here. Black-and-white photos of jazz giants line the walls, and a diverse crowd imbibes cocktail creations like Jazz Medicine (Jägermeister, sloe gin, Dubonnet, fresh blackberries, and angostura bitters). Really, it's medicine to recover from the snooty expressions of West End clubbers that make them look like they've just been ill.

▶ *i* ⊖Tottenham Court Rd. Turn onto Oxford St. with your back to ⊖Tottenham Court Rd., then turn left onto Soho St., right into the square, and right onto Frith St. Cove £10, more for big acts. Cocktail £8.50-9. ⏰ Open M-Sa 6pm-3am, Su noon-4pm and 6:30pm-midnight. Box office open M-F 10am-6pm, Sa noon-5pm.

The 606 Club   WEST LONDON
90 Lots Rd.
☎020 7352 5953 www.606club.co.uk

On quiet Lots Rd., opposite a foreboding abandoned factory, the 606 Club has been quietly hosting the best of the UK music scene since 1969. Properly underground (it's in a basement), the club is candlelit and closely packed. The music may be jazz, Latin, soul, gospel, R&B, and rock, and while the artists may be relatively unknown, they're almost always worth hearing.

▶ *i* Bus #22 from ⊖Sloane Sq. to Edith Grove/World's End. Continue walking on Kings Rd., turn left onto Tadema Rd., walk to the end, and turn right onto Lots Rd. Non-members have to eat in order to drink. Check website for special Su afternoon lunch and show. Cove £10-12. ⏰ Open M-Th 7pm-noon, F-Sa 8pm-1:30am, Su 12:30-4pm and 7-midnight.

Jazz Cafe   NORTH LONDON
☎020 7688 8899
☎ www.jazzcafe.co.uk

One of the better known jazz venues in London, the Jazz Cafe often surprises people with its expansive repertoire. It has hosted De La Soul and GZA as well as jazz luminaries; they've also got a good roster of Latin acts. Starting at 10:30pm every

Saturday night, they have DJs playing'80s hits, in addition to '90s hip hop every second Friday and '90s pop nights every fourth Friday.

▶ *i* ⊖Camden Town. Turn left onto ⊖Camden High St., then right onto Parkway. Tickets £5-40. Cover for DJ night £4-5. ⧖ Box office open M-Sa 10:30am-5:30pm. Shows generally start at 7pm; some nights have 2nd show at 11pm. DJ nights 10:30pm-3am.

FESTIVALS

▨ BBC Proms   SOUTH KENSINGTON AND CHELSEA
Kensington Gore
☎0845 401 5045 www.bbc.co.uk/proms

The Proms are a world-famous classical music festival put on by the BBC in the Royal Albert Hall. If you're thinking teen-agers in taffeta, think again. "Prom" stands for "Promenade Concert"—a performance at which much of the audience only has standing-room tickets. There's at least one performance every day at the Royal Albert Hall, plus around 70 other events throughout the city. All the performances are broadcast for free.

▶ *i* ⊖Knightsbridge. Turn left onto Knightsbridge, then continue onto Kensington Rd., which becomes Kensington Gore. Tickets fro £10. ⧖ Jul-Sept.

London Literary Festival   THE SOUTH BANK
Southbank Centre, Belvedere Rd.
☎0844 847 9939 www.londonlitfest.com

Some of the world's most famous poets, novelists, musicians, and scientists (it's quite the interdisciplinary fest) assemble at the South Bank Centre every July for this literary extravaganza. The festival also hosts writing workshops; you can download podcasts of past events on their website.

▶ *i* ⊖Waterloo. Rght onto York Rd. and then left onto Waterloo Rd. Look for the embankment before York Bridge. Ticket prices free £15. ⧖ Call daily 9am-8pm. Royal Festival Hall Ticket Office daily 10am-8pm.

Shopping

London is one vital quarter of the "Paris, New York, Tokyo, London" list that most major designers plaster on their store windows. Of course, most European capital high streets have some mix of Valentino, Burberry, and Hermes, so we'll skip to the singular: **Harrods** and **Harvey Nichols.** These megalithic department stores cater to the upper classes (the royal classes are more the custom-made type). It's not all for McQueen and the Queen, though—Soho is full of vintage clothing stores and independent record shops. The East End (when not tacitly ignoring its Urban Outfitters) is a reliable source of fun boutiques. As the eponymous movie showcases, Notting Hill has a gauntlet of secondhand shops. And for those who can't break in a city without scouring a bookstore, London has a litany of quirky independent retailers that round out the major chains like Waterstone's and Daunt.

BOOKSTORES

▓ John Sandoe Books   SOUTH KENSINGTON AND CHELSEA

10 Blacklands Terr.

☎020 7589 9473 www.johnsandoe.com

Undaunted by his father's vocal disapproval, John Sandoe founded this independent bookstore in 1957, and the bohemian writerly crowd of Chelsea adored it. Today, besides the modish, pretty covers that are hand-selected by edition, the store retains old-fashioned charm antithetical to the somewhat sterile displays at Waterstone's. Books are piled up on the sides of the staircase, moving shelves in the back leave more space for books, and the staff have read almost every title in stock.

▶ *i* ⊖Sloane Sq. Exit the Tube and go straight down Sloane Sq. Veer left onto King's Rd., and turn right at Blacklands Terr. ⏰ Open M-Tu 9:30am-5:30pm, W 9:30am-7:30pm, Th-Sa 9:30am-5:30pm, Su noon-6pm.

▓ Skoob   MARYLEBONE AND BLOOMSBURY

66 The Brunswick, off Marchmont St.

☎020 7278 8760 www.skoob.com

Evol: a palindromic ode to this secondhand bookstore that lionizes the written word. Amid the Brunswick complex—a series of stores posher than the next—walk down Skoob's stairs and prepare to be confronted with an astoundingly complete collection (unlike some secondhand bookstores, where there are only 10 copies of *Wuthering Heights* because no one liked it). Whether travel, science fiction, crime fiction, literary criticism, poetry or mathematics beckons to your sensibilities, expect to walk out pounds lighter and heavier.

▶ *i* ⊖Russell Sq. Turn right and then left up Marchmont St. Skoob is at the far end of Brunswick, on the right. ⏰ Open M-Sa 10:30am-8pm, Su 10:30am-6pm.

Taschen   SOUTH KENSINGSTON AND CHELSEA

12 Duke of York Sq.

☎020 7881 0795 www.taschen.com

With only 13 stores worldwide, this art book publisher made history with its publication of *GOAT (Greatest of All Time)*—a 700-page treatment of Muhammad Ali. Copies of *GOAT* go for $15,000, but the coffee table books in this shop are more along the lines of Impressionism surveys that cater to a Saatchi-visiting crowd. The company began as a comic publisher that brought lesser-known erotica to a larger audience; so, true to its roots, there's also a smattering of queer art and nudes galore.

▶ *i* ⊖Sloane Sq. Go straight down Sloane Sq., veer left onto King's Rd., and turn left onto Duke of York Sq. (it's the one by the Saatchi Art Gallery). Prices vary, but the books can be surprisingly inexpensive. ☎ Open M-Tu 10am-6pm, W 10am-7pm, Th-F 10am-6pm, Sa 10am-7pm, Su noon-6pm.

ART

Marcus Campbell Art Books   THE SOUTH BANK
43 Holland St.
☎020 7261 0111 www.marcuscampbell.co.uk

Of course, art books have a high level of intellectual buy-in. Terms like "post-postmodernism" and "neo-colonialist" get thrown around like Rihanna. And if you, like us, admit to just looking at the pictures, you're sure to solicit the judgmental stares of the staff. However, if you want to try to educate yourself nonetheless in the void of art, Marcus Campbell is the ultimate choice. Close enough in theme and proximity to the Tate Modern to be considered its unofficial bookstore, the shop sells a wide variety of exhibition catalogues (many fo £1-2) and rare and expensive art books (up t £3000).

▶ *i* ⊖Southwark. Turn left onto Blackfriars Rd., then right onto Southwark St. Then turn left onto Sumner and left onto Holland St. ☎ Open M-Sa 10:30am-6:30pm, Su noon-6pm.

Southbank Printmakers   THE SOUTH BANK
Unit 12 Gabriels Wharf, 56 Upper Ground
☎020 7928 8184 www.southbank-printmakers.com

If we had a piece of art for every piece of crap sold to a tourist on the South Bank, we could fill the Tate Modern for centuries. Southbank Printmakers is your antidote to the poison of generic shots of the London Eye. Why settle for a postcard of Trafalgar Square when you can support local artists with innovative designs for the same price? If you're ready to commit, larger prints are sold fro £40 and up.

▶ *i* ⊖Southwark. Turn left onto Blackfriars Rd., left onto Stamford St., and right onto Duchy St. ☎ Open in summer M-F 11:30am-6:30pm, Sa-Su 10am-8pm; in winter M-F 11:30am-5:30pm, Sa-Su 10am-7pm.

MUSIC

◧ Music and Video Exchange   HYDE PARK TO NOTTING HILL
42 Notting Hill Gate
☎020 7221 2793 www.mgeshops.com

Music and Video Exchange will provide hours (if not days) of entertainment to any audiophile. The staff engage in constant

Shopping

High Fidelity-esque conversations and practically ooze musical knowledge, while customers browse through vinyl, CDs, and cassettes in the bargain area. Upstairs in the rarities section, you can find anything from £12 original vinyl of the Rolling Stones' *Get Yer Ya-Ya's Out!* to the original German sleeve for the Beatles' *Let it Be*. Customers can trade their own stuff in exchange for cash or—in a move betraying MVE's cold-hearted understanding of a music-lover's brain—twice the cash amount in store vouchers.

▶ *i* ◉Notting Hill Gate. Walk out of the south entrance of the Tube and go down Notting Hill Gate. ⏰ Open daily 10am-8pm.

🎵 Sister Ray   THE WEST END
34-35 Berwick St.
☎020 7734 3297 www.sisterray.co.uk

An old-school record shop of the best kind, Sister Ray's stellar staff is adept at creating musical matches made in heaven. Hip, cheap books about music line the check-out counter, and listening stations are located throughout the store. And when they're not sellin £500 special edition LPs, the prices are quite cheap. The store also buys, so if you want to sell your classic punk records to fund the next leg of your vacation, this is the place for you.

▶ *i* ◉Tottenham Court Rd. Turn left onto Oxford St., left onto Wardour St., and left onto Berwick St. ⏰ Open M-Sa 10am-8pm, Su noon-6pm.

The Schott Music Shop   THE WEST END
48 Great Marlborough St.
☎020 7292 6090 www.schottmusic.co.uk

Opened in 1857, Schott is the oldest sheet music shop in London. This quiet, spacious store sells everything from the Beatles to Bartók. The expert staff is the type that knows not only all of the pieces but also different recordings and can help recommend the best. Especially notable for music-starved travelers are the three **practice rooms** beneath the shop (each with a baby grand Steinway) available to rent by the hour.

▶ *i* ◉Oxford Circus. Turn left onto Regent St. and left onto Great Marlborough St. 10% student discount on print music. Practice room £10 per hr. before noon £12 per hr. noon-6pm £15 per hr. after 6pm. ⏰ Open M-F 10am-6:30pm, Sa 10am-6pm.

BM Soho Music   THE WEST END
25 D'Arblay St.
☎020 7437 0478 www.bm-soho.com

A favorite of many local DJs, BM (still known to many by its former name, **Black Market**) sells all things house, dubstep, and drum and bass. And, of course, every subgenre of house you can imagine (deep acid jazz funky house, anyone?). DJ gear like slip mats and record cases are also sold. Check the website for occasional in-store appearances by famous DJs.

▶ *i* ⊖Tottenham Court Rd. Turn left onto Oxford St., left onto Wardour St., left onto Berwick St., and right onto D'Arblay St. 🕐 Open M-W 11am-7pm, Th-F 11am-8pm, Sa 11am-7pm, Su noon-6pm.

MARKETS

🏷 Borough Market   THE SOUTH BANK
Southwark St.
☎ www.boroughmarket.org.uk

Even though the advent of globalization has removed any excuse for horrible British food, it's still a stereotype that proves true. And if you come from a culture where fresh produce is taken for granted (basically any other culture), Borough Market is your gateway ticket to fresh French cheeses, English strawberries that wouldn't be caught dead in a Tesco's, and baked goods that were made for high tea. You can spend days (three per week to be precise) browsing the stalls, or you can pick the "I'm feeling lucky" option.

▶ *i* ⊖London Bridge. Exit the Tube and walk down Southwark St. away from the river. The market is on the right, starting where Southwark St. and Borough High St. split off. 🕐 Open Th 11am-5pm, F noon-6pm, Sa 8am-5pm.

Old Spitalfields Market   EAST LONDON
Commercial St.
☎ www.oldspitalfieldsmarket.com

This is the sort of market that clearly belongs in the East End, selling stylish vintage clothes, quirky antiques, and an array of art. It's a mix of stores and stalls offering everything from a quick manicure to a spicy kebab. Sort of like the Goldenrod City Underground in the second generation Pokémon games, they're not all open every day, but Sundays are the busiest and have the best variety of vendors. If you're looking for antiques, Thursday is your day.

▶ *i* ⊖Shoreditch High St. Make a left down Commercial St. 🕐 Opening times vary per vendor, but most are open daily 10am-5pm.

Shopping

DEPARTMENT STORES

▨ Harrods
SOUTH KENSINGSTON AND CHELSEA

87-135 Brompton Rd.

☎020 7730 1234 www.harrods.com

Pick your favorite trappings of capitalism. You can choose spectacle—the sight of thousands of tourists and the upper classes looking at the soles of Christian Louboutins and slipping on Helmut Lang. Or perhaps status symbols would suffice, for what will make you evolutionarily desirable more than casually buying a Patek Phillipe? As they say, you just hold onto it for the next generation.

▶ *i* ⊖Knightsbridge. Take the Harrods exit. ⏰ Open M-Sa 10am-8pm, Su 11:30am-6pm.

Liberty
THE WEST END

Great Marlborough St.

☎020 7734 1234 www.liberty.co.uk

For Americans, when the word "liberty" is spoken, it's usually in a "Give me liberty or give me death" sort of way. For the French, similar revolutionary connotations apply. For the English, freedom is apparently only found in expensive, high art arenas. We're honestly not that surprised. The store's epic Tudor venue has been presenting the best in art and design to its customers since the 19th century. Today, you can buy everything from clothes to plates bearing the store's iconic prints. Don't miss the array of ribbons, feathers, and tulle in the haberdashery section.

▶ *i* ⊖Oxford Circus. Go down Regent St. and turn left onto Great Marlborough St. ⏰ Open M-Sa 10am-8pm, Su noon-6pm.

Harvey Nichols
SOUTH KENSINGSTON AND CHELSEA

109-125 Knightsbridge

☎020 7235 5000 www.harveynichols.com

Whoever was looking for the Fountain of Youth clearly never checked out the ground floor of Harvey Nichols. This level is packed with women arming themselves for the battle against age. Foreigners can shop tax-free if they go to the fourth-floor customer services and fill out a form. And yes, the staff in black is really just paid to judge you.

▶ *i* ⊖Knightsbridge. Follow the signs out of the Tube station. ⏰ Open M-W 10am-6pm, Th 10am-8pm, F 10am-7pm, Sa 9am-7pm, Su 10:30am-5pm.

Excursions

If you ever feel like the grim weather, constant references to the Queen Mum and those screaming soccer hooligans are dampening your crumpets, it may be time to get out of the city. Fortunately, the grim weather is no match for the shining light of knowledge you will gain from touring the United Kingdom. Get a taste of medieval architecture and a modern metropolis while visiting the college courtyards of Oxford. After you've gotten your fill of the mystical stonecircle of Stonehenge, get back to learning with a trip to the nearby Cambridge and its beautiful colleges and exciting history. So get your hungover self out of bed, stop by the market for some tea and biscuits, and head to the train station—you have a date with some books under the shade of an historic building that has taught thousands of students for centuries. You may even learn something during your vacation. Don't be frightened, you can get back to partying later.

Excursions

OXFORD

If you find yourself in Oxford, then be aware that there is one seminal text that every student holds in the back of his or her mind: *Brideshead Revisited*. A conservative treatment of interwar Britain, Evelyn Waugh's novel portrays Oxford as a garden of sensory delights: endless champagne, cigarettes in the sun, and studying only as barest necessity. It's still true today, although the city is a little more commercialized and a little less homophobic. As a tourism destination and student hub, Oxford offers its inhabitants not only a nightlife scene that leaves Cambridge students to slowly sink with regret, but it also boasts a platter of cultural delights like the Ashmolean Museum and the Bodleian Library. Then there are also the colleges themselves: millennia-old testaments to academic might (a good indicator of a university's age is when you have a non-zero number of saints as alumni). All in all, Oxford is a universal reference point in the United Kingdom with posh associations and a fearsome historical legacy. And, let us reiterate, really great bars.

Accommodations

Compared to Cambridge, Oxford has a surprisingly good selection of budget accommodations. Establishments are clustered around the train station and on **Iffley Road;** the former are closer to town and the city's nightlife, but the latter are in a quieter and more sedate area near the shops and cafes on Cowley Rd. If you want to stay in the heart of town, the University of Oxford's conferencing website (www.conference-oxford.com) lists individual email contacts for B&B accommodations at the colleges. The process can be a hassle but is worth it if you'd like to stay in the medieval digs of one of the colleges. Easier to navigate, but generally pricier, is www.universityrooms.co.uk, which allows you to book B&B accommodations in some of the colleges. Prices usually start a £40 for a single.

▨ Central Backpackers   HOSTEL
13 Park End St.
☎01865 242 288 www.centralbackpackers.co.uk

True to its name, this hostel is not only central but also filled with friendly backpackers excited to experience the latter part of Oxford's "think and drink" culture. The rooftop garden is a lovely anomaly in the hostel scene, and the rooms are clean and not cramped. The clubs on the street level don't stop believing until 3am. However, you can usually find a group to tag along with and partake in the libations (there are also free earplugs).

▶ *i* From the train station, follow Botley Rd. east toward the town center; it becomes Park End St. Free Wi-Fi. Continental breakfast and lockers included. Laundry £3.50. Free luggage storage. Self-catering kitchen. 12-bed dorms £20; 8-bed £21; 6-bed women-only £22; 4-bed £24.

🖾 Oxford Backpackers   HOSTEL
9A Hythe Bridge St.
☎01865 721 761 www.hostels.co.uk

"Go into the first hostel you see after leaving the train station," said no one ever. Except for this one. While some of the university rooms can seem barren and lonesome, this hostel has all of the cheeriness of a junior common room without any of the pretension or just general tension.

▶ *i* From the Oxford train station, walk up Hythe Bridge St. The hostel is after the bridge on the left. Free Wi-Fi. Breakfast included. Kitchen available.18-bed dorm £17; 14-be £18; 10-be £19-20.50; 4-be £24; 4-bed female onl £26.50. 🕓 Reception open 8am-11:30pm.

Sights

Most people come to admire Oxford's dozen or so aesthetically pleasing colleges, and we advise you to look at the university's free info booklet, which details all of the colleges' opening hours and admission fees. You can find it on the university's website (www.ox.ac.uk) under "Visiting the University." However, due to conferences, graduations, and general eccentricity, the hours open to tourists might change without further notice, like your favorite bureaucratic Kafka novel. One of the best ways to get into the colleges for free—especially during term-time—is to attend a church service in the college chapels. Show up 15min. before a service starts and tell the people at the gate that you'd like to attend; they'll usually let you in for free.

🖾 Ashmolean Museum   MUSEUM
Beaumont St.
☎01865 278 000 www.ashmolean.org

The Ashmolean befits its dual honors of being the oldest university museum in the world and the most smorgasbordy collection in the UK (that's just our own award). While the British Museum is great for a survey of colonialism, the Ashmolean tries to work within a world narrative by organizing their collection into equal parts "Eastern," "Western," and "West meets East." As befits a university museum, the exhibits are highly educational; well-organized displays teach you about everything from the consolidation of northern European tribes to the decipherment of ancient Aegean scripts. As you feast on knowledge in this ivory tower, you can also feast on food, as the Ashmolean has Oxford's only rooftop restaurant.

▶ *i* From Carfax (at the west end of High St.), head up Cornmarket St., then turn left onto Beaumont St. Free lunchtime gallery talks for 1st 12 who express interest Tu-F 1:15-2pm; pick up tokens at the information desk. Free. Special exhibits £5-6. ☼ Open Tu-Su 10am-6pm.

🎨 Bodleian Library   LIBRARY
Broad St.
☎01865 277 178 www.bodleian.ox.ac.uk

The Bodleian is one of the greatest libraries in the world, holding millions of volumes, including the normal trifecta of rare manuscripts (Shakespeare's First Folio, the Gutenberg Bible, and the Magna Carta). However, there are also some neat deep cuts, like the oldest copy of The Song of Roland, the earliest surviving work of French Literature, and the Huntington MS 17, which is not a type of rifle but rather the oldest printing of the gospels in the West Nile dialect of Bohairic. The complex of 17th-century buildings surrounding the courtyard are impressive enough to justify the visit, but if you want to experience some inevitable Harry Potter déjà vu, you can take a tour. All tours go to the Divinity School, the oldest teaching room in the university; longer ones take you to the gorgeously ancient Reading Room and by the rotund Radcliffe Camera (a vital part of every TV serial that takes place in the city).

▶ *i* Entrances on Broad St., Catte St., and Radcliffe St.; take Catte St. off High St. Entrance to the courtyard free. Entrance to Divinity Hall £1. 30min. tour of Library and Divinity Hall £5, 1hr. tour £7, extended tour £13. Audio tour £2.50. ☼ Open M-F 9am-5pm, Sa 9am-4:30pm, Su 11am-5pm.

🏛 The Pitts River Museum   MUSEUM
Park Rd.
☎01865 270 927

There's no such thing as referencing colonialism too many times, so we're going to breach it once more. While not every one of the thousands of artifacts in Oxford's archaeological and anthropological museum was acquired by colonial shopping at a 1000% discount, at least they're not exploiting the items that were (admission is free). From macabre shrunken heads to provocative fertility statues, razor-like samurai swords to practical Maori spears, real Inuit furs to golden feathered cloaks, every shelf in every glass case teems with fresh wonders of the creativity and ingenuity of the human species. In classic Victorian style, every case is arranged not by culture, as is now the norm, but by theme, which brings the wonderfully stark comparisons to the dim, somber light around you. Giving you just enough information to whet your appetite for travel, understanding, and worldly experience, this is a must for any globetrotter.

▶ *i* From High St., take Catte St., which becomes Parks Rd. Walk through the Museum of Natural History on the right. Tours W 2:30 and 3:15pm. Audio tour £2. Free. ☑ Open M noon-4:30pm, Tu-Su 10am-4:30pm.

Modern Art Oxford   GALLERY
30 Pembroke St.
☎1865 722 733 www.modernartoxford.org.uk

Oxford's entire appeal is founded on the fact that it is not modern *at all*. It's such a creature of the past that you can barely go for a meal, drink, or piss without finding out that Tolkien ate, drank, and pissed there, too. That's why this is your antidote to leaving the town covered in a thin film of historical dust. The museum rotates exhibits that are equal parts bizarre and incomprehensible: documentary films on things you didn't even know you were interested in, strange series of short film collages, sculptures without plaques. Unlike the other Oxford museums, which justify their exhibits by over-explaining, the Modern Art museum justifies itself by not, and thus allows the visitor's mind to wander creatively.

▶ *i* From Carfax, walk down Queen St. Turn left onto St. Ebbe's St. Turn left onto Pembroke St. The gallery is on the left. Check online for current exhibits and night events. Bar open on event nights.Free. ☑ Open Tu-W 10am-5pm, Th-Sa 10am-7pm, Su noon-5pm.

Carfax Tower   TOWER
Junction of St. Aldate's, Cornmarket, High, and Queen St.
☎01865 792 633

This was the site of the former City Church of Oxford (St. Martin's Church). However, in 1896, university leaders decided that the bulk of the church needed to be demolished in order to make room for more traffic in the downtown area. Given the stagnant mass of tourist crowds that now mill around it below, that was probably a bad move. Despite its name soundinglike an auto insurance price quote company, it actually comes from the French *carrefour,* or "crossroads," which makes sense, as the tower marks the official center of Oxford. To prevent the Tower of Babel II (and thus more linguistic majors), no building in the city center may be taller; this means that from the top, you get an extraordinary view over the university's spires.

▶ *i* £2.20, under 1 £1.10. ☑ Open daily Apr-Sept 10am-5:30pm; Oct 10am-4:30pm; Nov-Mar 10am-3:30pm.

Oxford Castle   CASTLE
44-46 Oxford Castle
☎01865 260 666 www.oxfordcastleunlocked.co.uk☐

Sometimes disappearing down a dark passageway while following an underpaid, faux-torch-bearing actor is exactly what
the doctor ordered. Oxford Castle will remind you that this
hasn't always been the safe student haven it is today. A shot of
medieval intrigue and a sudden understanding of the immense
past behind every street corner can finely tune your appreciation for Oxford (even if it is done in costume and outrageously
overacted bits). Life was tough, no question. People were thrown
into dungeons, hanged, murdered, tortured, and even brought
back from the dead—all slightly more fun than clubbing in
Cambridge.

▶ *i* Directly behind the Castle St. bus stop. Tours approximately every 20min
£9.25, student £7.25. ☼ Open daily 10am-5pm; last tour 4:20pm.

Magdalen College   COLLEGE
High St.
☎01865 276 000 www.magd.ox.ac.uk

Magdalen is spelled differently from its Cambridge coun-
terpart, but pronounced in the same manner (MAUD-lin).
With its winding riverbanks, flower-filled quads, and 100-acre
grounds, Magdalen is possibly Oxford's most attractive college.
The contrast between the medieval quad and the 18th-century
New Building (where C.S. Lewis lived) also makes for some
impressive architectural observations. Magdalen boys have
traditionally been quite a catch—the college has housed seven
Nobel Prize winners, Dudley Moore, and Oscar Wilde—so put
your wooing cap on. The college also has a pleasant deer park,
where equally attractive deer have grazed aimlessly for centuries.

▶ *i* At the east end of High St., by the river £5, concession £4. ☼ Open
Jul-Sept daily noon-7pm; Oct-Jun 1-6pm or dusk.

Balliol College   COLLEGE
Broad St.
☎01865 277 777 www.balliol.ox.ac.uk

Along with Merton and University, Balliol, founded in the
1260s, has a legitimate claim to being the oldest college in
Oxford. Renowned for its PPE subject (Politics, Philosophy,
and Economics), Adam Smith, Aldous Huxley, Christopher
Hitchens, three British prime ministers, and six members
of the Obama administration were produced from Balliol's
mismatched spires. Its grounds feel impressively medieval, complete with crenellated parapets surrounding the first court (for a

less intimidating view, go through the hedges on the right-hand side, past the first court, for a picturesque garden).

▶ *i* From Carfax (at the west end of High St.), take Cornmarket St., then turn right onto Broad St £2, student £1. 🕐 Open daily 10am-5pm or dusk.

Merton College   COLLEGE
Merton St.
☎01865 276 310 www.merton.ox.ac.uk

Though Balliol and University were endowed before it, Merton has the earliest formal college statutes (1274), which helps to legitimize its boast of being the oldest college. Its traditions and high-achieving student body also give it a nerdy reputation. For example, the annual Time Ceremony has students dance around the Fellows Quad in full regalia, drinking port in celebration of the end of British Summer Time. J.R.R. Tolkien was the Merton Professor of English here and spent his time casually inventing the Elvish language and writing a well-received minor trilogy on the side. The college's 14th-century Mob Quad is Oxford's oldest and one of its least impressive, while the nearby St. Alban's Quad is home to some of the university's best gargoyles.

▶ *i* From High St., turn down Magpie Ln., then take a left onto Merton St £3. 🕐 Open M-F 2-5pm, Sa-Su 10am-5pm.

Food

Here's one major perk of visiting a student town:**kebab trucks.** These student favorites line High St., Queen St., and Broad St. (we recommend Hassan's on Broad St.), and stay open until 3am during the week and 4 or 4:30am on weekends.

🦪 The Vaults and Garden   CAFE $$
St. Mary's Church, Radcliffe Sq.
☎01865 279 112 www.vaultsandgarden.com

In the summer, this garden is hands-down the best place for lunch in the entire city. Based out of the University Church of St. Mary the Virgin, the large garden offers picturesque views of the Bodleian Library, Radcliffe Camera, and nearby colleges. You can stretch out and soak up the sun on picnic blankets while enjoying the Brideshead life (although the emphasis is less on champagne and strawberries than on scones and tea). Notwithstanding, the eponymous vaults are a worthy consolation prize if rain reigns. The organic, locally sourced menu changes daily, with fresh salads, sandwiches, and soups, as well as coffee, yogurt, and pastries.

▶ *i* Turn up St. Mary's Passage off Queen St. or High St. 10% student discount. Lunch entree £7-10. Tea item £2.20 each. 🕑 Open daily 8:30am-6:30pm.

Georgina's   CAFE $
Avenue 3, The Covered Market
☎01865 249 527

Hiding above the furor of the Covered Market sits this fantastically unpretentious coffee shop. The old movie posters papering the ceiling and the cluttered seating arrangements ensure that you can lounge here comfortably while tackling a large-portioned meal. If you need a solid breakfast after a regrettable late-night kebab run, their custom omelettes £4.75) are a solid victory in the eternal struggle against hangover.

▶ *i* From Carfax, walk down High St. Turn right and enter the Covered Market. Go onto Avenue 3 and look for a staircase about halfway down. Tends to be full or nearly full from noon-1pm.Bagels, ciabatta, and panin £3.20-3.95. 🕑 Open M-Sa 8:30am-5pm.

The Eagle and Child   PUB $
49 St. Giles'
☎01865 302 925

This pub was a favorite watering hole of J.R.R. Tolkien, C.S. Lewis, and the group of writers who dubbed themselves the"Inklings." However, while visiting a bar that a serial alcoholic like George Orwell or Charles Bukowski frequented is a legitimate chance to channel their energy, it's harder to link the author of "Mere Christianity" with a drinking establishment. This brick and wood pub is now more of a tourist destination than a charming bar, although the booths at the front can shield you from cameras and hushed awe.

▶ *i* From Carfax (at the west end of High St.), follow Cornmarket St., which becomes St. Giles'. Sandwiche £5.75-9.75. Burger £8-11.50. 🕑 Open M-Th 11am-11pm, F-Sa 11am-midnight, Su noon-10:30pm.

Mission Burritos   MEXICAN $$
2 King Edward St.
☎01865 722 020 www.missionburrito.co.uk

A lack of burritos has been a much decried truth of the late-night food scene in Oxford for some time, a problem Mission Burritos is, most assuredly, working on. The familiar sounds and smells of the burrito place, the savory carnitas, the mixed tang of salsas, and the creamy bite of guacamole and sour cream will keep you full from your usual 10pm meal to well after your 3am kebab.

▶ *i* From Carfax, walk down the High St. Turn right onto King Edward St. The restaurant is on the right. Order online to save time.Burrito £5.45-6. 🕑

Open M-W 11am-10pm, Th-Sa 11am-11pm, Su 11am-10pm.

Atomic Burger   BURGERS $$
96 Cowley Rd.

☎01865 790 855 www.atomicburger.co.uk

This funky, outer space-themed restaurant offers a pop culture laden litany of delicious burgers, sides, shakes, and drinks. You can blow out your brain's capacity *Hitchhiker's Guide*-style with Zaphod's Flaming Gargleblaster Margherita (tequila, triple sec, and absinthe £7.50) or *Pulp Fiction*-style with a Big Kahuna burger. The inside of the restaurant looks like the bedroom of a child yearning to be an astronaut (or that of an adult with arrested development), but the joint is so earnestly not self-conscious that it makes you forget the heavy use of Comic Sans.

▶ *i* Follow High St. past Magdalen College and across Magdalen Bridge and head down Cowley Rd. All burgers come with a free side. 10% discount on takeout. Gluten-free options, vegetarian options.Burger with 1 sid £6.75-9.25. ◎ Open M-F noon-10:30pm, Sa-Su 10am-10:30pm.

Freud   CAFE, BAR $
119 Walton St.

☎01865 311 171 www.freud.eu

We're pretty sure there's nothing in *Interpretation of Dreams* that explains what drinking and dancing in a cathedral means. Regardless of the inexplicable premise, Freud inhabits the vaulted interior of a 19th-century Greek Revival church, stained glass and all—if it wasn't for the cafe tables on the portico outside, you'd never guess that this place serves food. The cafe progresses into a cocktail bar at night, with a DJ on the weekends. That may explain the disco ball, but it doesn't make the presence of a cocktail menu above a church pew any morecomprehensible.

▶ *i* From the train station, follow Botley Rd. toward the town center, bear left onto Hythe Bridge St., then left onto Worcester St., which becomes Walton St. Freud is on the right, next to Radcliffe Infirmary.Sandwiches and pizz £5.50-8. Appetizers and snack £1.75-4.50. Cocktail £6-7. ◎ Open M 5pm-midnight, Tu 5pm-1am, W 10:30am-1am, Th-Sa 10:30am-2am, Su 10:30am-midnight. Kitchen open daily until 10pm.

Branca   ITALIAN $$
111 Walton St.

☎01865 556 111 www.branca-restaurants.com

At first, the leather seats and sleek chrome of this restaurant may seem at odds with Jericho's gritty student aura. Look in the back, however, and you'll discover colorful Art Nouveau posters, a paradise of a garden terrace, and an olive tree growing in the center of the dining room. The upscale food—creamy risotto, prawn bruschetta, pan-fried pork cutlets—is similarly balanced byBranca's student-friendly prices. On weekdays until 5pm, you can get pizza, pasta, or risotto with a beer or (generous) glass of wine for jus £7.95. You don't have to be reading maths at Oxford to know that's a good value.

▶ *i* From the train station, follow Botley Rd. toward the town center, bear left onto Hythe Bridge St., then left onto Worcester St., which becomes Walton St. Freud is on the right, next to Radcliffe Infirmary. Takeout available. Entree £8-16. ⓩ Open daily noon-11pm.

Nightlife

in itIf the London clubbing scene is a nice Talisker, Oxford is a fair glass of Pinot Blanco, and Cambridge is a paper bag that once had Rubinoff and now has piss in it. Point being, nightlife here doesn't incur the excitement of London, but it could be much, much worse.The main clubbing area in Oxford is near the train station, on **Park End** and **Hythe Bridge Streets.** Both of these split off from **Botley Road** (the train station's home). The center of town has little in the way of dancing, but its many excellent pubs are perfect for a more laid-back evening.

▧ Purple Turtle Union Bar   BAR, CLUB
Frewin Ct.
☎018 6524 7007 www.purpleturtlebar.com

Prepare yourself for claustrophobic tunnel vision as you consume enough flaming absinthe shots to become the green fairy incarnate. This underground bar is directly under the Oxford Union Debating Society, and true to form, you're probably going to host the largest internal debate of your life when trying to decide which one of the 40 shooter options (based on the personalities of the different colleges) is really you. We're going to put on our Sorting Hat and recommend the Slytherin shooter (green absinthe, apple sours) regardless. The dance floor can get a bit insanely cramped, but the DJs spin with a deft hand.

▶ *i* From Carfax, walk down Cornmarket St. Turn left onto Frewin Ct. Check online for special offers and weekly happy hours. Beer from £2. Shooters £2.50. Shots from £1.50. ⓩ Open M-Sa 8pm-3am, Su 8pm-2am.

▧ The Bear Inn   PUB
6 Alfred St.
☎018 6572 1783

The Bear may be the oldest pub in Oxford—the current building was built in the 18th century, but previous incarnations go all the way back to 1242 (and since bears in Oxford went extinct in the 10th century, who knows?). Anyway, the pub does show its age with low ceilings and rickety stairs that make it slightly perilous for the tall and/or clumsy patron. But don't let this put you off; the Bear is a great, unfussy place to enjoy a pint. The ties in the display cases have been given in exchange for half pints and hail from clubs and colleges around the world.

▶ *i* Off High St., just behind Christ Church. Pub quiz Tu 8:30pm. Live music W 9pm. Pints £3.50. ☎ Open M-Th 11am-11pm, F-Sa 11am-midnight, Su 11:30am-10:30pm.

The King's Arms   PUB

40 Holywell St.

☎018 6524 2369 www.kingsarmsoxford.co.uk

The King's Arms embraced only men from 1607-1973, and as befits an old-guard vestige of the patriarchy, there are enough leather-bound booths and pervasive whiffs of mahogany to sufficiently prove its masculinity. However, the various traditional rooms don't ooze the fabricated pubbiness of the chains, and it's no surprise that professors sometimes hold office hours here. Brass tacks, it's on students' list of reliable pubs to hit when a Royal Baby is born, when Andy Murray wins Wimbledon, or when anything that will make day-drinking more excusable occurs.

▶ *i* Across the street from the Bodleian Library. On the corner between Holywell St. and Park St. Beer fro £3.40. ☎ Open daily 10:30am-midnight. Kitchen open until 9:30pm.

Jericho Tavern   PUB, LIVE MUSIC

56 Walton St.

☎018 6531 1775 www.thejerichooxford.co.uk

Radiohead debuted here back in 1984; since then, Jericho Tavern has been sold and bought, remodeled and rebranded, but has always remained an indie favorite and a good spot to find live music in Oxford. The heated outdoor beer garden is also a plus, especially if you get a Fruli Strawberry Beer (or, you know, something less girly) to enjoy out there. There's live acoustic at 8pm on Sundays, and board games are available for further entertainment.

▶ *i* From Carfax, walk north on Cornmarket St., which becomes Magdalen St. Turn left onto Beaumont St., then right onto Walton St. The tavern is near the Phoenix Picturehouse.Pints aroun £3.50. ☎ Open M-F noon-midnight, Sa 11am-midnight, Su noon-midnight. Kitchen closes at 10pm.

The Cellar   LIVE MUSIC

Frewin Ct.

☎018 6525 0181 www.cellaroxford.co.uk

"Underground" music is one of those phraes that is immediately coded as"furtive," "obscure," and "authentic." But the Cellar brings it back to its roots by being very obviously underground, with tunnels echoing the newest, boldest rock groups and alternative DJs. Going through phases of greatness and less-than-greatness over the last few years, the Cellar is on the upswing again, clinging to its independent identity and subterranean culture. In other words, it has not sold out like the Bridge (which joins artists to corporations, obviously).

▶ *i* From the Town Center, walk down Cornmarket St. Turn left onto Frewin Ct. Check events online. Cove £5-12. ☾ Open M-Sa 10pm-3am, Su 10pm-2am.

The Turf Tavern   PUB

4-5 Bath Pl.

☎018 6524 4761 www.theturftavern.co.uk

Competing with the Bear for the title of Oxford's oldest drinking establishment, the Turf Tavern also holds the distinction of being named Britain's "Perfect Pub" in 2007. We can see why—from the sunny beer garden to the mix of students and faithful locals, it's a pretty inviting place. Supposedly, its location just outside the original walls of the city is due to the illegal gambling of its patrons (and their desire to avoid the local authorities). The legends of debauchery and excess don't stop there—this is where future Australian Prime Minister Bob Hawke set the world record for consuming a yard of ale in 11 seconds andis rumored to be where Bill Clinton "didn't inhale."

▶ *i* Follow Catte St. from High St., then right onto Holywell St. Bath Pl. is a tiny alley off Holywell St.Pints fro £3.20. ☾ Open M-Sa 11am-11pm, Su 11am-10:30pm. Kitchen open until 9pm.

Arts and Culture

▨ Oxford Playhouse   THEATER

11-12 Beaumont St.

☎01865 305 305 www.oxfordplayhouse.com

Known to locals as "The Playhouse," this independent theater hosts student and amateur dramas, contemporary dance and music, comedy, lectures, and poetry. Whether it's Philip Pullman and Neil Gaiman chatting or a production staged completely in the dark, whatever event is on will not be your average sit-and-pretend-to-appreciate-theater experience. In the summer, the theater puts on Shakespeare performances in the quad in front of the Bodleian Library (and also hosts Globe Theatre touring companies, meaning a trip to London is not necessary).

▶ *i* Down Beaumont St. from the Ashmolean Musem. Ticket prices vary.

Advance concessions £2 off. Student standbys available day of show for £9.50. 🕐 Box office open M-Sa 10am-6pm or until 30min. after curtain, Su from 2hr. before curtain to 30min. after (performance days only). Cafe open 10am-11pm (closes at 5:30pm on non-performance nights).

New Theatre   THEATER
George St.
☎01865 320 760,0844 847 1588 for booking www.newtheatreoxford.org.uk

Formerly known as the Apollo Theater, this is Oxford's main commercial theater. The Art Deco building is home to many visiting concerts, musicals, and dramas (as well as psychics and comedians)—often after they've been on the stages of London's West End.

▶ *i* From Carfax (at the west end of High St.), take Cornmarket St., then left on George St.Tickets anywhere fro £10-54. Concessions sometimes available for weekday shows. 🕐 Box office open M-Sa noon to 30min. after curtain, Su from 2½hr. before curtain to 30min. after.

The Sheldonian Theatre   THEATER
Broad St.
☎01865 277 299 www.ox.ac.uk/sheldonian

Described as a"Jewel of Oxford" in the same tone people use to say Stephen Fry is a "National Treasure," this theater does not have the amateur ease of the Playhouse. Instead, the curved sandstone façade inspires admiration and wonder at the gentle beauty of the building (as always, thank the omnipresent Sir Christopher Wren). Reserved for Oxford's more wordless performances, The Sheldonian is usually home to orchestral crescendos, from quartets to symphonies. The now-famous Oxford Philomusica usually performs here in, of course, the highest of style.

▶ *i* Directly next to the Bodleian Library on Broad St. Book events online through the Oxford Playhouse.Visitin £2.50 £1.50 concessions. Event ticket prices vary, though standby tickets may be available the day of the show. Visitor hours 10am-12:30pm. Mar-Oct 2 4:30pm, Nov-Feb 2-3:30pm. Check online for listings. Box office open M-Sa 10am-6pm (at the Oxford Playhouse).

Shopping

If you're tied to the old ball-and-chain store fashion, Cornmarket St. is here to fulfill your fast fashion dreams. **Jericho** has more alternative shopping, while shops on **High Street** and **St. Aldate's,** with their historic-looking decor, are generally aimed at tourists.

▨ Blackwell's   BOOKS

48-51 Broad St.

☎01865 792 792 www.bookshop.blackwell.co.uk

This is the Harrods of bookstores: sprawling, overwhelming, and full of strange finds among classic staples. And, fortunately for the student who only spends money on books, this is not nearly as expensive. It's silly to suggest a particular plan of attack, because we have no idea what type of books you like, but a universally nice option is to go on one of the literary walking tours that leaves from the shop. Perhaps it will give you some book recommendations.

▶ *i* From High St., take Catte St. Turn left onto Broad St. Blackwell's is 10m away on the right. Check online for event listings. ⏰ Open M 9am-6pm, Tu 9:30am-6pm, W-Sa 9am-6:30pm, Su 11am-5pm.

▨ The Albion Beatnik   BOOKS, CAFE

34 Walton St.

☎01865 511 345

The Albion Beatnik's inventory spans the Moloch of Milton to the Moloch of Ginsberg (with emphasis on the latter). Almost half of the space in this independent bookstore is dedicated to an impressive collection of Beat poetry and other Beatnik-related topics. Open up the well decorated cupboard in the back corner to find hundreds of jazz CDs. There's also a cafe of sorts inside, so you can settle into an armchair with a cup of tea and a book while Dylan and Coltrane play in the background.

▶ *i* Heading north on St. Giles', turn left onto Little Clarendon, then turn right at the end. New and secondhand books from £1. ⏰ Open M-Tu 11am-8pm, W-Sa 11am-11pm, Su 2-5pm.

Essentials

Practicalities

- **Tourist Offices:** The Tourist Information Centre (TIC) provides the free "What's On In Oxford" guide, sells discounted tickets to local attractions, and books rooms with a 10% deposit. (15-16 Broad St. *i* From Carfax, take Cornmarket St., then turn right onto Broad St. ☎01865 252 200 www.visitoxford.org ⏰ Open M-Sa 9:30am-5pm, Su 10am-4pm. Closes 30min. earlier in winter.)

- **Student Travel Offices:** STA Travel. (Threeways House, 36 George St. *i* From Carfax, take Cornmarket St. Turn left onto George St. The office is on the right. ☎0871 702

9839 www.statravel.co.uk ☼ Open M 10am-6pm, Tu-Th 9am-7pm, F 10am-7pm, Sa 10am-6pm, Su 11am-5pm.)

- **Tours:** The official Oxford University Walking Tour leaves from the TIC and provides access to some colleges otherwise closed to visitors. The 2hr. tours are capped at 19 people and are booked on a first-come, first-served basis. You can get tickets up to 48hr. in advance at the TIC, by phone, or online. (☎01852 726 871, ☎01865 252 200 to book tickets www.visitoxford.org *i* £8, children £4.50. ☼ Tours daily in summer 11am and 1pm (additionally 10:45am and 2pm on Sa). Themed tours, like the C.S. Lewis, Harry Potter and J.R.R. Tolkien Tours run on a varied schedule; check with the TIC. (*i* £15, concessions £10.)

- **Currency Exchange:** Banks line Cornmarket St. Marks and Spencer has a bureau de change with no commission. (13-18 Queen St. *i* From Carfax, walk down Cornmarket St. M&S is on the right. ☎01865 248 075 ☼ Open M-W 8:30am-6:30pm, Th 8:30am-7:30pm, F 8:30am-6:30pm, Sa 8:30am-6:30pm, Su 11am-4:30pm.) There is also a bureau de change with no commission attached to (but not affiliated with) the TIC.

- **Internet:** Free at Oxford Central Library; however, there is often a wait during prime hours. Some stations are open to pre-booking if you know exactly when you'd like to use it. (Westgate *i* From Carfax, walk down Queen St. The library is ahead. ☼ Open M-Th 9am-7pm, F-Sa 9am-5:30pm.) Offered for free at most cafes in the area.

- **Post Office:** 102-104 St. Aldate's. (☎01865 513 25 postoffice.co.uk *i* From Carfax, take St. Aldate's. Bureau de change inside. ☼ Open M-Sa 9am-5:30pm.

Emergency

- **Emergency Services:** In any emergency, dial ☎999. On the corner of St. Aldates and Speedwell St. (St. Aldates ☎08458 505 505 ☼ Open 24hr.)

- **Hospitals/Medical Services:** John Radcliffe Hospital. (Headley Way ☎01852 741 166 *i* Bus #13 or 14.)

Getting There

Botley Road Station (Botley Rd., down Park End St. ☎01865 484 950 ☼ Ticket office open M-F 5:45am-8pm, Sa 7:30am-

8pm, Su 7:15am-8pm) receives trains from: **Birmingham** £34 🕐 1hr., every 30min.); **Glasgow** £116 🕐 5-6hr., every hr.); **London Paddington** £23.40 🕐 1hr., 2-4 per hr.); and **Manchester** £62.80 🕐 3hr., 2 per hr.).

By Bus

Gloucester Green Station is the city's main bus station. The Oxford Bus Company (☎01865 785 400 www.oxfordbus.co.uk) runs the **Oxford Express** (*i* Free Wi-Fi. £14, students £11 🕐 1½hr., every 15-30min.) and the **X70 Airline** runs from Heathrow Airport. (*i* Free Wi-Fi. £23. 🕐 1½hr., every 30min.) It also runs the **X80 service** from Gatwick Airport. (*i* Free Wi-Fi. £28 🕐 2½hr., every hr.) It's best to book tickets in advance on the Oxford Bus website. The **X5 bus** connects Oxford with Cambridge. (*i* Free Wi-Fi. £12.50 🕐 3¼hr., every 30min.)

Getting Around

By Bus

Oxford Bus Company (☎01865 785 400www.oxfordbus.co.uk) provides service throughout the city. Fares vary depending on distance traveled. (*i* DayPass £4, weekly pass £14.) Weekly passes can be purchased at the Oxford Bus Company Travel Shop. (*i* 3rd fl. of Debenham's department store, on the corner of George St. and Magdalen St.🕐 Open M-W 9:30am-6pm, Th 9:30am-8pm, F 9:30am-6pm, Sa 9am-6pm, Su noon-4pm.) **Stagecoach** (☎01865 772 250 www.stagecoachbus.com) also runs buses in the city and to some surrounding villages. One-way tickets within the city usually cost £1.80. Buy a pass for a week of riding within Oxford for £16. Be careful when buying Day Passes because they don't apply to both companies. For real-time information on buses in Oxford, use www.oxontime.com.

By Taxi

Call **Radio Taxi**(☎01865 242 424) or **ABC** (☎01865 770 077) for taxis. There are taxi ranks at Oxford Station, Saint Giles, Gloucester Green, and in the evening at Carfax. Taxis may be hailed in the street.

By Bike

You can rent some wheels at **Cyclo Analysts.** (150 Cowley Rd. ☎01865 424 444www.oxfordcycles.com *i* Includes lock. £10, 2 days £18, 3 days £24, every additional day £3. 🕐 Open M-Sa 9am-6pm, Su 10am-4pm.)

CAMBRIDGE

Eight centuries of history, 31 colleges, and the energy of a living university town, all in one easily accessible package. It was here that James Watson and Francis Crick (with the oft-forgotten Rosalind Franklin's help) discovered the double helix, Sir Isaac Newton deduced gravity, Lord Byron and John Milton wrote their famous poetry, and Winnie-the-Pooh was born. The city is dominated by its eponymous university; the school's medieval buildings line the winding streets, and every pub, club, and cafe seems to exist to serve students. If you're looking for the definitive Cambridge experience, try the "P and P" formula: Punting and Pimm's—in American, boating and boozing. This is best done in the summer, when the banks of the Cam turn green and flowers bloom in the college gardens, but to get a sense of the real Cambridge, you'll have to come during term-time, when the town fills with its 18,000 students.

Accommodations

Budget lodging options in Cambridge are notoriously bad, as people who come to visit or live here either fall into the categories of "student with pre-arranged dorm room" or "parent with some dough to burn." There are few affordable rooms near the town center, and overpriced, occasionally sketchy bed and breakfasts fill the area to the north and south of town. In particular, B&Bs cluster on **Arbury Road** and **Chesterton Road** to the north; several can be found close to the station on **Tenison Road.** Bus #1 goes between Tenison Rd. and the town center, while bus #2 serves Chesterton Rd. When the university is not in session, many of the colleges offer their rooms (generally called "digs") at competitive prices (usuall £30-70 for a single); check www.cambridgerooms.co.uk for more information.

🏛 **Warkworth House** B&B $$$
Warkworth Terr.
☎01223 363 682 www.warkworthhouse.co.uk

Warkworth House—one of the few Cambridge accommodations that are both affordable and centrally located—can be found on a flower-filled residential block just a few minutes from the main colleges (and from appropriately named "Paradise" and "Eden" streets). Its rooms vary in style—from dark wood and exotic patterns in one to primary colors and lighter

finishes in another—but large windows and scrubbed wood
floors are a common theme.

▶ *i* Walk down Parkside away from the town center and turn left onto Warkworth Terr. Free Wi-Fi. Full English breakfast included. Laundry available. Singles £65-75; doubles £80-85; family rooms (for 4) £110-120.

🏠 Lynwood House   B&B $$$$
217 Chesterton Rd.
☎01223 500 776 www.lynwood-house.co.uk

This recently renovated B&B traded in predictable floral
motifs that commonly grace Victorian hotels for a bolder, modern theme. The rooms are nice, large, and well designed, with
rich, tasteful color combinations and great furnishings. Though
Lynwood House is a bit to the north of the city center, there's a
convenient cluster of pubs and stores nearby.

▶ *i* From the town center, take either Victoria Ave. or Bridge St., then turn right onto Chesterton Rd. Free Wi-Fi and ethernet. Breakfast included. Ensuite bathrooms. Often 2-night min. stay. Check website for details. Singles £65-85; doubles £85-120.

Tenison Towers   B&B $$
148 Tenison Rd.
☎01223 363 924 www.cambridgecitytenisontowers.com

The name would suggest a Dredd-style complex of 200 floors,
but this quaint establishment is quite the opposite. The guesthouse's theme is positively cute, with periwinkle blue and white
gingham lightening up the clean rooms. Even though it's a
15min. walk from the city, that really just gives you more of
a reason to pack in another incredible homemade muffin at
breakfast. The best aspect is the proximity to the train station,
a mere three-minute jaunt on foot.

▶ *i* From the train station, go down Station Rd. and turn right onto Tenison Rd. Free Wi-Fi. Breakfast included. Single £45; double £70.

YHA Cambridge   HOSTEL $
97 Tenison Rd.
☎0845 371 9728 www.yha.org.uk

The rooms at this YHA are fairly basic (wooden bunks, simple
carpeting), but they live up to the chain's standards for cleanliness and convenience. Common spaces abound—which is great
for the solo traveler looking for a friend to go pubbing with—
and include a game room with a pool table and multiple dining
rooms served by a cafe, self-catered kitchen, and small bar.

▶ *i* From the train station, head down Station Rd. and turn right onto Tenison Rd. Interne £1 per 20min. £5 per 24hr. £12 per 3 days £15 per week.Breakfas £4.95. Laundry facilities available. All dorms single-sex. 7-day max. stay. 8-bed dorm £19-22; doubles, quads, and 6-bed private £20 per person.

Acorn Guest House   B&B $$$
154 Chesterton Rd.
☎01223 353 888 www.acornguesthouse.co.uk

A lot of tourists have a Cambridge bike fantasy, where they roam the streets like a beautiful mechanical antelope. Maybe that's just us. If you do plan on biking around, Acorn's distance becomes less prohibitive and makes up for the trek with some nice touches. Silk bed canopies will make you feel like a classic royal, while hundreds of channels on the flat screen TVs will entertain you like a modern one. Most of the rooms are in a townhouse-like building, but a few newer ones are clustered in a separate unit in the back.

▶ *i* From the city center, take either Victoria Ave. or Bridge St. and turn right onto Chesterton Rd. Free Wi-Fi. Breakfast included. 5% surcharge if paying by credit card.Single £50-75; double £70-90; family room £95-140.

Sights

Cambridge is quite different from Oxford—its "peer institution"—in that the colleges are more homely, with a few grandiose exceptions like King's and Trinity. We've listed our favorites below, but all the city-center colleges are beautiful (the "new," 20th-century colleges can be skipped), but if you're only in town for a few days,you can take a punt and see six or seven of them from behind in one go. The town itself—which is a sight in its own right—has the close-to-the-ground feel of an agricultural market (quite a contrast from Oxford's warren of gothic castles). As for the museums, most showcase what Cambridge is famous for: excellence in the sciences, from the poles of botany to engineering.

🖾 King's College   COLLEGE
King's Parade
☎01223 331 100 www.kings.cam.ac.uk

Founded by Henry VI in 1441, King's College was the feeder school for Eton until it relaxed its admission policy in 1873 and reluctantly began to accept students from vastly inferior schools like Harrow. These days, King's draws more students from state schools than any other Cambridge college, and it has gained a reputation as the most socially liberal of the institutions. Still, you wouldn't guess that from the massive buildings and the rolling grounds that scream privilege. Catch a look from the other side of the river to see the college in all its glory, then come visit the Gothic King's College Chapel, where spidering arches and stunning stained glass will wow even the most church-weary tourist. King's alumni include John Maynard Keynes, E.M. Forster, and Salman Rushdie.

▶ *i* King's Parade is the western of the city center's 2 main avenues, the northern continuation of Trumpington St. £7.50, concessions and ages 12-18 £5, under 12 free. 🕐 Open during term time M-F 9:45am-3:30pm, Sa 9:30am-3:15pm; outside of term time M 9:45am-4:30pm, Tu-Su 9:30am-5pm. During term time, Evensong in chapel M-Sa 5:30pm; Su Eucharist 10:30am, Evensong 3:30pm.

🏛 Trinity College   COLLEGE

Trinity Ln.

☎01223 338 400 www.trin.cam.ac.uk

Welcome to the largest and richest college in Cambridge. Glib descriptions attribute its founding to Henry VIII, but it was really Catherine Parr who persuaded the ornery king to create a new college instead of destroying the whole Oxbridge system monastery-style. Now, Trinity is famous for its illustrious alumni, which include literati Dryden, Byron, Tennyson, and Nabokov; atom-splitter Ernest Rutherford; philosopher Ludwig Wittgenstein; and Indian statesman Jawaharlal Nehru. The epically beautiful Great Court is the world's largest enclosed courtyard—and also the track for young runners who attempt to beat the 12 strikes of the clock in under 43 seconds as shown in *Chariots of Fire* (even though it was filmed at Eton). The supposed great-great grandchild of the apple tree that inspired Issac Newton's theory of gravity stands near the gate; in the north cloister of nearby Neville's Court, Newton calculated the speed of sound by stamping his foot and timing the echo. In less practical exercises, Lord Byron used to bathe nude in the college's fountain and kept a pet bear because college rules forbade cats and dogs. The Wren Library houses alumnus A.A. Milne's handwritten copies of *Winnie-the-Pooh* and Newton's personal copy of his *Principia*. Trinity also has punts, available for rent by the river near Garret Hostel Ln.

▶ *i* Turn left off Trinity St. onto Trinity Ln. £3, children £1.50. Punts £14 per hr. with £40 deposit. 🕐 Courtyard open daily 10am-4:30pm. Wren Library open M-F noon-2pm. Hall open 3-5pm. Punts available spring-summer M-F 11am-5:30pm, Sa-Su 10am-5:30pm.

🏛 The Fitzwilliam Museum   MUSEUM

Trumpington St.

☎01223 332 900 www.fitzmuseum.cam.ac.uk

This grandiose revivalist museum has the variety of the British Museum without the crushing realization that all of the exhibits came about directly via colonialism (then again, an argument can be made for structural violence in the case of the absurdly wealthy British collector who started the museum). Loosely centered around "art and antiquities," the collection hosts a fearsome selection of Italian and French painters; Greek and Middle Eastern pottery; Egyptian sarcophagi; and illustrated medieval manuscripts. On the more modern side of things, there are some excellently preserved works by Thomas Hardy and Virginia Woolf as well.

► *i* Trumpington is the western of the 2 main roads in the city. If coming from the east, turn off Pembroke St.; if coming from the west, turn off Silver St. Free. Audio tours £3, students £2. Guided tours £4. 🕐 Open Tu-Sa 10am-5pm, Su noon-5pm. Guided tours depart from the courtyard entrance Sa at 2:30pm.

Excursions

St. John's College   COLLEGE
St. John's St.
☎01223 338 600 www.joh.cam.ac.uk

The motto of St. John's—*"souvent me souvient"*—is a triple pun, and none of them have to do with souvenirs. One meaning is "Often I remember," which is appropriate given that the college celebrated its quincentennial in 2011. William Wilberforce, William Wordsworth, Sir Cecil Beaton, and Douglas Adams are only a few of the students that have studied here through its history. A second meaning of the slogan is "Think of me often"—not difficult when considering the gorgeous chapel, Bridge of Sighs, or the 93ft.-long Fellows' Room where some of the D-Day planning happened. St. John's is also associated with its choir, which has been singing Evensong for over 300 years. The final pun is "I often pass beneath it," which could possibly be interpreted now as snooty Trinity College rivals passing by while humming "We'd Rather Be at Oxford than St. John's" (sung to the tune of "She'll Be Coming 'Round the Mountain").

► *i* Head north on Sidney St., which becomes Bridge St. Take a left onto St. John's St. £5, ages 12-17 £3.50, under 12 free. 🕐 Open daily Mar-Oct 10am-5:30pm; Nov-Feb 10am-3:30pm.

The Backs   VIEWS
Queen's Rd.

In the nostalgic retrospectives of Cambridge alums, The Backs almost always crops up à la, "We would button our blazers and take down a hamper from Harrods, then punt down the river while whiling away our education with champagne and folly." Intuitively, staring at the back of a building does not elicit particular excitement, but the row of colleges that face the River Cam proves a notable exception. If you can't bear the expense of a punt, the manicured fields opposite are an excellent place to have a picturesque picnic; the golden stone of the colleges is the perfect backdrop. Armed with a tartan blanket, enough alcohol to start your own off-license, and the sunbeams sifting through majestic clouds, you too can experience quintessential Cambridge.

▶ *i* From Queens' College bus stop, go around Cripps Court college and into the fields beyond. Occasionally closed for university purposes.Free. ⏲ Open 24hr.

Magdalene College   COLLEGE

Magdalene St.
☎01223 332 100 www.magd.cam.ac.uk

Magdalene College (pronounced MAUD-lin) was not only purposely built on the other side of the river in order to protect its Benedictine monks from the town's licentious crowd, but it was also the last Oxbridge college to admit women in 1988 (students protested vigorously by wearing black armbands). This is all a bit strange given the college's namesake, Mary Magdalene, and the fact that they host the most lavish May Ball every year (it's also the only college that insists on a white tie dress code). Academically, it's famous for the Pepys Library, which holds some of the diaries of C.S. Lewis, who, though an Oxford man, occasionally lived in Magdalene. The long riverfront area behind the main courtyards is technically closed to visitors, but some travelers report that if you look like a student—and act like you know what you're doing—it's possible to stroll unbothered along the willow-lined path.

▶ *i* Walk south down Huntington Rd. as it changes into Castle St., then into Magdalene St.Free. ⏲ Open daily until 6pm. Library open daily Apr 20-Aug 31 11:30am-12:30pm and 2:30-3:30pm; Oct 6-Dec 5 2:30-3:30pm; Jan 12-Mar 13 2:30-3:30pm.

Whipple Museum of the History of Science   MUSEUM

Free School Ln.
☎01223 330 906 www.hps.cam.ac.uk/whipple

The trope of "Oxford for humanities, Cambridge for sciences" goes a long way to explain the focus of this museum. Robert Whipple donated a collection of 1000 scientific devices to the university, and many of these are on display here. Newer additions include the Gömböc (a mathematically precise object that rolls to the same resting position no matter where you place it) and Fred, a 19th-century anatomical model whose parts have been mercilessly scattered across the museum. Several intriguing planetariums, some microscopes and telescopes, and a wealth of pocket calculators round out the quirkily fascinating collection.

▶ *i* Turn left off St. Andrew's St. onto Downing St. Follow it until it becomes

Pembroke and turn right onto Free School Ln.Free.   📷   Open M-F 12:30-4:30pm.

Scott Polar Research Institute   MUSEUM

Lensfield Rd.

☎01223 336 540 www.spri.cam.ac.uk

Modern British forays into the polar regions are a bit less harrowing (a great example is *Top Gear*'s casual drive to the magnetic North Pole in 2007) than when Robert Falcon Scott was tooling around the South Pole a century ago. But with all of this gear on display, one can just imagine a boisterous student thinking that the polar regions can't be that bad—after all, Cambridge has some frightful winters. If you're an extreme adventure type, you can spend a good chunk of time perusing the packed collection of memorabilia that includes everything from intricate Inuit art and artifacts, including some of the most exquisite scrimshaw ever collected, tomoving tales of men (and women) versus freezing nature.

▶ *i* From Cambridge station, the Institute is approximately a 10min. walk toward the city center. From Station Rd., turn right onto Hills Rd., then left onto Lensfield Rd. at the next crossroads.Free. 📷 Open Tu-Sa 10am-4pm.

Christ's College   COLLEGE

St. Andrews St.

☎01223 334 900 www.christs.cam.ac.uk

"Tempered to the Oaten Flute / Rough Satyrs danced and fauns with cloven heel" would be an epic testimonial on the "Is Christ's College Right For You?" admissions page. And indeed, that was how John Milton—called by his friends "The Lady of Christ's"—described the college in *Lycidas*. A portrait and bust in the Great Hall pay homage to Milton and another of Christ's famous alums: Charles Darwin, who didn't lionize the college nearly as much. Sacha Baron Cohen also graduated from Christ's, so we all look forward to the day when a picture of Borat will adorn the wall.

▶ *i* Continue north on Hills Rd. until it turns into Regent St., then into St. Andrew's St.Free. 📷 Open daily 9:30am-noon.

Jesus College   COLLEGE

Jesus Ln.

☎01223 339 339 www.jesus.cam.ac.uk

Yes, it's hard to keep all of the colleges straight when the names are only variations on a New Testament theme. A good memory aide is to think of Jesus being tempted to stay hours in this college's 25 acres of lovely gardens and courts. Keep an eye out for some strange art installations that include the annual Sculpture

Excursions

in the Close (when we visited, it was 10 mannequins re-enacting a crime scene). Attracting an eclectic set, the college's alumni include Thomas Cranmer, Samuel Taylor Coleridge, and Nick Hornby.

▶ *i* Go north on Sidney St. and turn right onto Jesus Ln.Free. 🕑 Open daily 8am-dusk.

Food

For a "college town," Cambridge has more upscale dining options than off-licenses and supermarkets. However, there are a number of cheap cafes that can set you up with a meal for less tha £5. The summer months see students camping out on one of the "Pieces" with wine and sandwiches or strolling the streets with wine and ice cream cones.

🔳 **The Eagle**   PUB $$
8 Bene't St.
☎01223 505 020

Even though Cambridge students might roll their eyes at this pub's high tourist profile, it remains genuine enough to still draw crowds of locals. Why the fame? It's a veritable monument to life and death. On February 28, 1953, Francis Crick and James Watson burst into the Eagle to announce their discovery of the "secret to life"—the double helix. And toward the back, look for the messages and squad numbers that RAF men scorched into the ceiling on the evenings before piloting missions during World War II. For your hopefully less dramatic purposes, the bar adds to its storied charm with affordable alcohol and classics of the pub food genre—sausage and mash or a steaming steak and ale pie.

▶ *i* Heading south on King's Parade, turn left onto Bene't St. Entrees £8-14. Pints around £3.50. Credit card min. £5. 🕑 Open M-Sa 10am-11pm, Su 11am-10:30pm.

🔳 **Stickybeaks**   CAFE $
42 Hobson St.
☎01223 359 397 www.stickybeakscafe.co.uk

There's something beautiful about a cafe that provides all of the white, blinding modern vibe of a gallery while serving you gourmet food as well. The menu items here are a bit fancier than your average ham and cheese toast (think more continental, like bruschetta and olives), but you can nab some heartier breakfast staples for cheap prices if you're not satisfied with the usual hostel corn flakes and toast.

▶ *i* Hobson St. splits off to the right of Sidney St., next to Christ's College. Breakfast dishes £1.50-3. Lunch dishes £4.50-7. 🕑 Open M-F 8am-5:30pm, Sa 9am-5:30pm, Su 10am-5pm.

Dojo's Noodle Bar   ASIAN $
1-2 Millers Yard
☎01223 363 471

The closest a dignified Cambridge student is going to come to a real dojo is in a Pokémon game, but the only things getting beaten to death in this establishment are noodle puns (place settings are bordered with "Noodfucius," little words of wisdom). Every imaginable Asian noodle dish is served here: Japanese, Chinese, Thai, and Malaysian are all fair game. The quick service, largeportions, and low prices make this a popular and worthy student haunt.

▶ *i* Turn onto Mill Ln. off Trumpington St., then left onto Millers Yard.Entrees fro £7-9. 🕙 Open M-F noon-2:30pm and 5:30-11pm, Sa-Su noon-11pm.

The Cow   PIZZA $$
Corn Exchange St.
☎01223 308 871 www.pizzakitchenbars.co.uk

This backstreet restaurant offers eclectic styles of stone-baked pizzas in a part pub, part cafeteria dining room. The pop art picture of a cow, replacing the more traditional coat of arms on the pub sign, is representative of the restaurant's contemporary twist on the normal pub experience. The theme continues with a rugged decor offset by modern additions in furniture and menu, making the dining experience a fun blend of old and new. As the evening wears on, the student atmosphere intensifies and the decent cocktail bar in the corner becomes a little more tempting than the menu's offerings.

▶ *i* From the Corpus Christi bus stop, walk up Trumpington St., which turns into King's Parade, and continue toward King's College. Turn right onto Be-ne't St., which becomes Wheeler St. The restaurant is on the corner at the end of the road. 2-for-1 on Tu.Pizz £4-8.50. 🕙 Open M-W noon-11pm, Th noon-midnight, F-Su noon-1am.

Rainbow Cafe   VEGAN, GLUTEN-FREE $$
9A King's Parade
☎01223 321 551 www.rainbowcafe.co.uk

In a world that glorifies the steak and ale pie that has staved off the wasting muscles of academics for centuries, contrarian vegetarians can find their pot of gold here. Rainbow is hands down the city's best place to explore a wealth of creative vegan, vegetarian, and gluten-free dishes inspired by cuisines from around the world.

▶ *i* On King's Parade, just across from the college gates. Entrees £8-10. 🕙 Open M 10am-4pm, Tu-Sa 10am-10pm, Su 10am-4pm.

Clowns Cafe   ITALIAN, CAFE $
54 King St.
☎01223 355 711

If you're ready to expatriate yourself to the continent, take out your euro (or pounds) and tuck into some delicious Mediterranean food. The effervescent Italian staff wave off the familiar customers and tell them to swing by later to pay the rest of the bill, while clusters of students order large cappuccinos and banter for hours. Those who have a fear of clowns may want to avoid this place, as paintings and figurines of the cafe's namesakes abound.

▶ *i* Turn right off Sidney St. onto Jesus Ln., then turn right onto Malcolm St. and continue until you hit King St. Entree £4-6.50. Full English breakfast £6. Cash only. ☑ Open daily 8am-11pm.

La Margherita   ITALIAN $$
15 Magdalene St.
☎01223 315 232

Run by an Italian family, La Margherita offers homey Italian food in a stylish dining room straight across from Magdalene College. The *spaghetti alla carbonara* and *risotto ai funghi* will make you miss your own (possibly imaginary) nonna, and the diverse pizza toppings will make you glad you skipped that frozen pie at Sainsbury's. The restaurant also serves the largest selection of delectable gelato in Cambridge, including an especially fantastic amaretto flavor.

▶ *i* Go south down Castle St., which becomes Magdalene St. Main courses and pizza £9-15. 2-course prix-fixe £10, 3-course £13. M and Su pizza £5 when you order a drink. ☑ Open M-F 10am-2:30pm and 6-10:30pm, Sa 10am-10:30pm, Su 11am-7:30pm. Prix-fixe menu available M-Th noon-2:30pm and 6-7pm, F-Su noon-3pm.

Nightlife

Nightlife in Cambridge is split between pubs that close at 11pm and clubs that don't get going until midnight. Clubs are generally reserved for extremely drunken student nights out, which, depending on what you're looking for, can either make for a great time or a total nightmare. The pubs tend to be of an extremely high quality—full of good beer (almost universally £3.50-4) and even better conversation. Keep in mind that, during term-time, colleges run their own bars, some of which are open to the public.

Excursions

⊠ The Maypole   PUB

20A Portugal Pl.

☎01223 352 999 www.maypolefreehouse.co.uk

This lively pub is known affectionately as "The Staypole" thanks to it being one of the few bars in Cambridge with a late-night license. It takes advantage of its status as a "free house" (meaning that it's independent from any brewery and can serve whatever beers it wants) by stocking a selection of a dozen rotating beers on draft and many more in bottles. It's a tremendously popular spot, where students drink pints and pitchers of cocktails late into the night.

▶ *i* When walking toward the river on Sidney St., turn right onto Portugal Pl. Pints from £3.50; pitchers £12-14. ☒ Open M-Th 11:30am-midnight, F-Sa 11:30am-1am, Su noon-11:30pm.

⊠ The Elm Tree   PUB

16A Orchard St.

☎01223 502 632 www.theelmtreecambridge.co.uk

The pub may look very English, but its specialty is Belgian beer. Over 50 brews are represented here, and as you step inside, you'll be offered an incredibly helpful menu. The two rooms hold dusty bottles and tables filled with locals, while pictures of drinking customers cover the walls. Outside, the smoking crowd spills out as the only acknowledgment there's a pub in the quiet area. Occasionally, the space hosts live music.

▶ *i* Walking south on Parker St., make a left onto Clarendon St. The pub is on the corner with Orchard St.Beer from £3.50. Cash only. ☒ Open daily 11am-11pm.

Hidden Rooms   BAR

7A Jesus Ln.

☎01223 514 777 www.hiddenthing.com□

The curtained booths and leather upholstery of this cocktail bar recall the days when Churchill and de Gaulle would meet in this underground lounge. Even if state-making isn't on the evening's agenda, you'll feel sufficiently sophisticated as you sip on one of the dozens of classic and unclassic cocktails twirled and poured behind the glamorous bar. When the ol' peripheral vision inevitably starts to go, make a beeline to the club room, which offers a darker, louder section with quickly changing tracks and dazzling light shows.

▶ *i* With the ADC Theater on your right, head to the end of Park St. Turn right onto Jesus Ln. The bar is on the right. 2-for-1 cocktails M-W.Cocktails £6.80-9.20. ☒ Open M-Sa 3pm-12:30am, Su 3-10:30pm.

The Free Press   PUB
Prospect Row
☎01223 368 337 www.freepresspub.com

Cell phones and music are banned at this old-school pub, making space for the pubby conversation that's missing at many modern establishments. Deriving its name from its former life as a newspaper printer, The Free Press pays homage to the drinking habits of journalists with cask ales and single malts.

▶ *i* From Parkside (when heading away from town center), turn left onto Warkworth Terr., then left onto Warkworth St. and right onto Prospect Row. Pints fro £3.50. ⏰ Open M-F noon-2:30pm and 6-11pm, Sa noon-11pm, Su noon-3pm and 7-10:30pm.

Fez Club   CLUB
15 Market Passage
☎01223 519 224 www.cambridgefez.com

Fezzes are cool, but Fez Club is mainly loud and cheesy. A student club if ever there was one, it's a great deal of fun if you just want to drink and dance, even if you might not be hearing the most innovative DJs. Tuesdays feature hip hop and R&B, Saturdays focus on house and trance, and the other nights play a mix of pop, indie, techno, and classic anthems. Fez offers significant drink specials and discounts to those with a student ID.

▶ *i* Turn left onto Market St. off Sidney St. and right onto Market Passage. Inquire about a free membership card and ask about student discounts. No sneakers allowed for men.Cover usually £5-7; students £3-5. Discounts if you sign up for the guest list. Drinks from £4, not including daily specials. Cover cash only. ⏰ Open M 10pm-3am, Tu 10:30pm-3am, W-Su 10pm-3am.

The Place   CLUB
22 Sidney St.
☎01223 324 600 www.theplacenightclub.co.uk

There's a certain degree of self-assuredness one needs to give an establishment such a vague and encompassing name. But spread over three floors of neon lighting and carefully selected graffiti, this is the major clubbing "place" in Cambridge. There is no doubt that this is a hot spot for the going-out student crowd. The actual atmosphere tends to be overwhelmingly inebriated students stumbling from floor to floor to bathroom, all to the soundtrack of underwhelming beats. Go for the atmosphere, if not for the experience.

▶ *i* Directly across the street from Holy Trinity Church. Check online for live music listings. Cove £5, but varies with night. ⏰ Open daily 10pm-4am.

Lola Lo   CLUB

1-6 Corn Exchange St.

☎01223 367 866 www.lolalocambridge.com

Recently opened Lola Lo aims to be a more upscale clubbing option in Cambridge devoid of young adults who haven't yet learned to make friends with their liver; nevertheless, it's still very much a student spot. The tiki-themed decorations and light-up dance floor will entertain you even if the crowd doesn't. Music is generally a variety of R&B, pop mashups, and dance hits.

▶ *i* Go down Downing St. and turn right onto Corn Exchange. Sa 21+. No sportswear allowed.Cover £3-9; usually £1 extra if non-student and/or after midnight. Bottled beer £4.50. Mixed drinks from £6. Frequent student and guest-list discounts. ☼ Open M 9pm-3am, W-Th 9pm-3am, F-Sa 6pm-3am

Arts and Culture

🔣 ADC Theatre   THEATER, COMEDY, DANCE

Park St.

☎01223 300 085 www.adctheatre.com

"It was grown-up and polished, yet at the same time bashful and friendly; it was sophisticated and intelligent but never pretentious or pleased with itself; it had authority, finish, and quality without any hint of self-regard, vanity, or slickness," wrote Stephen Fry of the first Cambridge Footlights show he saw. The "Arts Dramatic Club" is the student-run theater that hosts the Footlights, which launched the comedic careers of Hugh Laurie, Fry, and half of Monty Python. Many other famous actors who attended Cambridge—including Ian McKellen, Emma Thompson, and Rachel Weisz—performed here as well. During term-time, there are usually two performances per day, while out of term there are still shows most days. There are occasional dance shows in addition to the usual theater and comedy.

▶ *i* Head away from town center and take a left off Jesus Ln. to get to Park St. Tickets £5-10, concessions sometimes available. ☼ Box office open Tu 12:30-7pm, W-Th 3-7pm, F 12:30-7pm, Sa 3-7pm.

🔣 Scudamore's   PUNTING

Quayside

☎01223 359 750 www.scudamores.com

For North Americans, punting is solely related to kicking a football across half a stadium. For Cantabrigians (excluding the Boston variety), it is glamorously sticking a pole in mud and

Excursions

vaulting your way along the river Cam. Unless you're an old hand or an idiot, it's best to avoid the self-hire option and get a tour guide to regale you with over-the-top accounts of alumni and their youthful exploits. Scudamore's is the gold standard, with a small kiosk on the river and a fleet of attractive men roaming around the banks aggressively advertising the punting experience.

▶ *i* Underneath Magdalene Bridge. Take a right off Bridge St. Another location is at the end of Mill St. Self-hir £22 per hr., students £16; plus £90 deposit taken in the form of an imprint of your credit or debit card. Guided tours £16, concessions £14.50, under 12 £8. Discounts if you buy tickets online. Private and specialty tours can be pre-booked. ☒ Open daily 9am-dusk.

Cambridge Corn Exchange   LIVE MUSIC

Wheeler St.

☎01223 357 851 www.cornex.co.uk

Probably the largest music venue in Cambridge, the Corn Exchange has hosted most of the big-name musical acts that come through Cambridge, from the Beatles and Pink Floyd to The Smiths and Oasis. It also presents musicals, dance performances, and opera. The 19th-century building was established as a space for merchants to trade grain; nowadays, it serves as an exam room for the university when it's not being used for concerts (sadly, they don't play "School's Out" when you finish).

▶ *i* Heading south on King's Parade, turn left onto Bene't St. and go straight until it becomes Wheeler St. Prices vary. Occasional student discounts. ☒ Open M-Sa 10am-6pm.

Essentials

Practicalities

- **Tourist Offices:** The Tourist Information Centre at Peas Hill has National Express tickets, discounted punting tickets, and sightseeing bus tickets and also offers accommodations bookings and an access guide to the city for disabled visitors. (☎0871 226 8006 www.visitcambridge.org ☒ Open M-Sa 10am-5pm, Su 11am-3pm.)

- **Student Travel Offices:** STA Travel (38 Sidney St. ☎0871 702 9809 www.statravel.co.uk ☒ Open M-Th 10am-7pm, F-Sa 10am-6pm, Su 11am-5pm.)

- **Internet:** Jaffa Net Cafe. (22 Mill Rd. ☎01223 308 380 *i* £1 per hr. ☒ Open daily noon-midnight.)

- **Post Offices:** Bureau de Change. (9-11 St. Andrew's St. ☎ Open M 9am-5:30pm, Tu 9:30am-5:30pm, W-Sa 9am-5:30pm.)

Emergency

- **Police:** on Parkside. (☎0345 456 4564 ☎ 8am-10pm.)

- **Hospitals/Medical Services:** Addenbrookes Hospital. (Hills Rd., by the intersection of Hills Rd. and Long Rd. ☎01223 245 151)

Getting There

By Train

The only significant starting point for trains to Cambridge is London. Trains arrive at **Station Road.** (*i* 20min. walk southeast from the town center. ☎ Ticket office open M-Sa 5:10am-11pm, Su 7am-10:55pm.) You can catch trains at London King's Cross £22. ☎ 50min., 2 per hr.) and **London Liverpool Street.** £15.30. ☎ 1¼hr., 2 per hr.).

By Bus

The bus station, mostly for short-distance buses, is on **Drummer Street.** (☎ Ticket office open M-Sa 9am-5:30pm.) Airport shuttles and buses to more distant destinations run from **Parkside.** Buses arrive from: London Victoria (*i* Transfer at Stansted. £12.70. ☎ 3hr., every hr.); Gatwick £34. ☎ 4hr., every 2hr.); Heathrow £28.60. ☎ 3hr., every hr.); Stansted £10.50. ☎ 50min., every 2hr.); Oxford. (*i* Take the X5 bus. £12.50. ☎ 3¼hr., every 30min.)

Getting Around

By Bus

CitiBus runs from stops throughout town, including some on **Saint Andrew's Street, Emmanuel Street,** and at the train station. The most useful routes are C1 (from the station) and C2 (goes out along Chesterton Rd.). Single rides cost £2.20. **Dayrider Tickets** (unlimited travel for 1 day; £3.90) can be purchased on the bus; for longer stays, you can buy a **Megarider** ticket (unlimited travel for weeks; £13 per week).

Excursions

By Taxi

For a taxi, call **Cabco.** (☎01223 312 444 🕐 Open 24hr.)

By Bike

You'll see students on bikes everywhere in Cambridge. To fit in, go to **City Cycle Hire.** (61 Newnham Rd. ☎01223 365 629 www.citycyclehire.com *i* £7 for 4hr., £10 for 8hr., £12 for 24hr., £17 for 2-3 days, £25 for 4-7 days, £35 for 2 weeks, £80 for up to 3 months. 🕐 Open Easter-Oct M-F 9am-5:30pm, Sa 9am-5pm; Nov-Easter M-F 9am-5:30pm.)

BATH

As a tourist, going to Bath is like taking a trip to Disney World: Ancient Rome. During the day, thousands of tourists putz over the city's cobblestone hills and wait in line for the Roman Bath Pump Room; ubiquitous, costumed street performers are your Esmeraldas, and human statues are the gargoyles. At night, the vines and hops are brought out en masse for the debasement of hen and stag parties from all over the UK. While this is all very exciting, there are few respite periods if you are looking for a vacation rather than a sightseeing bonanza. Sundays and Mondays are good bets for a quiet stay (when most of the museums are closed.) If you're looking for a spa day, we're happy to inform you that, while the spa waters were closed for decades because of an algae infection, the Thermae spa opened in 2008 and harnesses the only geothermal spring in Britain for a reasonable price.

Orientation

A good central point to use is the **Bath Abbey** and **Pump Room.** In this square, you can find the tourist information center (just to the right of the abbey when facing it). While the city is heralded as an architectural marvel, it's not a city-planning one; your best bet is to just wander around the square formed by the Bath Spa train station in the south, the river Avon in the east, Gay St. in the west, and hills in the north (literally, when it starts getting too steep, that's when you know to quit). Moving up north on Gay St., you will pass by a slice of the era that launched a thousand Harlequin novels, with the Jane Austen Centre, the Regency Tea Room, the Regency Circus, and the Royal Crescent.

Accommodations

YMCA   HOSTEL $$

International House, Broad St. Pl.
☎01225 325 900 www.bathymca.co.uk

This large and spacious complex has the best of both worlds when it comes to location. Primarily, it's near the nightlife of George St., which is great for prime bar-hopping action. But a quiet night can also be had in the scenic courtyard dotted with picnic tables. The dorms are clean and fairly spacious, and you'll find an older crowd here, some of whom left their party hostel card at the door a long time ago.

▶ *i* From the bus or train station, walk north up Manvers St. Pass Bath Abbey on your left and, keeping the River Avon on your right, continue via Orange Grove (on left) and High St. to Walcot St. or Broad St. There are entrances to the YMCA, which is within a courtyard, from Broad St. (next to a haridresser's) or Walcot St. (close to Harvest Food Shop), up a flight of steps. Look out for signs pointing to YMCA. Free Wi-Fi downstairs. Continental breakfast included. Laundry service available. Luggage storage at receptio £1 per 24hr. Lockers available for purchase. Bike racks. Health and fitness center available for guest use £4 for full-day access. Single-sex dorms available. Dorm £15-23; single £32; double £56-64; triple £69-75; quad £88-96. Weekly rates available by phone booking. ⏲ Reception 24hr. Restaurant open daily for breakfast and M-F noon-2pm.

Bath Backpackers   HOSTEL $

13 Pierrepont St.
☎01225 446 787 www.hostels.co.uk

Bath's most colorful hostel is made memorable by the bright paintings on its walls, its dark, late-night "dungeon" (i.e., windowless basement), and unique room names ("Divas," "Brutus"). This is definitely a true backpackers' home, and yes, that subtly implies all the normal trappings of the hostel experience, including close quarters and weekend comings and goings. However, if carrying your life on your back has made you empathize with Igor, the hostel is only a three-minute walk from the bus and train stations.

▶ *i* From the train station, go straight down Manvers St. 400m, past the police station and church on the right side. The hostel is on the left side, just before the 2nd set of traffic lights on the same street. Breakfast included. Laundr £3.50. Luggage storag £1. Wi-F £2.50 for full stay. Interne £1 per 30min. Self-catering kitchen. Single-sex dorms available. Online and weekly discounts available. Dorm £13-23. ⏲ Reception 8am-midnight.

St. Christopher's Inn   HOSTEL $$

9 Green St.

☎01225 481 444 www.st-christophers.co.uk

Centrally located near Bath's major sites and with a young crowd of partiers, St. Christopher's sports simple dorm rooms that don't have room for much else other than the beds. There's a cute attic with a TV, movies, and microwave that functions as the hostel proper's common space. Most of the social action occurs, as in all St. Christopher's establishments, at the downstairs bar, where patrons can purchase heavily discounted food.

▶ *i* Past the Podium, Green St. is to the left. On top of Belushi's Bar. Reception is at the bar. Free Wi-Fi. Continental breakfast included. Laundry service available. Discounts when you book online. Dorm £16-26.

Sights

🖾 Roman Baths   BATHS

Abbey Church Yard

☎01225 477 785 www.romanbaths.co.uk

Brits like their warm and warming liquids, and who can blame them? In a cold and damp nation, the 115°F (46°C) water that spews from the country's only hot springs is the faint proof that a warm core exists beneath a foggy, frosty exterior. For 400 years during the colonial glory days (how does it feel now, Britain?), the Romans harnessed Bath's bubbling natural springs, and since their rediscovery in the 1800s, the baths have been the city's biggest tourist attraction. The city even erected an elaborate Roman-style balcony around them, complete with statues of the Roman gods. Speaking of paganism, Bath itself was original called Sulis Minerva in tribute to the Goddess of Wisdom. There are really no alternative ways to witness Bath's signature sight other than paying a handsome fee: views of the actual baths are inaccessible from the city streets. Make sure you hold onto your ticket and head over to the elegant Pump Room next door: entrance to the site includes a free glass of mineral water (not the green stuff) that comes directly out of the fountain from the Baths. It might not be the best tasting aqua you've ever tried, but "taking the waters" is sort of a rite of passage, and those fish and chips provide nowhere near your daily value of minerals.

▶ *i* In the center of Bath. Entrance in Abbey Church Yard. Tickets include audio tour and free guided tours of the Bath area; depart hourly £12.75, concession £11; joint ticket with the Museum of Fashio £16.25/14. ⏰ Open Jul-Aug 9am-10pm, Sept-Oct 9am-6pm, Nov-Feb 9:30am-5:30pm, Mar-Jun 9am-6pm. Last entry 1hr. before close.

Bath Abbey
ABBEY

12 Kingston Buildings

☎01225 422 462 www.bathabbey.org

Occupying the site where King Edgar was crowned the first king of all England in 973 CE (check out the Edgar window, which depicts the ceremony of his crowning), the 140ft. Bath Abbey stands proudly in the city center. This is the most-visited parish church in the UK, with about 300,000 visitors each year, and if you come in the summer, you'll believe it. Thus, photography real estate really is hard to procure when tourists are angling all around you to get a picture of the stained glass mural depicting 56 scenes of the life of Jesus. However, it gets even madder underground: there are believed to be 3000-4000 bodies squished together and buried directly underneath the abbey floor. For a hefty price, wealthy believers could have their remains placed in the church up until an 1853 Act of Parliament prohibited the practice on the grounds of danger to public health.

i The Abbey is next to Orange Grove, off of Manvers/Pierrepoint St., and on the other side of the Roman Baths. Suggested donatio £2.50. Tower tour £5. ⏰ Open Apr-Oct M-Sa 9am-6pm, Su 1-2:30pm and 4:30-5:30pm; Nov-Mar M-Sa 9am-4:30pm, Su 1-2:30pm and 4:30-5:30pm.

Fashion Museum and Assembly Rooms
MUSEUM

Bennett St.

☎01225 477 173 www.fashionmuseum.co.uk

Looking at hoop skirts, corsets, and garter belts can either leave women feeling relieved that they don't have to wear such instruments of torture today or scared that their high heels and bandage dresses look eerily as constricting. This museum hosts a vivacious parade of four centuries of catwalk styles and charts the sartorial evolution of everything from pockets to gloves. Also on display is the famed silver tissue dress, an exquisite survivor from the 1660s, and a mini replica of an 18th-century court dress. As befits a fashionable, modern museum, the curators try to keep current with rapidly-changing fashion trends.The museum hides in the basement of the Assembly Rooms, which are not the birthplace of a Ford Fiesta but once held fin-de-siècle balls and concerts. You can still take tea here, although the patrons' dress and the building's state have both been damaged by the war.

▶ *i* In the Assembly Rooms, next to the Royal Crescent and Circus in Bath's Upper Town. Follow black pedestrian signs £7.75, concession £7; joint ticket with the Roman Bath £16.25/14. Audio tour included. ⏰ Open daily Mar-Oct 10:30am-6pm; Nov-Feb 10:30am-5pm. Last entry 1hr. before close.

Excursions

Jane Austen Centre   MUSEUM

40 Gay St.

☎01225 443 000 www.janeausten.co.uk.

Jane Austen is one of Bath's most famous residents, though, ironically, she loathed living here—she found the city to be the leading cause of a five-year period of writer's block, a span of time during which she managed only one attempt at a novel, *The Watsons* (note: not an anachronistic piece of Sherlock Holmes fanfiction), which she abandoned after 17,000 words. Even though Austen wrote of "happy feelings of escape" when she departed Bath for good in 1806, the city had notable influences on her work and was referenced in many of her novels, particularly in *Persuasion* and *Northanger Abbey*. The Jane Austen Centre stands just a few blocks from her former dwellings. Exhibits tell the story of Austen's experiences in Bath and also explain the atmosphere of Bath during her day.

▶ *i* £8, concession £4.50.Tours of Bath sights mentioned in Austen's books and her family's homes are also available. ⏰ Open daily summer season 9:45am-5pm; winter season 11am-4:30pm. Walking tours Sa-Su 11am.

Stonehenge

As the Stonehenge audio tour will explain, Stonehenge is not only an enigma, but a mystery (jury's out on whether either one is wrapped in the other). But the question remains: what is it all for? Is it a calendar? A status symbol? A sacrificial altar? Proof of extra-terrestrials? We're sad to inform you that merely visiting will not leave you with one definitive answer. However, whatever its purpose or maker, the stone circle really does inspire a sense of wonder—and that's enough of a reason for 21st-century tourists to visit.

🏛 Stonehenge   MONUMENT

Amesbury

☎019 8062 2833 www.english-heritage.org.uk

A trip to Stonehenge paired with a stop in Salisbury—the nearest major city—is a full-day event that basically repeats the message of Ken Follett's *The Pillars of the Earth*: building stuff is hard. Stonehenge itself is a tricky customer. While only 30 years ago, the place was an out-of-the-way tourist spot that only very thorough travelers would attempt to visit, there are now bus tours that drop thousands of visitors next to the highway that Stonehenge overlooks. For casual appreciation of pagan architecture, an hour is all you need; the audio tour will walk you through the materials, construction, layout, and purpose of the pi-shaped masonry. Surprisingly, even though you'll share your magical experience with hundreds of people, the design of the walkway is expertly shaped so that you can get as many mystical selfies as your heart deigns without someone in a red windbreaker wandering into the shot. If you have more time and money saved up, traveling here via Salisbury instead of via the A303 is a nice way to get a more rounded survey of British history (and pre-history).

▶ *i* By train: take the National Rail from Waterloo to Salisbury (aroun £40). Once in Salisbury, the Stonehenge Bus leaves from the train station for the site every 30min. from about 9:30am-6pm in summer and 10am-2pm in winter £12). By bus: tours leave the city £30 with price of admission). Adult £8, concessions £7.20. By barge, with 50-ton rocks: leave that to the pagans. ⏰ Open daily Jan-Mar 15 9:30am-4pm; Mar 15-May 9:30am-6pm; Jun-Aug 9am-7pm; Sept-Oct 15 9:30am-6pm; Oct 15-Dec 9:30am-4pm.

Getting to Stonehenge

There is no public transportation that runs from Bath to Stonehenge National Heritage Site. (☎01722 343 834 wwww.english-heritage.org.uk/stonehenge *i* £8, £7 concessions. Price includes a guided audio tour. ⏰ Open daily June-Aug 9am-7pm; Sept-Oct 9:30am-6pm; Oct-Mar 9:30am-4pm; Mar-May 9:30am-6pm.) The vast majority of visitors who decide to make a trip to Stonehenge use one of the tour companies from in town. They run every day of the year, and prices include full transport to and from the site, along with guides and commentary.

Food

🏛 Bath Guildhall Market   MARKET $$
High St.
☎01225 460 808 www.bathguildhallmarket.co.uk

Bath's historic market (dating to the 16th century) boasts a slew of delicious eats, including a cheese shop, an espresso snack bar, a fruits and veggies specialty shop, and the "Bath Humbug" shop featuring a selection of snacks and chocolates (better than tears and capitalism). While you're here, check out the market's original 1863 design: the impressive dome, created by Hicks and Isaac, contains intricate floral moldings and high, iron-framed windows.

▶ *i* High St., between Northgate St. and Grand Parade. ⏰ Open M-Sa 8am-5:30pm. Individual shop hours may vary.

▨ Regency Tea Room   TEA ROOM $$

Jane Austen Centre, 40 Gay St.
☎01225 443 000 www.janeausten.co.uk/tearooms

The best place in town to take authentic afternoon tea is the lovely
Georgian townhouse that hosts the Jane Austen Centre. Unlike
the Centre's exhibits, however, entrance to the Tea Room is free.
Even though you might initially scoff at the idea of partaking in
the dance of high tea, you will inevitably fall in love with the "Tea
with Mr. Darcy" £15), which, as high tea, includes cheese and cucumber finger sandwiches, cakes, scones with cream and jam, and
a tea of your choice from the varieties of loose-leaf on the menu.
Even if you make onl £10,000 a year, you can try smaller bites, like
the Bath Bun with tea for £5.50 as light lunch. Given that some
character or other in every single Jane Austen novel has said, "You
must drink tea with us," just succumb to the imperative.

▸ *i* Enter the Jane Austen Centre, then head upstairs to the 2nd floor. 10%
off voucher available on website. Sandwiche £5.65. Toastie £6.50. Cake
£3.75. Tea £2.25-2.75. ◷ Open Apr-Oct daily 9:45am-5:30pm, Nov-Mar
M-F 11am-4:30pm, Sa 9:45am-5:30pm, Su 11am-4:30pm.Last entry 50min.
before close.

The Eastern Eye   INDIAN $$$

8a Quiet St.
☎01225 422 323 www.easterneye.com

Yeah, we forgot to mention this to you in the introduction, but
Bath also has a giant Ferris Wheel—ahem, sorry—"Observation Wheel." Okay, we jest. But the Eastern Eye does have
something reflective of London: wonderful, award-winning
Indian food. Previously a casino, ballroom, and auction house,
this polished Georgian building is now the Eye's long-time
home. Check out the intricate murals coloring the walls and the
famous, three-domed ceilings. Zesty tandoori, meat, poultry,
seafood, and vegetarian dishes are available.

▸ *i* Green St. and Wood St. become Quiet St. Entree £8-17 ◷ Open daily
noon-2:30pm and 6-11:30pm.

Cafe Retro   CAFE, TAKEOUT $$

18 York St.
☎01225 339 347 www.caferetro.co.uk

"Retro" does not mean lots of Elvis tributes or, really, anything
other than "not contemporary." Instead, it's a mix of Regency
architecture, stained glass, large windows for people watching,
and an eclectic mix of French, British, and American favorites.

▸ *i* From train station, turn left off Pierrepoint. Sandwiche £4.40-6.70.
◷ Open M-F 9am-4pm, Sa 9am-5pm, Su 10am-5pm.

Scoffs   SANDWICHES, DELI $

9 Terrace Walk
☎01225 471 137

This local sandwich shop scoffs at your Tesco Egg and Prawn
on White and raises you a sandwich creation completely crafted
on-site (with the exception of the fresh bread, which comes from
a bakery up the street). Grab a fish, veggie, or meat sandwich of
choice and a slice of cake and sit outside (re: judge passersby) on
the nearby green of Orange Grove or by the River Avon, just a
2min. walk away.

▶ *i* East on York St., toward North Parade. Sandwiche £3.50-7. 🕑 Open
M-Sa 8am-5pm, Su 9am-4pm.

Boston Tea Party   CAFE $$

19 Kingsmead Sq.
☎01225 313 901 www.bostonteaparty.co.uk

The name doesn't just stop at a cute reference: this really is a
radical, modern departure from the solidly Georgian style of
most other restaurants in Bath. The main draw is the excellent
coffee, and at the early dawn of summer, this is one of the first
places open (with a lovely outdoor seating area where you can
enjoy your breakfast in peace).

▶ *i* Kingsmead Sq. is at the intersection of Avon, Westgate, and Monmouth
St. Free Wi-Fi. Salad £6.85. Burger £7.25-7.50. 🕑 Open M-Sa 7:30am-
7pm, Su 9am-7pm.

Yak Yeti Yak   NEPALESE $$

12 Pierrepont St.
☎01225 442 299 www.yakyetiyak.co.uk

Sometimes, when the British go on holiday, they start believing
that they are undertaking a massive endeavor that involves scal-
ing the M4, leaving the children to dye their nanny's hair blue,
and camping out in period piece flamboyance. Just go to this
Nepalese restaurant instead to ground yourself into realizing
that it's just Bath and not something actually terrifying (like
dying alone in the mountains). The basement venue swims with
local music playing in the background, and the owners display
diverse miscellany picked up from years of travel around the
Himalayas, including a pair of boots that reached the summit
of Everest. If you feel like getting into the atmosphere, try the
kukharako thukpa, the national dish of the Sherpas, and request
seating in the side room.

▶ *i* Next to Bath Backpackers, underground. Vegetarian options available.
Entree £5.69-8.90. 🕑 Open M-Sa noon-2pm and 6-10:30pm, Su noon-
2pm and 6-10pm.

Nightlife

The Pig and the Fiddle   PUB
2 Saracen St.
☎01225 460 868 www.thepigandfiddle.co.uk

Pub names are often so bizarre that they say nothing about the
joint's character (only about the eccentric owner's). However,
the image of a jovial, fiddle-playing pig is ideal for this well-fre-
quented, massive streetside pub. On the fiddle side, the pub is
known for its lively atmosphere, with quiz and open mic nights.

▸ *i* Off Broad St. Free Wi-Fi. Pints aroun £3.Credit cards accepted for food
only. 🕐 Open M-Sa 11am-11:30pm, Su noon-10:30pm. Kitchen open M-F
11am-6:30pm, Sa-Su noon-6pm.

Coeur de Lion   PUB
27 Northumberland Pl.
☎01225 333 639

Bath's self-proclaimed smallest pub is hidden off an alley in
a corner that tourists seem weirdly immune to, Leaky Caul-
dron-style. It takes advantage of its pocket-sized interior nicely,
outfitting it with snug, red velvet-covered wooden booths and
mirrors that make the room look bigger, making for a cozy
atmosphere. Try a pint of Abbey Ales' Bellringers £3)—a cruel
reminder of a Sunday morning hangover if we ever heard of one.

▸ 🕐 Open M-Th 10:30am-11pm, F-Sa 10:30am-late. Kitchen open M-Th
10:30am-3pm and 5:30-8:30pm, F-Sa 10:30am-5pm.

Adventure Cafe Bar   BAR
5 Princes Building, George St.
☎01225 462 038

This is the Prancing Pony of Bath drinking establishments:
you're all ready to go on a big adventure, so where do you start?
Adventure Cafe transitions slowly from daytime restaurant to
nighttime pre-game central. Blasting music and cocktails bring
out the wild sides in the young clientele, who depart much more
jovially than they arrived.

▸ *i* 6-9pm pizz £6. 🕐 Open daily 8am-midnight. Kitchen open until 9pm.

Arts and Culture

Theater

Little Theatre Cinema   ST. MICHAEL'S PLACE
St. Michael's Pl.
☎330 817 www.picturehouses.co.uk

This local theater has two screens showing off-beat mainstream movies, art house films, and recorded operas. Take a break from sightseeing and relax in this building, which is owned by the same Bath family that opened the cinema in 1936.

▶ *i* Corner of St. Michael's Pl. and Bath St. Ticket £8.60, student £5.60. 🕐 Box office open 15min. before 1st curtain, closes 15min. after last curtain. Generally M-Th 9:30am-11:15pm, F-Sa 12:30-11:30pm, Su 9:30am-11:15pm.

Classical Music

Theatre Royal   CITY CENTER
Sawclose
☎01225 448 844 www.theatreroyal.org.uk

This highly vaunted theater sees pre-West End tours come to Bath, along with dramas, music performances, operas, and classical music.

▶ *i* Standby tickets available in person starting at noon £6 for specific areas in the theater. Ticket £15-35. Student concessions available M-Th evening shows and Sa matinees; usuall £1 off. 🕐 Box office open M-Sa 10am-8pm, Su noon-8pm.

Shopping

Books

📓 Mr. B's Emporium   CITY CENTER
14-15 John St.
☎01225 331 155 www.mrbsemporium.com

When your personalized "Buy this next" list on Amazon has you regretting your purchase of *50 Shades of Grey,* "just to see how bad it was," head to the greatest recommender in the word: the knowledgeable bookstore employee. And Mr. B's are the prime example of personalized care. For example, if the hostel experience is making you want to crawl back into your mother's womb just for some peace and quiet, take up their "Reading Spa" bibliotherapy service £55), where a member of the team listens to your woes and returns with a stack of books for self-medication £40 of the fee can be used to buy recommended books). For a free literary experience, try the bathroom instead, which is covered from floor to ceiling with articles, poems, and covers of *The London Review of Books.*

▶ *i* Behind Jolly's, opposite the "Salamander" pub. 🕐 Open M-Sa 9:30am-6:30pm, Su 11am-5pm.

Souvenirs

The Glasshouse   CITY CENTER
1-2 Orange Grove
☎01225 463 436 www.bathaquaglass.com

The Glasshouse can turn your relatives' ashes into a gorgeous paperweight or fill a commission to fashion the stained glass for that cathedral you've had your eye on. More universally, it sells jewelry, blown glass, mirrors, and hangings, and all products are made in local Bath factories. Glassblowing demonstrations are available at the company's "Theatre of Glass" on 105-107 Walcot St. (01225 428 146), which offers interactive presentations Monday through Friday at 11:15am and 2:15pm £4.50, concessions £3) and production viewing at 10:15am, 12:15pm, and 3:15pm £2.50, concession £1.50).

▶ *i* Orange Grove. 🕐 Open M-Sa 9:30am-6pm, Su noon-6pm.

Essentials

Practicalities

- **Tourist Office:** The TIC is at Abbey Chambers, Abbey Yard. Town maps and mini-guide are for sale for £1. Use of books rooms is free with a 10% deposit. (☎0906 711 2000, ☎0870 420 1278 for accommodation bookings. wwww.visitbath.co.uk. 🕐 Open Jun-Sept M-Sa 9:30am-6pm, Su 10am-4pm, Oct-May M-Sa 9:30am-5pm, Su 10am-4pm.)

- **Tours:** Several companies run tours with diverse themes to introduce tourists to the city. **Bizarre Bath** tours leave from Huntsman Inn, North Parade Passage. This isn't your most accurate history lesson, but the guides will keep you smirking with their tricks and ad-libbing as they poke fun at their own city. (☎01225 335 124 wwww.bizarrebath.co.uk *i* £8, concessions £5. 🕐 Nightly 90min. tours leave at 8pm.) **Ghost Walks of Bath** tours leave from Garrick's Head Public House, next to Theatre Royal. (☎01225 461 888 wwww.ghostwalksofbath.co.uk *i* £8, concessions £5. 🕐 90min. tours Th, F, Sa at 8pm.)

- **Internet:** Free Wi-Fi at **Central Library** and throughout the Podium Shopping Center. You can also get access at **Internet Cafe.** (13 Manvers St. ☎01225 312 685 *i* £1 per 20min. 🕐 Open daily 9am-9pm.)

- **Post Offices:** Visit 27 Northgate St. (☎08457 223 344 🕐 Open M 9am-5:30pm, Tu 9:30am-5:30pm, W-Sa 9am-5:30pm.), Postal Code: BA1 1AJ.

Emergency

- **Pharmacy:** **Boots** in Southgate Shopping Centre. (New Marchant Passage. 🕐 Open M-Sa 8am-7pm, Su 11am-5pm.)

- **Hospital:** **Royal United** at Coombe Park in Weston. (Take bus #14 ☎01225 428 331). For non-emergencies, visit the NHS Walk-In Centre in Riverside Health Centre. (James St. ☎01225 478 811 🕐 Open daily 8am-8pm.)

Getting There

By Bus

The bus station has **National Express** buses going to London £10-28.20. 🕐 3hr., every 2hr.) and Oxford £12.70. 🕐 2hr., 1 per day). The ticket office is open M-Sa 9am-5pm.

By Train

Trains run from Bath Spa Station on Manvers Street to Cardiff £18.70. 🕐 2 per hr.); Bristol £5.80. 🕐 every 10-15min.); London Paddington £30.50, 🕐 1-2 per day.); Chippenham £5.10. 🕐 2 per hr.); Birmingham £53. 🕐 2 per hr.); Salisbury £16.40. 🕐 1-2 per hr.); and Oxford £16.20. 🕐 every hr. with change at Didcot Parkway). Buy at the ticket office. (🕐 Open M-F 5:30am-8:30pm, Sa-Su 7:30am-8:30pm.)

Getting Around

By Bus

First buses (☎0871 200 2233) run throughout the city and to the surrounding areas. Day Passes £4.40 peak, £4.20 off-peak) are available for purchase on the bus for unlimited travel within Bath. (Churchill Bridge. 🕐 Office open M-Sa 9am-5pm.)

By Taxi

For a taxi call Abbey Radio (☎01225 444 444) or V Cars (☎01225 464 646). There's a taxi stand outside of Bath Spa Station.

Essentials

You don't have to be a rocket scientist to plan a good trip. (It might help, but it's not required.) You do, however, need to be well prepared, and that's what we can do for you. Essentials is the chapter that gives you all the nitty-gritty you need to know for your trip: the hard information gleaned from over 50 years of collective wisdom and several months of furious fact-checking. Planning your trip? Check. Where to find Wi-Fi? Check. The dirt on public transportation? Check. We've also thrown in communications info, safety tips, and a climate chart, just for good measure. Plus, for overall trip-planning advice from what to pack (money and as little underwear as possible) to how to take a good passport photo (it's physically impossible; consider airbrushing), you can also check out the Essentials section of www.letsgo.com.

So flick through this chapter before you leave so you know what documents to bring, while you're on the plane so you know how you'll be getting from the airport to your accommodation, and when you're on the ground so you can find a laundromat to solve all your 3am stain-removal needs. This chapter may not always be the most scintillating read, but it just might save your life.

RED TAPE

Documents and Formalities

We're going to fill you in on visas and work permits, but don't forget the most important one of all: your passport. Don't forget your passport!

Visas

Those lucky enough to be EU citizens do not need a visa to globetrot through Britain. You citizens of Australia, Canada, New Zealand, and the US do not need a visa for stays of up to six months. Those staying longer than six months may apply for a longer-term visa; consult an embassy or consulate for more information. The rules for citizens of other non-EU countries vary. Check to find out what you need to do.

Work Permits

Admittance to a country as a traveler does not include the right to work, which is authorized only by a work permit.

Embassies and Consulates

- **British Consular Services in Australia:** Consulate General. (Level 16, Gateway Bldg., Macquarie Pl., Sydney, NSW 2000 ☎02 9247 7521 ⏰ Open M-F 9am-12:30pm and 1:30-5pm.)

- **British Consular Services in Canada:** Consulate General. (777 Bay St., Ste. 2800, College Park, Toronto, ON M5G 2G2 ☎416-593-1290 ⏰ Open M-F 9am-4:30pm.)

- **British Consular Services in Ireland:** Embassy. (29 Merrion Rd., Ballsbridge, Dublin 4 ☎01 205 3700 ⏰ Open M-Th 9am-12:45pm and 2-4:15pm, F 9am-12:45pm and 2-5pm.)

- **British Consular Services in New Zealand:** High Commission. (44 Hill St., Wellington, 6011 ☎04 924 2888 ⏰ Open M-F 8:45am-5pm.)

- **British Consular Services in the US:** Consulate General. (845 Third Ave., New York, NY 10022 ☎212-745-0200 ⏰ Open M-Th 9am-noon, Th-F 9am-noon.) Other consulate generals in Atlanta, Boston, Chicago, Denver, Houston, Los Angeles, Miami, and San Francisco, and the embassy in Washington, DC.

- **Australian Consular Services in London:** High Commission. (Australia House, Strand ☎020 7379 4334 ⏰ Open M-F 9am-5pm.)

- **Canadian Consular Services in London:** High Commission. (Macdonald House, 1 Grosvenor Sq. ⏰020 7258 6600 ⏰ Open M-F 9:30am-1pm.)

- **Irish Consular Services in London:** Embassy. (17 Grosvenor Pl. ☎020 7589 8450 ⏰ Open M-F 9:30am-5pm.)

- **New Zealand Consular Services in London:** Embassy. (New Zealand House, 80 Haymarket ☎020 7839 4580 ⏰ Open M-F 9am-5pm.)

- **American Consular Services in London:** Embassy. (24 Grosvenor Sq.]020 7499 9000 ⏰ Open M-F 8:30am-5:30pm.)

MONEY

Getting Money from Home

Stuff happens. When stuff happens, you might need some money. When you need some money, the easiest and cheapest solution is to have someone back home make a deposit to your bank account. Otherwise, consider one of the following options.

Wiring Money

Arranging a bank money transfer means asking a bank back home to wire money to a bank in London. This is the cheapest way to transfer cash, but it's also the slowest and most agonizing, usually taking several days or more. Note that some banks may only release your funds in local currency, potentially sticking you with a poor exchange rate; inquire about this in advance.

Money transfer services like Western Union are faster and

more convenient than bank transfers—but also much pricier. Western Union has many locations worldwide. To find one, visit www.westernunion.com or call the appropriate number: in Australia ☎1800 173 833, in Canada ☎800-235-0000, in the UK ☎0808 234 9168, in the US ☎800-325-6000. Money transfer services are also available to American Express cardholders and at selected Thomas Cook offices. Remember to bring your ID to receive the money!

US State Department (US Citizens Only)

In serious emergencies only, the US State Department will help your family or friends forward money within hours to the nearest consular office, which will then disburse it according to instructions for a US$30 fee. If you wish to use this service, you must contact the Overseas Citizens Services division of the US State Department. (☎+1-202-501-4444, from US ☎888-407-4747)

Withdrawing Money

To use a debit or credit card to withdraw money from a cash machine (ATM) in Europe, you must have a four-digit Personal Identification Number (PIN). If your PIN is longer than four digits, ask your bank whether you can just use the first four or whether you'll need a new one. Credit cards don't usually come with PINs, so if you intend to hit up ATMs in Europe with a credit card to get cash advances, call your credit card company before leaving to request one.

One of the most expensive cities on the planet, London is chock-full of ATMs. Don't worry—there will most likely be an ATM near to you if you plan on staying within the city limits. A capitalist's heaven, London is also home to some of the biggest bosses in the banking business such as Barclay's, Natwest, Lloyd's, and the Royal Bank of Scotland. For tourist purposes, these are all essentially the same, unless your home bank has a special relationship with one of them.

Tipping and Bargaining

Tips in restaurants are sometimes included in the bill (sometimes as a "service charge"). If gratuity is not included, you should tip your server about 10%. Taxi drivers should receive a 10% tip, and bellhops and chambermaids usually expect £1-3. To the great relief of many budget travelers, tipping is not expected at pubs and bars in Britain (unless you are trying to get jiggy with the bartender). Bargaining is practically unheard of in the upscale shops that overrun London. Don't try it (unless you happen to be at a street market, or feel particularly belligerent).

Taxes

The UK has a 20% value added tax (VAT), a sales tax applied to everything but food, books, medicine, and children's clothing. The tax is included in the amount indicated on the price tag. The prices stated in *Let's Go* include VAT. Upon exiting Britain, non-EU citizens can reclaim VAT (minus an administrative fee) through the Retail Export Scheme, although the process is time-consuming, annoying, and may not be worth it, except for large purchases. You can obtain refunds only for goods you take out of the country (not for accommodations or meals). Participating shops display a "Tax-Free Shopping" sign and may have a minimum purchase of £50-100 before they offer refunds. To claim a refund, fill out the form you are given in the shop and present it with the goods and receipts at customs upon departure (look for the Tax-Free Refund desk at the airport). At peak times, this process can take up to an hour. You must leave the country within three months of your purchase in order to claim a refund, and you must apply before leaving the UK.

GETTING THERE

By Plane

London's main airport is **Heathrow** (LHR ☎0844 335 1801 www.heathrowairport.com), commonly regarded as one of the world's busiest airports. The cheapest way to get from Heathrow to central London is on the Tube. The two Tube stations servicing Heathrow form a loop at the end of the Piccadilly line, which runs to central London. (⏱ 1hr.; every 5min. M-Sa 5am-11:54pm, Su 5:46am-10:37pm.) Heathrow Express (☎084 5600 1515 www.heathrowexpress.com) runs between Heathrow and Paddington station four times per hour. The trip is significantly shorter (though comparably pricier) than many of the alternatives, clocking in at around 15-20min. (*i* £20 when purchased online, £25 from station. ☎ 1st train departs daily around 5:10am.) The Heathrow Connect also runs to Paddington but is cheaper and takes longer, since it makes five stops on the way to and from the airport. There are two trains per hour, and the trip takes about 25min.

The National Express bus (☎08717 818 178 www.nationalexpress.com) runs between Victoria Coach Station and Heathrow three times per hour. Though cheap and often simpler than convoluted Underground trips, the buses are subject to the travails of London traffic. Posing a similar traffic threat, taxis from the airport to Victoria cost around £60 and take around 45min. In short, they aren't worth it.

Getting to Gatwick Airport (LGW ☎0844 335 1802 www.gatwickairport.com) takes around 30min., making it less convenient than Heathrow but less hectic, too. The swift and affordable train services that connect Gatwick to the city make the trip a little easier. The Gatwick Express train runs nonstop service to Victoria station. You can buy tickets in terminals, at the station, or on the train itself. (☎0845 850 1530 www.gatwickexpress.com *i* 1-way £19.90; 2-way £34.90. Round-trip ticket valid for a month. ☎ First train at 3:30am, then 4:30am, then every 15min. from 5:00am-11:45pm., then last trains at midnight and 12:30am.)

National Express runs buses from the North and South terminals of Gatwick to London. The National Express bus (☎0871 781 8178 www.nationalexpress.com) takes approximately 1½hr., and buses depart for London Victoria hourly. Taxis take about 1hr. to reach central London. easyBus (☎084 4800 4411 www.easybus.co.uk) runs every 15min. from North and South terminals to Earls Court and West Brompton. (Tickets from £2. ☎ 65min., every 15min.)

By Train

Europeans are far ahead of Americans in terms of train travel, and London offers several ways to easily reach other European destinations. Multiple train companies pass through the city. The biggest are Eurostar (☎08432 186 186 www.eurostar.com), which travels to Paris and Brussels, and National Rail (☎08457 48 49 50 www.nationalrail.co.uk), which oversees lines running throughout the United Kingdom. Train travel in Britain is generally reliable but can be unreasonably expensive. Booking tickets weeks in advance can lead to large savings, but spur-of-the-moment train trips to northern cities could cost more than £100.

By Bus

Bus travel is another (frequently cheaper) option. Eurolines (☎08717 818 181 www.eurolines.co.uk ☼ Open 8am-8pm) is Europe's largest coach network, servicing 500 destinations throughout Europe. Many buses leave from Victoria Coach Station, at the mouth of Elizabeth St. just off Buckingham Palace Rd. Many coach companies, including National Express, Eurolines, and Megabus, operate from Victoria Coach. National Express is the only scheduled coach network in Britain and can be used for most intercity travel and for travel to and from various airports. It can also be used to reach Scotland and Wales.

GETTING AROUND

Though there are daily interruptions to Tube service, the controlling network, Transport of London, does a good job of keeping travelers aware of these disruptions to service. Each station will have posters listing interruptions to service, and you can check service online at www.tfl.gov.uk or the 24hr. travel information service (☎0843 222 1234). The website also has a journey planner that can plot your route using any public transport service ("TFL" is a verb here). Memorize that website. Love that website. Though many people in the city stay out into the wee hours, the Tube doesn't have the same sort of stamina. When it closes around midnight, night owls have two choices: cabs or night buses.

Travel Passes

Travel passes are almost guaranteed to save you money. The passes are priced based on the number of zones they serve (the more zones, the more expensive), but Zone 1 encompasses central London, and you'll rarely need to get past Zone 2. If someone offers you a secondhand ticket, don't take it. There's no real way to verify whether it's valid—plus, it's illegal. Under 16s get free travel on buses. Passengers ages 11-15 enjoy reduced fares on the Tube with an Oyster Photocard. Students 18 and older must study full-time (at least 15hr. per week over 14 weeks) in London to qualify for the Student Photocard, which enables users to save 30% on adult travel cards and bus passes. It's worth it if you're staying for an extended period of time (study abroad kids, we're looking at you).

Oyster cards enable you to pay in a variety of ways. Fares come in peak (M-F 6:30-9:30am and 4-7pm) and off-peak varieties and are, again, distinguished by zone. Oysters let you "pay as you go," meaning that you can store credit on an as-needed basis. Using an Oyster card will save you up to 50% off a single ticket. Remember to tap your card both on entering and leaving the station. You can use your card to add Travelcards, which allow unlimited travel on one day. This will only be cost-effective if you plan to use the Tube a lot. They cost £8.80 for anytime travel or £7.30 for off-peak travel. You can top up your Oyster at one of the infinite off-licenses, marked by the Oyster logo, that are scattered throughout the city.

Season Tickets are weekly, monthly, and annual Travelcards that work on all public transport and can be purchased inside Tube stations. They yield unlimited (within zone) use for their duration. (*i* Weekly rates for Zones 1-2 £30.40, monthly £116.80.)

By Underground

Most stations have Tube maps on the walls and free pocket maps. The Tube map barely reflects an above-ground scale, though, and should not be used for even the roughest estimation of walking directions (seriously). Platforms are organized by line and will have the colors of the lines serviced and their names on the wall. The colors of the poles inside the trains correspond with the line, and trains will often have their end destination displayed on the front. This is an essential service when your line splits. Many platforms will have a digital panel indicating ETAs for the trains and sometimes type and final destination. When transferring within a station, just follow the clearly marked routes.

The Tube runs from Monday to Saturday from approximately 5:30am (though it depends on the station and line) until around midnight. If you're taking a train within 30min. of these times (before or after), you'll want to check the signs in the ticket hall for times of the first and last train. The Tube runs less frequently on Sunday, with many lines starting service after 6am. Around 6pm on weekdays, many of the trains running out of central London are packed with the after-work crowd. It's best to avoid these lines at this time of day.

You can buy tickets from ticket counters (though these often have lines at bigger stations) or at machines in the stations. You need to swipe your ticket at the beginning of the journey and then again to exit the Tube. Random on-train checks will ask you to present a valid ticket to avoid the £80 penalty fee (reduced to £40 if you pay in under 21 days).

The Overground is a new addition to the London public transportation scene. It services parts of the city past Zone 1, where Tube lines are sparse, and is particularly useful in East London. Fares and rules are the same as the Tube; you can just think of it as another line, except with a better view.

By Bus

While slower than the Tube for long journeys (thanks to traffic and more frequent stops), buses are useful for traveling short distances covered by a few stops (and several transfers) on the Tube.

Bus stops frequently post lists of buses servicing the stop as well as route maps and maps of the area indicating nearby stops. These maps are also very helpful for finding your way around a neighborhood. Buses display route numbers.

Every route and stop is different, but buses generally run every 5-15min. beginning around 5:30am and ending around midnight. After day bus routes have closed, night buses take over. These typically operate similar routes to their daytime equivalents, and their numbers are usually prefixed with an N (N13, for instance). Some buses run 24hr. services. If you're staying out past the Tube's closing time, you should plan your night bus route or bring cab fare. (*i* Single rides £2.40, Oyster card £1.40.)

PRACTICALITIES

- **TOURIST OFFICES:** The main central tourist office in London is the Britain and London Visitor Centre (BLVC). (1 Regent St. www.visitbritain.com *i* ⊖Piccadilly Circus. ⊠ Open Apr-Sept M 9:30am-6pm, Tu-F 9am-6:30pm, Sa-Su 10am-4pm; Oct-Mar M 9:30am-6:30pm, Tu-F 9am6pm, Sa-Su 10am-4pm.) Also useful is the London Information Centre. (Leicester Sq. ☎020 7292 2333 www.londoninformationcentre.com *i* ⊖Leicester Sq. 🕗 Open daily 8am-midnight.)

- **TOURS:** Original London Walks offers walking tours with themes like "Jack the Ripper" and "Harry Potter." (☎020 7624 9255 www.walks.com *i* £9, students and over 65 £7.)

- **CURRENCY EXCHANGE:** Thomas Cook. (30 St James's St. ☎084 5308 9570 🕗 Open M-Tu 10am-5:30pm, Th-F 10am-5:50pm.)

- **CREDIT CARD SERVICES:** American Express (www.amex-travelresources.com) has locations at 78 Brompton Rd. (☎084 4406 0046 *i* ⊖Knightsbridge. 🕗 Open M-Tu 9am-5:30pm, W 9:30am-5:30pm, Th-F 9am-5:30pm, Sa 9am-4pm.) and 30-31 Haymarket. (☎084 4406 0044 *i* ⊖Piccadilly Circus. 🕗 Open M-F 9am-5:30pm.)

- **GLBT RESOURCES:** The official GLBT Tourist office offers information on everything from saunas to theater discounts. (25 Frith St. www.gaytouristoffice.co.uk *i* ⊖Leicester Sq.) Boyz (www.boyz.co.uk) lists gay events in London as well as an online version of its magazine. Gingerbeer (www.gingerbeer.co.uk) is a guide for lesbian and bisexual women with events listings. *Time Out London's* magazine and website (www.timeout.com/london) also provide a good overview of the city's GLBT establishments and the city in general.

- **TICKET OFFICES:** Albermarle of London agency provides official tickets for all major West End theater productions. Book tickets via web, phone, or visiting the office. (5th fl., Medius House, 63-69 New Oxford St. ☎020 7379 1357 www.albemarle-london.com 🕗 Open M-F 8am-8:30pm, Sa 8:30am-8pm, Su 10am-6pm.)

- **INTERNET:** Wi-Fi abounds in this technologically advanced city. Most cafes provide internet access. Chains like Starbucks (www.starbucks.co.uk) and McDonald's (www.mcdonalds.co.uk) almost always have free Wi-Fi. Other chains with Wi-Fi include the Coffee Republic (www.coffeerepublic.co.uk), Wetherspoon (www.jdwetherspoon.co.uk), Pret a Manger (www.pret.com), COSTA (www.costa.co.uk), and Caffé Nero (www.caffenero.co.uk). Public areas also have Wi-Fi. The area between Upper Street and Holloway Road, also known as The Technology Mile, is

Essentials

the longest stretch of free internet in the city.

- **POST OFFICES:** Trafalgar Square Post Office. (24-28 William IV St. ☎020 7484 9305 *i* ⊖Charing Cross. ⏰ Open M 8:30am-6:30pm, Tu 9:15am-6:30pm, W-F 8:30am-6:30pm, Sa 9am-5:30pm.)

EMERGENCY

- **EMERGENCY NUMBERS:** ☎999. City of London Police. (37 Wood St. ☎020 7601 2455 ⏰ Open M-F 7:30am-7:30pm.) Metropolitan Police. (☎030 0123 1212)

- **RAPE CRISIS CENTER:** Solace. (136 Royal College St. ☎0808 802 5565 www.rapecrisis.org.uk)

- **HOSPITALS/MEDICAL SERVICES:** St. Thomas' Hospital. (Westminster Bridge Rd. ☎020 7188 7188) Royal Free Hospital. (Pond St. ☎020 7794 0500) Charing Cross Hospital. (Fulham Palace Rd. ☎020 3311 1234) University College Hospital. (235 Euston Rd. ☎0845 155 5000)

SAFETY AND HEALTH

General Advice

In any type of crisis, the most important thing to do is stay calm. Your country's embassy abroad is usually your best resource in an emergency; registering with that embassy upon arrival in the country is a good idea. The government offices listed in the Travel Advisories feature at the end of this section can provide information on the services they offer their citizens in case of emergencies abroad.

Police

Police are a common presence in London, and there are many police stations scattered throughout the city. There are two types of police officers in Britain: regular officers with full police powers, and police community support officers (PCSO), who have limited police power and focus on community maintenance and safety. The national emergency number is ☎999.

Drugs and Alcohol

The Brits love to drink, so the presence of alcohol is unavoidable. In trying to keep up with the locals, remember that the Imperial pint is 20 oz., as opposed to the 16oz. US pint. The legal age at which you can buy alcohol in the UK is 18 (16 for buying beer and wine with food at a restaurant).

Despite what you may have seen on *Skins,* use and possession of hard drugs is illegal throughout the country. Do not test this—Britain has been cracking down on drug use for young people in particular over the past few years. Smoking is banned in enclosed public spaces in Britain, including pubs and restaurants.

Specific Concerns

Terrorism

The bombings of July 7, 2005 in the London Underground revealed the vulnerability of large European cities to terrorist attacks and resulted in the enforcement of stringent safety measures at airports and major tourist sights throughout British cities. Though nearly a decade has passed, security checks are still as thorough as ever. Check your home country's foreign affairs office for travel information and advisories, and be sure to follow the local news while in the UK.

Pre-Departure Health

Matching a prescription to a foreign equivalent is not always easy, safe, or possible, so if you take prescription drugs, carry up-to-date prescriptions or a statement from your doctor stating the medications' trade names, manufacturers, chemical names, and dosages. Be sure to keep all medication with you in your carry-on luggage.

Immunizations and Precautions

Travelers over two years old should make sure that the following vaccines are up to date: MMR (for measles, mumps, and rubella); DTaP or Td (for diphtheria, tetanus, and pertussis); IPV (for polio); Hib (for Haemophilus influenzae B); and HepB (for Hepatitis B). For recommendations on immunizations and prophylaxis, check with a doctor and consult the Centers for Disease Control and Prevention (CDC) in the US (☎+1-800-232-4636 www.cdc. gov/travel) or the equivalent in your home country.

KEEPING IN TOUCH

By Email and Internet

Hello and welcome to the 21st century, where you're rarely more than a 5min. walk from the nearest Wi-Fi hot spot, even if sometimes you'll have to pay a few bucks or buy a drink for the privilege of using it. Internet cafes and free internet terminals are listed in the Practicalities section above. For lists of additional cyber cafes in London check out www.cybercaptive.com.

Wireless hot spots make internet access possible in public and remote places. Unfortunately, they also pose security risks. Hot spots are public, open networks that use unencrypted, un-secured connections. They are susceptible to hacks and "packet sniffing"—the theft of passwords and other private information. To prevent problems, disable "ad hoc" mode, turn off file sharing and network discovery, encrypt your email, turn on your firewall, beware of phony networks, and watch for over-the-shoulder creeps.

By Telephone

Calling Home from London

If you have internet access, your best—i.e., cheapest, most conve-nient, and most tech-savvy—means of calling home is probably our good friend Skype (www.skype.com). Calls to other Skype users are free; calls to landlines and mobiles worldwide start at US\$0.023 per minute, depending on where you're calling.

For those still stuck in the 20th century, prepaid phone cards are a common and relatively inexpensive means of calling abroad. Each one comes with a Personal Identification Number (PIN) and a toll-free access number. You call the access number and then follow the directions for dialing your PIN. To purchase prepaid phone cards, check online for the best rates; www.calling-cards.com is a good place to start. Online providers generally send your access number and PIN via email, with no actual "card" involved. You can also call home with prepaid phone cards purchased in London.

Sir Giles Gilbert Scott's swanky red-box phone booths still line the London streets. Adapted to the modern age, the public phone booths now accept both coins and cards. As with most former crown property, the price of modernization was privatization, with British Telecom now in charge of the operation and maintenance of these more modern, utilitarian boxes.

Cellular Phones

Cell phones are everywhere in the UK, although the Brits call them "mobile phones." Competitive, low prices and the variety of calling plans make them accessible even for short-term, low-budget travelers. For most visitors to the UK, a pay-as-you-go plan is the most attractive option. Pick up an eligible mobile (from £25) and recharge, or top up, with a card purchased at a grocery store, online, or by phone. Incoming calls and incoming text messages are always free. Vodaphone (www.vodaphone.co.uk) and T-Mobile (www.t-mobile.co.uk) are among the biggest providers.

TIME DIFFERENCES

Great Britain is on Greenwich Mean Time (GMT) and observes Daylight Saving Time. This means the Brits are 5hr. ahead of New York City and 8hr. ahead of Los Angeles. Note that Australia and New Zealand observe Daylight Saving Time from October to March, the opposite of the Northern Hemisphere—therefore, Sydney is 9hr. ahead of Britain from March to October and 11hr. ahead from October to March. Don't accidentally call your mom at 5am!

CLIMATE

We'd love to tell you that everything you've heard about British weather is false...but we're not here to lie to you. Britain is traditionally cool and summertime precipitation is considerably higher than other European destinations. Don't let the weather keep you from traveling to this wonderful country, but be prepared for some damp, chilly days during your stay. The silver lining is that there are few extremes either, so you're unlikely to melt, freeze, or be blown away by a freak storm during your trip.

MONTH	AVG. HIGH TEMP.		AVG. LOW TEMP.		AVG. RAIN-FALL		AVG. NUMBER OF WET DAYS
Jan	6°C	43°F	2°C	36°F	54mm	2.1 in.	15
Feb	7°C	45°F	2°C	36°F	40mm	1.6 in.	13
Mar	10°C	50°F	3°C	37°F	37mm	1.5 in.	11
Apr	13°C	55°F	6°C	43°F	37mm	1.5 in.	12
May	17°C	63°F	8°C	46°F	46mm	1.8 in.	12
June	20°C	68°F	12°C	54°F	45mm	1.8 in.	11
July	22°C	72°F	14°C	57°F	57mm	2.2 in.	12
Aug	21°C	70°F	13°C	55°F	59mm	2.3 in.	11
Sept	19°C	66°F	11°C	52°F	49mm	1.9 in.	13
Oct	14°C	57°F	8°C	46°F	57mm	2.2 in.	13
Nov	10°C	50°F	5°C	41°F	64mm	2.5 in.	15
Dec	7°C	45°F	4°C	39°F	48mm	1.9 in.	15

To convert from degrees Fahrenheit to degrees Celsius, subtract 32 and multiply by 5/9. To convert from Celsius to Fahrenheit, multiply by 9/5 and add 32. The mathematically challenged may use this handy chart:

°CELSIUS	-5	0	5	10	15	20	25	30	35	40
°FAHRENHEIT	23	32	41	50	59	68	77	86	95	104

MEASUREMENTS

Like the rest of the rational world, Great Britain uses the metric system. The basic unit of length is the meter (m), which is divided into 100 centimeters (cm) or 1000 millimeters (mm). One thousand meters make up one kilometer (km). Fluids are measured in liters (L), each divided into 1000 milliliters (mL). A liter of pure water weighs one kilogram (kg), the unit of mass that is divided into 1000 grams (g). One metric ton is 1000kg. It'll probably just be easiest if you check out this chart:

MEASUREMENT CONVERSIONS	
1 inch (in.) = 25.4mm	1 millimeter (mm) = 0.039 in.
1 foot (ft.) = 0.305m	1 meter (m) = 3.28 ft.
1 yard (yd.) = 0.914m	1 meter (m) = 1.094 yd.
1 mile (mi.) = 1.609km	1 kilometer (km) = 0.621 mi.
1 ounce (oz.) = 28.35g	1 gram (g) = 0.035 oz.
1 pound (lb.) = 0.454kg	1 kilogram (kg) = 2.205 lb.
1 fluid ounce (fl. oz.) = 29.57mL	1 milliliter (mL) = 0.034 fl. oz.
1 gallon (gal.) = 3.785L	1 liter (L) = 0.264 gal.

London 101

From Westminster Abbey to Abbey Road, from the Queen of England to Elton John, from bangers 'n' mash to chicken tikka masala, London has something to satisfy every taste. To help you navigate through it all, London 101 is here to fill you in on the city's past and present. If the diversity of British food is overwhelming at first, don't fret, just check out the lowdown in our Food and Drink section. We'll also demystify the world of football without helmets and crickets that don't chirp in our Sports and Recreation section, and tell you when you should say "pissed" and shouldn't say "biggie" in Customs and Etiquette. Finally, we'll fill you in on all the Holidays and Festivals so you don't miss out on the Queen's Birthday festivities. Here we give you all the basics you need to make the most out of your London experience, whether it's three days or three months.

HISTORY

Birthday (43-410 CE)

London was actually founded in 43 CE by the Romans (they called it Londinium then), just seven years after their conquest of Britain. It was meant to be a civilian town, as opposed to the military outposts the Romans had previously built in this restive northern frontier. Seventeen years later, the Celtic Warrior-Queen Boudica burned Londinium to the ground during her campaign to expel the Romans from her island. But the pesky foreigners came back and the town was rebuilt, now with city walls! (These old Roman walls still demarcate the historic City of London at the center of the now-sprawling metropolis.) The town grew in size and importance and became the capital of the Roman province of Britannia.

I Want You (She's So London) (410-1215)

In 410, after years of fighting British "barbarians," the Romans cleared out, in order to battle other "barbarians" (this time, of the German variety) on their home turf. Once the Romans were gone, Britain fell into a period of flux, with Saxons, Vikings, and Danes fighting over the city—until the Normans arrived in 1066 and showed everyone who was boss. William the Conqueror, who demolished his competitors for the crown at the Battle of Hastings, treated London with special attention. William transformed London into his capital by building three new castles (one of these is now known as the Tower of London). Westminster, the enormous abbey that Edward the Confessor built just before the Normans took over, became the fiscal and legal center of the nation. London's status as the largest and wealthiest city in Britain made it a kingmaker in every disputed succession (trust us, there were a lot of these). Prospective monarchs had to make sure that they had London's support, or their heads would most likely end up on a pike.

Helter Skelter (1215-1666)

But political power doesn't make a city invincible. The city's densely-packed population and booming commerce made it highly susceptible to plagues and fires. The Black Death hit London in 1369 and killed more than half of the population. In 1665, the Black Plague reared its ugly head again and carried off about 100,000Londoners. Then came the Great Fire of 1666, which leveled more than 60% of the city, including the original St. Paul's Cathedral and Royal Exchange. This time, many decided to rebuild in stone.

It's Getting Better All the Time (1666-1900)

In spite of its devastating destruction, the Great Fire helped make London the modern city it is today. Over the next 20 years, streets were widened, new stone houses were built, and the city began to assume the character of a modern metropolis. By the end of the 18th century, Samuel Johnson could say without a hint of irony, "when a man is tired of London, he is tired of life; for there is in London all that life can afford."

Despite losing its North American colonies in 1776, England became the most powerful country in the world. Having defeated France in the French-Indian and Napoleonic Wars, it was the ultimate colonial power. The spoils of its worldwide empire all poured back to London. Over the next century, Big Ben and the Houses of Parliament were built, the National Gallery was erected, a police force was established by Sir Robert Peel (hence the nicknames "bobbies and "peelers"), and a sewage system was put into place to spare Londoners a repeat of the Great Stink of 1858 (and prevent the cholera outbreaks that followed the habit of dumping an entire city's raw sewage in the Thames). The Underground, the first subterranean rail line in the world, opened in 1863. Within a few months, it was carrying more than 25,000 passengers a day.

The Industrial Revolution brought huge numbers of rural peasants to work in factories in the capital. London's population passed one million around 1800, and it remained the largest city in the world for much of the 19th century. By 1900, 6.7 million people called London home.

Magical Mystery Tour (1900-today)

Over the course of the 20th century, London survived two world wars, two Olympics, and Johnny Rotten. During WWII, German planes bombarded London in an eight-month Blitz, intended to terrorize Britons into submission. Beginning on September 7, 1940, the Luftwaffe bombed the city for 57 consecutive days. Children were evacuated, and more than 150,000 people camped out in the Underground each night. (The government explicitly forbade this practice, but people got around this by going to the extreme measure of…purchasing a ticket.) The Blitz destroyed more than a million houses, and left an enduring mark on the city.

By the 1960s, in the Swinging London period, the city really had its mojo back. Jean Shrimpton became one of the world's first supermodels, the Beatles ensconced themselves in Abbey Road Studios, The Who's Pete Townshend smashed up his guitar and shattered conventions, and hipsters were known as mods. It was a good time to be in London.

Since then, the city has only become more multi-ethnic, more artistic, and more tourist-friendly. In 2000, Ken Livingstone—a man who said, "If voting changed anything, they'd abolish it"—became London's first elected mayor. Under his watch, London won its bid to host the 2012 Olympics (see Arts and Culture), introduced a motorist fee to cut down on congestion in the city, and gave the Underground a facelift. Though riots in the summer of 2011 were a symbol of the difficult times faced by post-economic crisis Britain, the city's residents roundly rejected the anarchy of the rioters and pulled together to reassert their community. Now London excitedly prepares for its third Olympics, an honor no city has ever received before.

CUSTOMS AND ETIQUETTE

Brits and Americans may both speak English, but that doesn't mean that they can always understand each other. As George Bernard Shaw once remarked, "America and Britain are two nations separated by a common language." Here are some phrases you should know not to mix up:

- **Biggie:** Carries the double-meaning of "doo-doo," what a child calls number two, and an erection. Watch out, the reflexive "no biggie" could take on a whole new world of significance.

- **Blow me:** Not the euphemism that we're used to, it's merely an exclamation of surprise in this land.

- **Fags:** Not a gay slur, but merely cigarettes.

- **Football:** There are no touchdowns or field goals in this game. Remember, don't talk about "soccer" here, or you might bring the wrath of legendary football hardman Vinnie Jones upon you.

- **Pissed** :Means drunk, not angry.

While we're at it, here's a short guide to some other English slang worth knowing:

- **Aggro:** Short for aggravation.

- **All right?:** Used a lot around London and the south to mean, "Hello, how are you?"

- **Barmy:** If someone tells you that you're barmy, they mean you have gone mad or crazy (e.g. you'd have to be barmy to visit England without trying black pudding).

- **Belt up:** Shut up.

- **Cock up:** A mistake.

- **Dekko:** Borrowed from Hindi, this means to take a look at something.

ALL IN THE (ROYAL) FAMILY

Even though your odds of casually running into a royal (perhaps excepting Prince Harry) are the same as Nick Clegg becoming prime minister, there's no harm in knowing a little bit about one of the world's most famous families.

- **Queen Elizabeth II.** Queen since 1952, she is the second longest-reigning monarch in British history. Untouchable in classiness, she's also legitimately untouchable, so no handshakes/pats/hugs/half-Nelsons unless you're a really cute seven-year-old.

- **Prince Philip.** Elizabeth's husband and *not* King. Basically the English Joe Biden, he once told some British students in China, "If you stay here much longer, you'll be all slitty-eyed."

- **Prince Charles.** The Prince of Wales, he is the first in line to the throne.

- **Prince William.** Second in line to the throne after his father, he recently married his sweetheart Catherine Middleton and spends most of his time proving his manliness by serving

London 101

with the Royal Air Force in Wales and fathering children.

- **Prince Harry.** Nazi costumes and strip billiards aside, the second son of Princess Diana now can breathe more easily now that he is fourth in line. From now on, his royal duties primarily include being a cool uncle.

- **Prince George.** As William and Kate's son, he is the newest addition to the royal family. He shares a number of hobbies with his grandfather—most notably, babbling to himself incoherently.

FOOD AND DRINK

British food often gets a bad rap, probably because of English favorites with names like jellied eel and spotted dick. But many traditional standards are actually quite delicious, and no visit to London is complete without sampling some fish 'n' chips, Yorkshire pudding (fried batter), or bangers and mash (sausage and mashed potatoes).

In your English travels, you're almost certain to find a "full breakfast" (eggs, sausage, beans, fried tomato, and buttered toast) or a "ploughman's lunch" (cheese, onions, pickles, and a hunk of bread) at any pub. The customary tea takes place between three and five in the afternoon. Head to a hotel lobby or a sit-down cafe and they'll surely have cucumber sandwiches and scones with clotted cream and jam, not to mention the actual namesake beverage.

One of the advantages of having a global empire was the ability to pick and choose all the best foods the world had to offer. Even with the empire gone, London is still an international city, and its food reflects that. Chicken tikka masala has become, by some accounts, the most popular English dish. (Chicken tikka is an Indian dish to which cooks added gravy to satisfy the British desire for meat with gravy. In 2001, the UK's Foreign Secretary, Robin Cook, proclaimed it "a true British national dish," calling it "a perfect illustration of the way Britain absorbs and adapts external influences.")

The sun has long since set on the days when sandwich meant two pieces of Wonderbread, some mayo, and a thin piece of meat. Now, you're more likely to find yourself being treated to a Vietnamese bánh mì or a Middle Eastern falafel. South Asian curries, Caribbean roti, Chinese dim sum, Spanish paella, and everything in between can be found on London's streets.

SPORTS AND RECREATION

Football

Soccer is king here, but don't call it that: football rules the roost. The English boast that the game was created here and whether that's true or not, they certainly act as if it is. Pubs are packed every Saturday and Sunday as football supporters (not fans) gather to cheer for their favorite team in the domestic leagues: the Premiership, the Championship, League 1, and League 2. Pubs are packed again on midweek evenings as the supporters of those lucky seven clubs that made the European leagues cheer on their teams' charge for continental glory. The passion felt for the clubs is nothing compared with how people feel about the national team: the Three Lions. The football team is perpetually star-crossed, but, despite its constant surfeit of incredible talent, it has not won the World Cup since 1966; the team always seems to do just well enough to cause national heartbreak each time they lose in spectacular fashion.

Cricket

For those not of the footy persuasion, there's cricket, a game that we yanks just don't get. There's a pitcher (who they call a bowler), a batter (sorry, a batsman), and innings (one or two depending on the game). Beyond that it all gets rather opaque. It's like a longer, slower version of baseball—games can last up to five days!—if the creator of baseball had gotten bladdered at the pub and thought two batsmen running between two wickets was equivalent to rounding the bases and that it was a good idea to have a position called "Silly Mid-Off."

Beyond Tourism

If you're ready to hop the pond and not hop back, to perfect your British accent, or to pull a Beatles in reverse and take London by storm with your electro-funk country band (you know they're ready for it), then this is the section for you. We've got you non-tourist visitors covered for places to study, volunteer, and work (they'll warm to your music eventually, but you need some ca$h money in the meantime).

STUDY

Nothing exemplifies the phrase "just a stone's throw away" like world-class universities in London; they are as abundant as the stones you're throwing.

- **University College London (UCL):** Known as "London's global university," UCL has top marks in both student satisfaction and quality of teaching. Together with King's College, UCL formed the foundation of the University of London system back in 1836. (www.ucl.ac.uk)

- **King's College London:** You'll be steeped in history both royal and pop at this college, which is the third oldest university in England and an inspiration for Dan Brown's imagination. (www.kcl.ac.uk)

- **Imperial College London:** If you're having trouble distinguishing this from the previous two "Regal-Sounding-Word College London" schools that also form a point in the "golden triangle" of British universities, just remember that it's the one that got away—or the awkward third wheel that joined the party late and left early (if said party is the University of London system, that is). (www.imperial.ac.uk)

- **Royal Holloway University:** If you want to get out of the center of London and into the countryside, but you also want to attend a top research university, Royal Holloway University is the place for you. (www.rhul.ac.uk)

- **London School of Hygiene and Tropical Medicine (LSHTM):** The most intriguingly named school in the University of London system, LSHTM is also a top postgraduate school in the fields of public health and tropical medicine. (www.lshtm.ac.uk)

- **Trinity Laban Conservatoire of Music and Dance:** As the label "Conservatoire" would suggest, this is a place to develop highly specialized artistic skills. However, the school also offers some classes that are open to the public. (www.trinitylaban.ac.uk)

- **University of the Arts London:** Go here to become a doctor. (www.arts.ac.uk)

VOLUNTEER

The following opportunities are the second-best thing to being employed.

- **Museum of London:** What could be cooler than spending your free time learning to work with artifacts and archiving historical objects? (www. museumoflondon.org.uk/Get-involved/Volunteers)

- **The Conservation Volunteers:** If you've got a green thumb and have already checked with the doctor that it's not gangrene, put your unusual pigmentation to good use greening urban spaces and "reclaiming green spaces." (http://www.tcv.org.uk)

- **Zoological Society of London:** Think less Eliza Thornberry and more Lyra Belacqua when she's in Oxford; volunteer positions do not generally involve contact with animals. (http://www.zsl.org/membership/volunteering)

Beyond Tourism

- **Kew Royal Botanical Gardens:** The Gardens are like the Museum of London, but for plants and plant lovers. (www. kew.org/support-kew/volunteer/index.htm)

- **Spitalsfield City Farm:** A "community farm only a stone's throw from the city of London," Spitalsfield City Farm is a respite from city living. (http://spitalfieldscityfarm.org/get_ involved/volunteering)

- **London Health Sciences Center:** If you have a lot of joy and a big heart, there's no better way to share it than with people whose health is not as strong.(http://www.lhsc.on.ca/ About_Us/Volunteer_Services)

- **Natural History Museum:** What better way to get in touch with London's natural history roots than to volunteer at the Natural History Museum. (www.nhm.ac.uk/support-us/ volunteer)

- **English Heritage:** If you're looking to connect with London's history and roots beyond what's Natural, check out this organization. (www.english-heritage.org.uk/caring/ get-involved/ volunteering)

- **Dogs Trust:** That's right, there's a charity that lets you hang out with dogs (walk them, play with them, cuddle with them) in your free time. (www.dogstrust.org.uk/giving/ supportyourcentre/volunteer)

WORK

Finding employment in London may be easier than in other European countries because of the whole English thing, but as a foreigner, you'll still face a lot of roadblocks when looking for employment because of the whole Europe thing.

- **Recruitment Agencies:** One of the best ways to locate where the jobs are in London is to visit a recruitment agency specific to your field. (www. agencycentral.co.uk)

- **Government-Run Job Centers:** Another avenue to tracking down jobs in your area of interest and expertise, though if you want to snag that job, best start referring to these as government-run job "centres." (https://www.gov.uk/jobsearch)

- **Newspaper Postings:** You can never go wrong with some good, old-fashioned scouring of the classifieds. Try The Guardian jobs, for instance. (http://jobs.theguardian.

com/jobs/uk/england/greater-london)

- **Peek-a-Boo Childcare:** Au pair gigs are like free homestays, but with way more responsibility. They are a great way to learn about London culture while also making lifelong bonds with a family. Check out Peek-a-Boo Childcare for a reputable and established au pair agency based in London. (www.peekaboochildcare.com/for-au-pairs.aspx)

- **Greater London Tutors:** Knowing English is not exactly a marketable skill in London, so teaching English is not a great way to make money here, but tutoring other subjects is a viable option. (www.greaterlondontutors.com)

Index

Index

RESEARCHER WRITER

Christine Ann Hurd

One of Let's Go's most beloved veterans, Christine returned to Europe this summer, taking her wit and droll humor to Great Britain, the country that invented them. After researching Eastern Europe in 2012, Christine traded palinka for Pimm's and wiener schnitzel for fish 'n' chips. In addition to writing a book, Christine also found time to stalk Benedict Cumberbatch and pay a requisite visits to 221B Baker St. and the BBC Headquarters.

LET'S GO

Director of Publishing: Michael Goncalves
Product Manager: Luis Duarte
Editorial Director: Claire McLaughlin
Research Manager: Christopher Holthouse
Marketing Directors: Nina Kosaric, Angela Song

President: Patrick Coats
General Manager: Jim McKellar

LONDON ACKNOWLEDGEMENTS

Claire Thanks: Chris, for all the music, screencaps, and laughs and for being the best RM/team mom/pod partner I could have asked for. Never forget that LA is a fortress city. Christine, for two summers of truly phenomenal copy and friendship; thanks for all the *Sherlock* references and for seeing *The Great Gatsby* with me. Michael, for being a great Boss Michael and an even greater Friend Michael—there's no one with whom I'd rather spend three hours at Crema. Luis, for all the late-night hours spent watching "8 Out of 10 Cats," "Countdown," and "8 Out of 10 Cats Does Countdown." Mackenzie, for always being game for everything from assassins to weeknight karaoke to too many BeTos. Thanks to the third floor for being the best floor; because I know most of you will never pick up this book, I don't feel obligated to recognize any of you by name. Thanks to a vending machine full of Coke Zero for providing me with cheap energy and aspertame. Thanks to Jim, Pat, Andy, and all of HSA for the empowerment and #unity. And thanks to my parents for liking me better than Sam and Jack.

Chris Thanks: Claire, for being the best team dad a team mom could ever ask for. Thanks for showing me the ropes, being a great friend, and making me a flipbook in your spare time. Could not have done this summer without you, partner. See you in Khouse. Michael for taking us out for sushi, reminding me to pay our RWs, and for being an all-around incredible boss. Christine, for being our rock, pushing your boundaries with UK copy (and nailing it), and keeping us laughing/googling your pop-culture references throughout the summer. Luis, for that hug on my last day. I still get butterflies about it. Mackenzie, for sharing music, cookies, and personal space with a smile and ever-ready water gun. Angela and Nina, for sacrificing your room on multiple occasions. Marketing pod, for being a stellar bunch and a great place to take five (or ten). The market on Brattle, for knowing "the usual" and always being open. Mom, Dad, Luke, and Roman, for planning your summer around my schedule and for being just the greatest. Love you guys.

ABOUT LET'S GO

The Student Travel Guide

Let's Go publishes the world's favorite student travel guides, written entirely by Harvard students. Armed with pens, notebooks, and a few changes of clothes stuffed into their backpacks, our student researchers go across continents, through time zones, and above expectations to seek out invaluabletravel experiences for our readers. Because we are a completely student-run company, we have a unique perspective on how students travel, where they want to go, and what they're looking to do when they get there. If your dream is to grab a machete and forge through the jungles of Costa Rica, we can take you there. If you'd rather bask in the Riviera sun at a beachside cafe, we'll set you a table. In short, we write for readers who know that there's more to travel than tour buses. To keep up, visit our website, www.letsgo.com, where you can sign up to blog, post photos from your trips,and connect with the Let's Go community.

Traveling Beyond Tourism

We're on a mission to provide our readers with sharp, fresh coverage packed with socially responsible opportunities to go beyond tourism. Each guide's Beyond Tourism chapter shares ideas about responsible travel, study abroad, and how to give back to the places you visit while on the road. To helpyou gain a deeper connection with the places you travel, our fearless researchers scour the globe to give you the heads-up on both world-renowned and off-the-beaten-track opportunities. We've also opened our pages to respected writers and scholars to hear their takes on the countries and regionswe cover, and asked travelers who have worked, studied, or volunteered abroad to contribute first-person accounts of their experiences.

Fifty-Four Years of Wisdom

Let's Go has been on the road for 54 years and counting. We've grown a lot since publishing our first 20-page pamphlet to Europe in 1960, but five decades and 60 titles later, our witty, candid guides are still researched and written entirely by students on shoestring budgets who know that train strikes, stolen luggage, food poisoning, and marriage proposals are all part of a day's work. Meanwhile, we're still bringing readers fresh new features, such as a student-life section with advice on how and where to meet students from around the world; a revamped, user-friendly layout for our listings; and greater emphasis on the experiences that make travel abroad a rite of passage for readers of all ages. And, of course, this year's titles are still brimming with editorial honesty, a commitment to students, and our irreverent style.

The Let's Go Community

More than just a travel guide company, Let's Go is a community that reaches from our headquarters in Cambridge, MA, all across the globe. Our small staff of dedicated student editors, writers, and tech nerds comes together because of our shared passion for travel and our desire to help other travelers get the most out of their experience.We love it when our readers become part of the Let's Go community as well—when you travel, drop us a postcard (67 Mt. Auburn St., Cambridge, MA 02138, USA), send us an email (feedback@letsgo.com), or sign up on our website (www.letsgo. com) to tell us about your adventures and discoveries.

For more information, updated travel coverage, and news from our researcher team, visit us online at www.letsgo.com.